The Emotion

The Emotional Learner combines practical advice with the latest evidence to offer essential guidance on how to understand positive and negative emotions. Taking its reader on a tour of the most significant research from psychology, neuroscience and educational studies, it reveals that in order to ensure educational success, teachers must have a deeper understanding of how and why emotional states manifest themselves in the classroom.

Written by experienced teacher and psychologist Marc Smith, the book examines the complex relationship between cognition and emotion, clearly and thoughtfully exploring:

- What we mean by 'emotions' and why they are important to learning
- Understanding master and performance learning orientations
- Cognition, emotion, memory and recall
- Personality and motivation
- Dealing with boredom in the classroom
- Activating and deactivating emotional states
- Navigating the teenage years
- Understanding the positive and negative impact of anxiety and stress
- Fear of failure, how it evolves and how to combat it.

The Emotional Learner is a compelling, accessible introduction to understanding that how we feel is intricately linked to how we learn. It will help all those involved in teaching children and young adults to challenge common-sense assumptions about the role of positive and negative emotions, showing its reader how to teach 'with emotions in mind' and ensure positive academic outcomes.

Marc Smith is a freelance writer, Chartered Psychologist and Associate Fellow of the British Psychological Society. He has taught in secondary schools across the north of England since 2004 and writes for publications including the *TES* and *The Psychologist*.

The Emotional Learner

Understanding Emotions, Learners and Achievement

Marc Smith

Routledge
Taylor & Francis Group

LONDON AND NEW YORK

First published 2018
by Routledge
2 Park Square, Milton Park, Abingdon, Oxon OX14 4RN

and by Routledge
711 Third Avenue, New York, NY 10017

Routledge is an imprint of the Taylor & Francis Group, an informa business

© 2018 Marc Smith

British Library Cataloguing in Publication Data
A catalogue record for this book is available from the British Library

Library of Congress Cataloging in Publication Data
A catalog record for this book has been requested

ISBN: 978-1-138-05957-3 (hbk)
ISBN: 978-1-138-05959-7 (pbk)
ISBN: 978-1-315-16347-5 (ebk)

Typeset in Galliard
by Swales & Willis Ltd, Exeter, Devon, UK

Contents

It's not easy being a Vulcan

> May I say that I have not thoroughly enjoyed serving with humans? I find their illogic and foolish emotions a constant irritant?[1]
>
> (Spock)

Despite never having considered myself a *Trekkie*, I have always possessed a certain degree of admiration for the Vulcan race, and Mr Spock specifically. Star Trek has been in my life for as long as I can remember, from the original 1960s show with the wonderfully ham James T. Kirk through its many incarnations on the small screen to the more recent blockbuster movies. I can't speak Klingon and I've never been to one of those conventions where people dress up as Andorians or Ferengi or any other alien species represented in the Star Trek universe, but there was always something about Spock that appealed to me. The appeal was that Spock had the ability to control his emotions to such an extent that he appeared totally devoid of them. Vulcans do experience emotion (and more extremely than humans) but over time they have learned to suppress them in order to live more productive and harmonious lives. Certainly, Spock was right when he claimed that emotions are irritating; they often get in the way, alter our behaviour, force us to act in irrational ways and disturb us, but as for being illogical?

Emotions are far from illogical, even though they may at times be very painful. Dale Carnegie, the grandfather of the self-improvement movement, suggested that humans are ultimately emotional rather than logical creatures, which is perhaps why Spock found them so frustrating. Carnegie certainly had a point. American psychologist Drew Western (author of *The Political Brain*) has spent most of his academic career studying the voting habits of the US electorate, concluding that people rarely make logical decisions when it comes to choosing their government. On the contrary, voting behaviour is much more likely to be an emotional response rather than a logical one, a phenomenon that appears to have had at least some impact on the 2016 UK referendum on European Union membership. If our voting habits are fuelled by emotions, it's highly likely that other decisions are too.

Of course, we would be poorer in spirit if emotions did not reside within us. Without emotions we would never be able to experience joy or lose ourselves in awe at the first sight of our newborn child; we would never be able to engage in fits of laughter that cause our cheeks to ache and tears to flow from our eyes. Conversely, without emotions we could never experience the bitter pain of sorrow, the yearning for someone lost or the sharp pangs of empathy at the sight of another in distress. I would not want to be like Spock, lacking the capacity that not only makes me human but also makes me who I am. The point Spock misses (and yes, I do understand that he is a purely fictional character) is that emotions serve a purpose, they aren't simply an evolutionary hiccup; on the contrary, they are necessary for human survival. Emotions let us know when there is danger, or when a close friend requires our understanding and support. Indeed, those humans who display a lack of emotion are seen as somehow lacking in basic human function. Emotionless individuals are often viewed as abnormal or suffering from some kind of psychological deficiency because society values emotions and views them as a basic human quality.

Emotions also have their dark side. Anger and rage can be destructive and result in harm to oneself and to others who dare to get in our way. Extreme sadness can lead to some individuals harming themselves or withdrawing from society, neglecting the basic human need to connect with others. According to the mental health charity Young Minds, one in every ten children aged between 5 and 16 years suffers from a clinically diagnosable mental disorder. Let's put that into context shall we? In every school classroom there are around three children who are struggling due to some kind of mental health problem. For every 12 to 15 children in any classroom, at least one child will have deliberately self-harmed. In fact, over the last ten years figures indicate that there has been a 68 per cent increase in the number of young people admitted to hospital because they have deliberately harmed themselves in some way. I could quote even more harrowing statistics, but I expect you've got the message by now.

These statistics highlight the power of emotional responses to external events. Emotions guide and often determine behaviour, raising us up and then allowing us to crash back down to earth. This book isn't about adolescent mental health, it's about the normative and the ordinary rather than the extreme. Nevertheless, it's worth taking a couple of steps back in order for us to think about the emotional lives of learners and survey our surroundings. If we consider the extreme end of the emotional continuum, three children in a class have some kind of diagnosable mental illness (one that might have gone undiagnosed). How, we might ask, does this impact on their educational progress? Children who are struggling with their own emotions may well be diverting precious cognitive resources to simply surviving from day to day and so are unlikely to be fully engaged in the learning process. It might appear that a particular child isn't paying attention or seems disengaged, quiet or withdrawn; it might be that problems manifest themselves in disruptive behaviours and defiance. What about the student who constantly worries about passing a test or getting a good mark for their homework, or the child so overcome with anxiety that they fall apart when asked even the simplest of questions in class? Teachers are familiar with the often unusual responses they receive from students; some are fleeting while others seem ingrained and habitual. When I was young I would rarely volunteer answers in class due to anxiety (a condition I have struggled with for most of my life), which inevitably made me a target for some teachers who felt that it was their duty to bring me out of my 'shell'. The truth was that I liked my shell very much because it made me feel safe. Furthermore, I knew that if I drew attention to myself I would become flustered and turn the most startling shade of crimson. The fear of looking incompetent (or resembling a tomato) caused me to withdraw even further so that by the time I was asked a question in class, I had already become a quivering wreck of nerves and anxiety.

These anxieties fade but never quite disappear. As someone who displays introvert characteristics (I'll avoid claiming to be 'an introvert' for a number of reasons I describe in Chapter 5), I also know that I approach new places, people and situations very cautiously, over-vigilance being one of the traits associated with introversion. When I became a teacher I almost forgot about how anxious I was as a child and, much to my shame, assumed that my students somehow didn't suffer from those same anxieties. It took me a few years to really find my feet as a teacher, but eventually I managed to establish some kind of rapport with most of my students (some students will simply hate you regardless and this, in itself, came as somewhat of a shock). I believe that some people are natural teachers while realising that this view isn't uniformly held. Although I always saw myself as approachable, as time passed it became clear that I was grossly mistaken. It took a 17-year-old student named Emily to make me fully aware of this.

Emily always seemed very able and confident and gave the impression that her positivity knew no bounds. When her grades began to fall and she began to miss lessons I decided we needed a chat. It transpired that Emily had felt she had been struggling for some time but didn't feel that she could ask me for help. 'You think I'm so clever but I'm not', she said, 'How could I tell you that I was struggling?' I'm not claiming that this exchange was some kind of revelation, an epiphany that would shape the rest of my career, but it did make me pause and take stock and think about how I labelled pupils in both positive and negative ways. Emily had become a prisoner to her anxieties about her own potential failure and falling from the pedestal I had placed her on. She became preoccupied with not failing and, as we will see in Chapter 10, fear of failure can lead to some very destructive behaviours.

Anxiety is perhaps the most obvious choice of negative emotion here, and there has been substantial research conducted on its impact on learning. Like the younger me, anxious children become more flustered; they forget the material they have been given to learn, misunderstand instructions and constantly fear being asked questions in class. They may even become temporarily mute if challenged to produce an answer. The immediate solution might be to help the student relax or assist them in the nurturing of positive emotions. However, the relationship between positive and negative emotions is a complex one and some areas of research have erroneously linked positive emotions with positive academic outcomes and negative emotions with poor outcomes (Chapter 3). Disentangling this complex relationship constitutes a weighty task and it will no doubt be some time before we have a clearer understanding of how these constructs operate. For now, however, we can attempt to piece together what we currently understand about the ways in which emotions (both positive and negative) impact learning and why being a Vulcan doesn't necessarily make you more successful.

Emotions aren't illogical

Spock was wrong – emotions aren't illogical. Humans are emotional beings, so how individuals recognise and regulate these emotions can have a major impact on future trajectories. Psychologists use the somewhat awkward term 'affect' to describe our experience of emotions and recognise that affect can be both positive and negative. The term 'affect' is useful, simply because it sidesteps the tricky question of whether emotions actually exist. This might seem an odd statement (especially when you consider the topic of this book), but the subjective nature of emotions can mean that their very existence can be challenged. You'll probably find that I use the term affect and emotion interchangeably, just be aware that I am (usually) referring to the same thing but, for convenience, I'll use both affect and emotion despite their differences. Emotions effect people in different ways, and while some are guided more by their emotions, others might be more logical and pragmatic in their approach. Emotions are also ingrained deeply into language, in that we might be an emotional person or someone who is 'in touch with their emotions' or someone who values their 'gut instincts' that often defy any logic. Others might be said to allow their emotions to 'get in the way' of rational and logical decision-making and there are some occupations where being able to keep emotions in check is preferable to the alternative.

During the early days of psychology there was a great deal of interest in emotions, but its reliance on introspection resulted in its decline as a serious area of research as psychology fought to claim its place as a serious scientific discipline. For many years, emotions were not seen as a particularly suitable area of research, perhaps in part due to their subjective nature and the fact that they are quite slippery things – they move about, darting from one extreme to another. They are also quite difficult to quantify in any meaningful way because we can never really be sure that the emotion I feel is the same as the one you feel in the same situation. People react differently in different situations and our behaviour can, at times, run counter to social norms, especially in traumatic situations. Despite these problems, research is now returning to the study of emotions as new technologies and research techniques provide more effective ways of understanding their role in people's lives. Furthermore, a growing number of scientists are now investigating the link between emotion and cognitive function (that is, aspects related to memory, learning and attention), and this new field of investigation is beginning to inform us about how emotions affect the way we think and learn as well as how they arise in the first place. Others are investigating how emotions impact on future success and failure in work, sports and life in general and are asking questions about how factors like emotional regulation influence our future.

Learning is more than cognition

Learning is a complex process and is much more than just the process of storing information in long-term memory for it to be retrieved at a later date – memory doesn't work like that anyway. To say that learning is just about cognition is like saying that riding a bike is only about pedalling.

When we learn to ride a bike, one of the main skills we need to learn is to pedal, but we also need to balance and apply the brakes when necessary to avoid collisions and to bring the bike to a stop. The process of learning certainly requires the engagement of cognitive processes, but without other so-called non-cognitive processes learning simply won't take place. The process of learning, therefore, involves cognitive, emotional as well as social processes.

Cognitive processes

This is perhaps the most important. Cognition is all about the thought and regulatory processes involved in the recognition, storage and retrieval of information. Committing information to memory also includes other cognitive processes such as perception and attention. However, basic forms of learning can take place without memory (as has been seen in individuals with severe memory deficits), and memories themselves are often highly inaccurate.

Emotional processes

How we feel during the learning event can enhance or impair the way in which we attend to such events, how we store information received during the event and the ability to retrieve stored information after the event. Specific emotions such as curiosity can enhance while others such as boredom can impair.

Social processes

Learning cannot take place in a vacuum. Relationships can make or break the ability to engage in any learning event. This is particularly important during the early stages of learning when children are developing their social skills and gradually beginning to understand what it is to be part of a group.

Although this book is specifically about emotional processes in learning, in reality all three components (cognitive, emotional, social) operate together.

Cognitive or non-cognitive?

As the pressure increases on students to achieve in high stakes exams and the wellbeing of our young people decreases (and mental health issues rise), investigating the role of that basic of human qualities seems an obvious road down which to travel. Certainly, the research base already exists in direct and indirect ways, but has so far failed to reap any real rewards in the classroom. Recently, certain skills have been identified as 'non-cognitive' in an attempt to distinguish them from those more directly related to aspects of learning such as memory and attention. These non-cognitive skills relate to attributes including resilience, character and grit, and while it can be argued that all personal attributes involve some kind of cognitive regulation and control, the label provides a useful way of distinguishing one group of skills from another. The number of interventions designed to measure and build on the attributes continues to grow, but, unfortunately, many are rarely implemented in a uniform way and definitions are often used differently. For example, a review of resilience programmes in UK schools published in 2013 found that many interventions used the term 'resilience' in such a vague way that the authors of the report were unable to identify exactly what was being measured (Hart & Heaver, 2013). Indeed, the role of emotions and emotional regulation forms a key component in our ability to cope with setbacks and deal with failure, so there is an intricate relationship between emotions and cognitions. One resilience intervention that does appear to include emotional characteristics is also the most widely used. The Penn Resiliency Programme, designed by leading psychologists at the University of Pennsylvania, is based around the optimism character strength, and suggests that by encouraging an optimistic and positive outlook on life and learning we can improve wellbeing and 'inoculate' individuals against helplessness.

The positive 'revolution'

Unfortunately, we rarely discuss the emotional lives of learners unless their negative emotions are a cause for concern (such as extreme anxiety or debilitating depression). Rarely do we link emotions to the learning process and rarely does it occur to us that many emotional reactions might be caused by the learning process itself. In fact, when we talk of teaching and learning there is scarcely any mention of the role emotion might play in success and failure beyond the occasional discussion over the existence or otherwise of concepts such as emotional intelligence. In a similar way, psychology is still often concerned with the treatment of mental illness rather than the prevention of it. This situation has started to change with the rise of what is known as 'Positive Psychology', associated with the study of happiness and wellbeing. While the principles of Positive Psychology remain well intentioned, there has been a growing concern about its methodology and scientific rigour, despite the movement being populated by some of the leading figures in psychology. The Penn Resiliency Programme, for example, arose from Positive Psychology and there have been further theories and ideas (some of which I will discuss later) that have grown out of this movement. However, the mistaken premise of the pursuit of happiness has forced the movement to shift its emphasis over the years. While research conducted under the Positive Psychology banner can certainly be useful, it can also often prove detrimental.

Should we 'emotionalise' education?

One concern that inevitably arises when we bring up the whole topic of emotions within an education setting relates to what has become known as the 'emotionalisation of education'. The concerns centre on the idea that we are taking normal life difficulties and somehow reframing them in terms of some kind of psychological deficit, following the shift seen in Anglo-American societies towards a more therapeutic ethos. Anxiety and fear are normal everyday emotions experienced by students even before formal education became the norm. When I was at school there was no talk of children with special educational needs, there were no teaching assistants to help the weaker students and there were certainly no interventions to help with exam anxiety. Back in those dark days teachers taught and, while there were a few who could be relied on to support children emotionally, many teachers rarely even thought about how their students were coping in that way. Now, of course, the shelves of our bookshops are filled with self-help guides and pop psychology – personal development is big business and the rise in psychological intervention programmes bears witness to such changes. Education is becoming more concerned with relieving stress, teaching coping skills and ways of dealing with the ups and downs of daily life. Even in our work as teachers we are more aware of wellbeing and work–life balance than ever before, and we hear more and more about character development, mindfulness and resilience training.

The emotionalisation of education is a response to changes within education and the pressures that didn't exist 30 or 40 years ago. I recall very little pressure to do A-levels or to go on to university so, consequently, I left school at 16 with a handful of rather poor exam results. Today I see the pressure placed on students that I never had, plus the pressures on teachers that didn't seem to exist when I was at school. League tables have placed pressure on schools, and these pressures are often passed down to students who are issued with target grades and expected grades and a constant flow of data that is expected to show linear progression. There is the expectation that the majority of those leaving school will go to university (whether they want to or not), placing pressure on them to get this grade or that grade in their A-levels. The reality is that there is certainly more pressure on young people today than three or four decades ago and this pressure appears to be increasing as the reliance on high stakes exams increases. Such pressure begins early and there is evidence that children as young as 6 or 7 are already beginning to compare themselves with their peers (they appear to be developing a *performance goal orientation* which I discuss in Chapter 2), for example, by writing themselves off in some subjects because they have been placed in low ability sets.

I stress that teachers are not mental health professionals (and shouldn't be expected to act as if they were), but they do come into contact with young people more often than any other group. It would therefore make sense for the profession to be aware of emotional issues and the ways in which they impact on learning. I say 'aware' because dealing successfully with extreme emotional issues is a job for trained professionals, and teachers are trained in teaching, not in dealing with mental health issues. However, while there is some debate surrounding the existence of a child mental health crisis, there is certainly a wellbeing issue to be tackled, certainly in the UK where our children are some of the unhappiest in Europe. While this book does touch on some issues at the extreme end of the spectrum, its primary aim revolves around the normative functions of emotion and learning.

Emotions are related to goals

There is a growing body of evidence indicating that emotions arise as a result of appraisals related to our goals – more precisely, achievement goals. This is also more relevant to education and learning as goals play a major role in the learning process. If we accept the premise that human actions are goal directed (and there is little to suggest that they aren't) then it must logically follow that goals underpin actions, thoughts and emotions. Lisa Linnenbrink-Garcia, an educational psychologist at the University of Michigan, has extended this argument by suggesting that goals are central to linking motivation, cognition and emotion (see, for example, O'Keefe and Linnenbrink-Garcia, 2014). Others, such as Reinhard Pekrun at the University of Munich, have further hypothesised that emotions arise from judgements about how successful we are at achieving our goals, the importance of these goals, how much we feel in control and how able we feel to handle any problems that arise (Pekrun *et al.*, 2007). Of course, the assumption here is that all goals are achievement goals (and these are certainly the most relevant in respect to teaching and learning), but other goals may also play an important part. Schools are more than just about learning and academic achievement, and other goals such as a sense of belonging play a part in both wellbeing and academic success. The feeling of belonging to a school, a year group or a particular class might lead to greater feelings of wellbeing and consequently a greater desire to engage in the learning process.

Hopefully I am winning the battle to convince you that emotions are a crucial and inescapable part of the learning process. No more obvious is this than in the part played by emotions such as anxiety (Chapter 6). In societies that rely heavily on the use of regular high stakes testing, those students who are unable to cope with even minor levels of anxiety will suffer more than those who are less anxious. Test anxiety has been found to have a detrimental impact on a specific form of memory known as working memory. Working memory is a type of short-term storage used for manipulating information that has been drawn from our long-term memory store. If you close your eyes and count the number of windows in your house, you are taking the memory of your house from the long-term memory store and transferring it into working memory. Once there, you can picture each part of the house and keep a tally of the number of windows. This is the same place where we engage in mental arithmetic and all types of problem solving from complex instructions to crosswords and Sudoku. It is also the place where we keep the instructions given to us by other people. So, a teacher might ask the class to finish writing the sentence they are on, put their pens down and bring their work to the front of the class. Children with specific problems with their working memory might have difficulties following such instructions because their working memory simply doesn't have the capacity. As a result, they might forget to finish the sentence and put their pen down and, instead, simply bring their work to the front of the class. Those children who suffer from anxiety might experience similar problems, not because of the working memory per se, but because their anxiety is impairing their ability to hold on to the information. In a system where students are expected to rely more and more on their ability to remember huge amounts of information, anxiety can mean the difference between success and failure. Researchers have even found that anxiety negatively predicts lower GCSE scores (Putwain, 2008). With a system where schools are judged so heavily on exam results, it's a wonder more of them don't spend more time identifying test anxious students and supporting them with appropriate interventions.

So, what are emotions anyway?

I've rambled on quite a bit about some of the ways emotions can impact learning and introduced the idea that emotions as we understand them might not exist at all. However, if we assume that they do exist (rather than simply being a statistical abstraction), we need to be as clear as we can about what they are. There's an assumption here that we all understand what an emotion is and is not; we seem to instinctively know what emotions are without having to define them in any kind of formal way. At this point I must confess that I like definitions; I like to know that my understanding of a concept is the generally held view and I think this is necessary because it avoids confusion and crossed wires. Common sense often guides our understanding of concepts, and emotions are no different. Emotions impact on and often guide our behaviour (as I have already discussed); they produce physical responses (such as crying or laughing), psychological responses (they might cause us to take stock of ourselves as individuals) and social responses (we use emotions to place ourselves within a wider social context).

Many researchers view emotions as three separate but interrelated constructs: affective tendencies, core affect and emotional experiences:

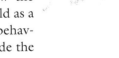

- *Affective tendencies* provide a lens through which we view our relationship with the world; in other words, how we view the world and our place within it. For example, if we see the world as a frightening and threatening place, then our transactions or behaviours will be based on the tendency of fear (this would include the school environment). These tendencies develop through a number of pathways, such as socialisation, individual beliefs, approach avoidance motives and personality.

- *Core affect* refers to how we feel at any particular point in time. Researchers measure core affect through a combination of valence (a continuum from pleasant to unpleasant) and arousal (the range of activation measured from low to high). For example, we might measure the experience of a formal exam as unpleasant (valence) but high in arousal (raised heart rate, increased adrenaline secretion, etc.).

• **_Emotional experiences_** represent the socially constructed and personally acted ways of being. These are formed through conscious and unconscious judgements about our perceived success at attaining goals or maintaining our standards and beliefs. If we view our goals as the difference between where we are and where we want to be, then our core affects will tend to become our emotional experience via our appraisals and attributions about what is happening during a particular episode and based on our goals, values, beliefs and social networks.

So how do we distinguish an emotion from a non-emotion? Thankfully, there is some consensus when it comes to defining an emotion, and there is (general) agreement that emotions represent coherent clusters of components based around a number of features. Just how many of these features should be present for these clusters to be termed an emotion is open to some debate. There certainly seems to be a consensus that there are at least five, including distinctive facial and vocal expressions, distinctive physiology, rapid onset and brief duration. For our purpose, I shall yield to the five definitions adopted by Sandi Mann in her wonderful little book _Emotion: All That Matters_ (2014): cognitions (what we think), feelings, physiological reactions, behaviour and expressions (although emotions can occur in the absence of outward expression – even though, I suspect, some expressions would occur at a micro-level).

Emotions, then, can be seen in others as well as experienced by the individual – if we are sad then we might cry; if we are angry we might screw up our faces. Facial expressions, however, can cause a particular problem, and many researchers claim that they aren't necessary in order to classify an event as an emotion. Extreme emotions like pleasure and plain, for example, appear to result in startlingly similar facial expression.

For an emotion to be an emotion it should include the above features – if it doesn't then it's something else. This leads us to the more problematic

question of how many emotions there are. As far as emotion researchers are concerned, there is no real consensus. Some say that there are six
(anger, disgust, fear, happiness, sadness and surprise), with others claiming
that there are eight (the previous six plus joy and anticipation) with all
other emotions being a combination of these core emotions. This is certainly problematic for those researchers who investigate emotions absent
from the list such as boredom and interest. The thing is, we kind of know
when an experience involves an emotion even if we can't quite decide on
what emotion that is. Because of this subjectivity, labelling emotions isn't
really essential. We might experience emotion and just think 'oh, I feel
really out of sorts today' or 'I'm just in a funny mood'. Emotions are as
much about having the language to describe them as having an objectively based label for them. There is, however, a way out of this empirical
dilemma. American psychologist Robert Plutchik proposed that there are
eight basic emotions that he groups in pairs of opposites (Plutchik, 2001).
According to the Plutchik model, the eight basic emotions can be blended,
just like colours, in order to produce a large number of related yet distinct
emotions. This helps us because we can then include more learning-
appropriate emotions such as interest, boredom and curiosity into our
discussion without having to worry too much about whether these constructs can be thought of as true emotions – we can widen our definition to
include 'basic' and 'blended' emotions. Furthermore, the ability to blend
emotions allows us to widen the emotion definition and account for pretty
much every word we use to label the multitude of subjective feelings experienced over a seemingly infinite number of personal experiences. With
regards to learning, it allows us to identify emotions specific to the learning
process such as interest, distraction and boredom.

We can see that however we decide to categorise emotions, they are
linked in some way to our personal goals, and the relationship between
emotions and goal achievement becomes more obvious when we start
looking into the role of failure (Chapter 10). The road to achieving our
goals is rarely a straightforward one (unless we set ourselves unrealistically low goals) and it's a road full of potholes, bumps and nasty mud
patches that can so easily derail us or send us off in unexpected directions before we reach our final destination. Progress is rarely linear and

there is likelihood that those students who do make sustained linear progression do so because they have set (or have been set) goals that are below their abilities. The idea that progression is linear and that students should make progress day on day and week on week is quite simply inaccurate and incredibly unhelpful because there are so many factors at play here. In fact, data from Education Datalab (a group involved in education research) indicates that fewer than ten per cent of students in UK schools make linear progress between key stages (Education Datalab, 2016). If we think of emotions as being linked to progress goals then, as educators, we begin to better understand how they impact learners on their long and very winding road. Emotional responses experienced as we get closer to achieving our goals or suffer setbacks, are crucial to motivation, resilience and mental toughness or 'grittiness' (our dogged determination to get there in the end no matter what life throws at us). Furthermore, certain emotions will hold us back at different points and in different circumstances – a student might lose confidence in a particular area and develop a fear of failure, or might react badly to a change of teacher or class. Some emotions are perhaps more relevant to teaching and learning than others. Nevertheless, they all play a role. Fear, anxiety, anger, boredom, interest, curiosity and so many others will help and hinder at different times, ultimately impacting on long-term goals which, in a system dominated by high stakes testing, translates into exam grades.

What's the point of emotions?

Emotions exist because they serve an evolutionary purpose. In other words, emotions have some kind of adaptive value – otherwise, evolution being the clever thing that it is, would have deleted them a long time ago. Even Vulcans have emotions; they have just learned to control them. Emotions help us deal with life tasks and help our species survive; this is the reason they share certain characteristics and common elements despite individual and cultural differences. That is, even in the most diverse of cultures, emotions will display certain similarities that can't be explained through socialisation or learning that takes place within that specific society or culture. If emotions are evolutionary, we should also be able to detect them in other primates even though certain emotions might be unique to humans. First and foremost, emotions are a biological response to a situation (be it good or bad) and the speed at which our biological system reacts can often be mesmerising. Our biology reacts by setting in motion a set of involuntary changes in both our expression and our physiology; so our facial expression might change even before we are aware of our response (as can often be seen with an emotion like disgust). In relation to learning, a student might be struck dumb or freeze when asked a question in class and, while some might interpret this as defiance or ignorance, the student might not be fully aware of their response. In this case, the experience of an emotion (anxiety) is seen as happening to them rather than something chosen by them. In the same way, we might see a face 'light up' at the suggestion of a topic a student finds particularly interesting.

Psychologist James Averill agrees that emotions fulfil vital biological functions for the survival of the species. According to Averill (1980), basic emotions should be universal – they should be seen in non-human primates and should be heritable. The problem here is that there is little consensus across cultures of what these basic emotions are; not only do they vary between cultures, they also vary within cultures over time. While it's clear that emotions are evolutionary, exactly what constitutes a basic emotion can be thought of as socially constructed. Furthermore, the most basic of basic emotions are likely to be psychological in nature, in that they have a transformative capacity in terms of our sense of self. This is important to the learning process because it suggests that constructs such as self-esteem and self-worth are guided by emotions and the ability to enhance and transform the way in which we see ourselves, as well as our beliefs about how others see us. Let's take the example of the anxious student being asked a question in class. The teacher says the student's name and asks a question. The first component of any emotion is subjective – the personal experience of being singled out and quizzed. The second component is physiological (raised heart rate, increased perspiration, raised blood pressure and so on). The final component is a behavioural one and for our over-anxious student this might manifest itself in silence, fidgeting or even crying. To the teacher asking the question, this might seem like a highly irrational response to a simple question, but to the student a complex set of variables are being played out, based on a number of largely psychological factors. The student has become overwhelmed by their emotional response to the situation – anxiety has been 'done to them'; it is not a course of action they have chosen.

Regulating emotions

People react in different ways to the many emotions they experience. We can respond to these emotions in both positive and negative ways, but as we mature we tend to become better skilled at expressing emotions in more constructive ways. Young people are often more impulsive, quicker to anger and sometimes more prone to certain negative emotions brought on by their experiences. The more emotions we experience over time, the better we become at what is termed 'emotion regulation'. Psychologist James Gross defines emotion regulation as 'the process by which individuals influence which emotions they have, when they have them, and how they experience and express them' (Gross, 2002, p.282).

More specifically, emotion regulation involves being able to think constructively about how to cope with feelings, not being overwhelmed by emotion. This would include feeling discouraged but not giving up, feeling anxious but not allowing that anxiety to limit your daily life and getting excited but not getting so carried away that you resort to poor judgement when making important decisions. While many theories of emotion regulation stress the use of cognitive processes, the setting of limits and the development of self-control, psychologist Kenneth Barish suggests that it's more important to ensure that people, and especially children, feel confident that their feelings will be heard. Barish goes on to claim that when there is an expectation from the child that their feelings and concerns will be appreciated and understood, problematic emotions become less urgent and, consequently, this reduces the pain of disappointment and frustration (see, for example, Barish, 2012). This might not be a popular notion amongst some teachers, yet it helps us to at least consider wider possibilities beyond simple rewards and punishments.

Unfortunately, many of the strategies people use to deal with emotions are often maladaptive. Appropriate emotion regulation has been linked to higher levels of personal wellbeing and academic success, but often the strategies we use have a deeper emotional impact. Maladaptive behaviours include:

- *distraction* – trying not to think about what is causing the distress;
- *rumination* – continually going over the problem in our mind and revisiting the distress it causes us;
- *worry* – focussing on the negative aspects of the problem;
- *thought suppression* – redirecting our attention away from the problem and focussing on other content. Thought suppression often leads to a greater focus on the distressing emotion.

Students who, for example, suffer with test anxiety may well ruminate on an impending exam and worry about failing or looking stupid in front of their peers. Others might forego exam preparation in order to distract them from the negative emotions associated with exam taking. Younger children may even ruminate out loud while others might use internal dialogue in an attempt to regulate their emotions, that is, they might talk to themselves. Talking to oneself isn't necessarily a sign of maladaptive or worrying behaviour and can actually serve an important adaptive function dependant upon its context. Those who are able to employ more adaptive strategies are said to display greater emotion regulation and function in a more positive way.

The implications of adequate emotion regulation have been demonstrated in a number of interesting ways. A series of studies that offer insights into how young children do this was conducted by Walter Mischel during the late 1960s and early 1970s. Commonly known as the Marshmallow Experiment (but actually a series of experiments), Mischel and his team tested the ability of 4-year-old children to delay gratification of a desired object – in this case, a marshmallow. The child was seated next to a table upon which had been placed a marshmallow.

The experimenter then told the child that they had to leave the room for a few moments and that the child must not eat the marshmallow. The child was also told that if they didn't eat the marshmallow, they would be allowed to eat two marshmallows on the experimenter's return. For an in-depth discussion of this and other studies, I would highly recommend *The Marshmallow Test* (Mischel, 2015), which provides an excellent analysis of the many studies Mischel and his colleagues conducted.

The studies revealed two important findings:

1. Children were able to wait longer if they could distract themselves from the marshmallow or if they thought about the marshmallow's more abstract qualities (size and shape rather than taste). Some of the children would distract themselves from the desired object by turning away from it, sitting on their hands or even talking to it; most, however, gave in to temptation and devoured it. Blakemore and Frith (2005) explain this behaviour in terms of brain development, specifically the development of the frontal lobes. The brain at this age still has a long way to go before it is fully developed, and the frontal lobes (the part that helps us to control our impulses and resist temptation) are no exception (see Chapter 9 for a more detailed discussion on the developing brain).

2. Perhaps the most interesting yet controversial finding was that when the children who displayed the greatest level of restraint grew into teenagers, they were found to be more successful at school when compared to the more impulsive children. They scored better on tests of perseverance, concentration and on cognitive logic tests, suggesting that emotion regulation and impulse control play an important role in later academic success. There could, of course, be other reasons for this, but it's likely that being able to delay gratification played a role.

Being able to control and express emotions in acceptable ways, therefore, impacts heavily on the ability to learn, and those students who are able to learn how to self-regulate are better equipped to succeed.

Additionally, the ability to delay gratification by, for example, completing an assignment before engaging in social activities unrelated to school places students in a more advantageous position. No emotion is inherently good or bad (or positive or negative), rather the most important skill is one that involves being able to ensure that emotions are used effectively and efficiently.

Why teachers need to be emotion aware

Teachers witness first-hand the impact emotions have on student behaviour (and, indeed, their own), but rarely do we see emotions as a roadblock to learning. While the statistics quoted earlier from Young Minds are harrowing, is this not a mental health issue rather than a learning issue? Furthermore, aren't teachers responsible for learning and not the psychological problems faced by students? We are perhaps entering dangerous territory here. Most teachers have neither the experience nor the training to deal with mental health problems, and I would always advise teachers to refer pupils on if they suspect deeper emotional or behavioural problems. Teachers are responsible for teaching, certainly, but there is also a part to play in nurturing effective learners, young people who are able to deal with information they are presented with and process this information in effective ways. The roadblocks learners face must be overcome if they are to succeed academically and this belongs firmly within a teacher's remit. Teachers should not only teach but also nurture student potential. In a perfect world all young people would start their education on a level playing field, creating a true meritocratic system, but we know this is far from the realities of the situation. Just like socioeconomic status, gender and upbringing, the psychological make-up of learners plays a part in their present and future trajectories, whether they are plagued by anxiety, lack confidence or harbour a near-pathological fear of their own failure.

While nurturing positive emotions and recognising damaging negative emotions can help, it is also necessary to recognise those negative emotions that can help and when positive emotions are hindering achievement. Emotions can aid wellbeing but they can also scupper it, and we now have adequate evidence to start to put this complex jigsaw together. Be mindful, however, that the world of emotion research remains a dark and uninviting place, populated with theories and research findings that are often contradictory in nature. All research must be open to critical debate (this is the only way science moves forward), and the research visited in the following pages is no exception.

The purpose of this book

The following chapters will attempt to answer a number of interrelated questions as well as offer some advice on how we can teach with emotions in mind. The most important questions are:

1. Do emotional experiences (what students are feeling before, during and after a learning episode) shape the way they deal with learning environments?
2. Do those learners with a propensity towards positive affect cope better and ultimately achieve greater success than those learners who display a tendency towards negative affect?
3. If positive emotions enhance learning, then does it make sense to nurture such emotions in students?
4. Do negative emotions always hinder learning, and do positive emotions always help?

What this book will help you to do

- Gain a greater understanding of how everyday emotions impact learning.
- Understand how common-sense views of positive and negative emotions are often inaccurate.
- Offer advice on how teachers and educators can nurture those emotions that have been found to result in positive academic outcomes.

- Offer advice on how to deal with low-level emotional responses that could hamper academic achievement.
- Gain a greater understanding of the research that underpins our understanding of emotions and learning.

What this book will not help you to do

- Deal with severe forms of anxiety and other mental health issues.
- Use quick fixes that provide only short-term benefits.

Note

1 For those with a particular penchant for Star Trek, the quote appears in the 1968 episode, *Day of the Dove*.

References

Averill, J.R. (1980). A constructivist view of emotion. In P. Plutchik & H. Kellerman (eds) *Emotion: Theory, Research and Experience* (pp.305–339). New York: Academic Press.

Barish, K. (2012). *Pride and Joy: A Guide to Understanding Your Child's Emotions and Solving Family Problems*. Oxford, UK: Oxford University Press.

Blakemore, S. & Frith, U. (2005). *The Learning Brain*. London: Blackwell.

Education Datalab (2016). *Seven Things You Might Not Know About Our Schools*. Available at www.educationdatalab.org.uk/wp-content/uploads/2016/02/EduDataLab-7things.pdf.

Gross, J.J. (2002). Emotion regulation: affective, cognitive, and social consequences. *Psychophysiology* 39(3), pp.281–291.

Hart, A. & Heaver, B. (2013). Evaluating resilience-based programs for schools using a systematic consultative review. *Journal of Child and Youth Development* 1(1), pp.27–53.

Mann, S. (2014). *Emotion: All That Matters*. London: Hodder & Stoughton.

Mischel, W. (2015). *The Marshmallow Test: Understanding Self Control and How to Master It*. London: Corgi.

O'Keefe, P.A. & Linnenbrink-Garcia, L. (2014). The role of interest in optimizing performance and self-regulation. *Journal of Experimental Social Psychology* 53, pp.70–78.

Pekrun, R., Frenzel, A.C., Goetz, T. & Perry, R.P. (2007). The control-value theory of achievement emotions: An integrative approach to emotions in education. In P.A. Schutz & R. Pekrun (eds) *Emotion in Education* (pp.13–36). San Diego, CA: Academic Press.

Plutchik, R. (2001). The nature of emotions: Human emotions have deep evolutionary roots, a fact that may explain their complexity and provide tools for clinical practice. *American Scientist* 89(4), pp.344–350.

Putwain, D.W. (2008). Test anxiety and GCSE performance: The effect of gender and socio-economic background. *Educational Psychology in Practice* 24(4), pp.319–334.

2 | Masters and performers

If you had to choose, which would it be? Loads of success and validation or lots of challenge?

(Carol S. Dweck)

In 1964 a young psychologist named Martin Seligman was about to begin his doctoral studies in experimental psychology at the University of Pennsylvania. At the time, psychology found itself on the cusp of a theoretical shift that would see behaviourist views of human action replaced with ideas influenced by thought processes, or 'cognitions'. Spurred on by the development of the microprocessor, human behaviour and action began to be compared with the functioning of a computer where information went through input, processing and retrieval processes, rather than conditioned responses, a view that had dominated psychology since the 1920s.

Seligman, along with Steve Maier and Bruce Overmier, would eventually play a part in dismantling the foundations of the ideas laid down by early behaviourists such as Ivan Pavlov, John Watson and B.F. Skinner who had asserted that behaviour was the product of simple stimulus response associations. In his book *Authentic Happiness* (2002), Seligman describes the laboratory in which he arrived as in 'uproar'. The graduate students were busy conducting experiments with dogs, using the principles of Pavlovian conditioning where a signal was paired with an electric shock. The dogs were later put in a chamber where running to the other side would turn off the shock. The problem was that the dogs made little or no attempt to escape the pain that the administered electric shock induced, resulting in the experiments grinding to a halt because the dogs refused to display the expected behaviour – even when they were given a means of escape, the dogs didn't take it, choosing instead to simply sit passively without moving.

Rather than sharing their annoyance, Seligman was fascinated by the behaviour the graduate students observed. While his studies into this seemingly unusual response continued over the following few years, psychologists began to learn a great deal about the psychology behind giving up and how both human and non-human animals learn to become helpless. The studies began as an investigation into classical conditioning, an area pioneered by the now famous experiments conducted by the Russian physiologist Ivan Pavlov at the beginning of the twentieth century. Like Pavlov, Seligman and his colleagues were attempting to pair a signal with a response (in Seligman's case an electric shock) to see if a signal, such as the ringing of a bell, would allow the animal to anticipate the coming pain of the shock. True to form, the dogs would react to the signal in the same way they reacted to the electric shock, flinching and displaying distress even before the shock had been administered. Seligman then put these dogs into what he called a 'shuttle box', essentially a large crate divided by a low fence (low enough for the dog to easily jump over). The floor on one side of the shuttle box was electrified and there was an assumption that when the dog experienced the pain of the live floor it would jump over the low fence to the safety of the other side. But this didn't happen – the dogs that, if you recall, had previously been given shocks from which they couldn't escape, simply stayed put and accepted their fate. Furthermore, when Seligman tried the experiment on a fresh set of dogs that hadn't been involved in the first part of the study, he found that they would successfully escape to the side of the box without the electrified floor.

Just like humans who give up when faced with uncontrollable negative events, the dogs had given up on their attempts to escape. Even more than that, they didn't even try because the first part of the experiment had taught them that there was no means of escape. This phenomenon became known as 'learned helplessness', and Seligman,

Maier and Overmier would spend the next five years attempting to find a way to prevent it. What so frustrated the behaviourists about learned helplessness was that behaviourism viewed animals and people as stimulus response machines and as such were unable to learn abstractions. In other words, the realisation that 'nothing I do matters' just didn't fit with behaviourist principles; behaviourism would suggest the dogs would learn how to escape the pain of the shocks habitually. The discovery that their actions had no effect and that there was no point in trying, suggested a more cognitive appraisal of the situation in which they found themselves. To clinical psychologists, learned helplessness looked like depression and the dogs' behaviour mirrored depressive symptoms.

Seligman concluded from this that human beings learn to give up based on their past experiences – the more you get knocked down, the less likely you are to bother getting up. People who suffer the often debilitating and emotionally painful symptoms of depression look at yesterday and see only the bad things; look at the present and see the same; assume that tomorrow (and all their tomorrows) will be equally miserable. Even when they are thrown a lifeline, they rarely grab hold of it, deciding instead to remain in the familiarity of their misery.

Students who fail view failure as the normal state of affairs and are much less likely to try and succeed. The theory of learned helplessness has informed much of what we now understand about depression, as well as providing a useful foundation on which to build upon our knowledge of resilience and perceptions of failure. In this respect, models used to explain and prevent depression can be used to further understand the nature of academic failure and student motivation. A student who works hard but fails to achieve the goals set, develops a way of thinking which assumes that failure is inevitable and that there is no use in even trying. Even more damaging is that even when offered help students will refuse to accept it because in their own minds there is no way out of the situation in which they find themselves. This behaviour may manifest itself in procrastination, disengagement and withdrawal from the learning process, behaviours also seen in people suffering from depression. In a more subtle way, students can feel helpless when the support they had been given previously is then taken away.

The system often creates helpless students

The increase in high stakes testing, an obsession with league tables and the like, combined with the increasing levels of often inappropriate accountability measures, produce pressures on both student and teacher. Practice tests, revision sessions, catch-up classes and so on have become the staple of a teaching profession determined to get students through their exams and other progress checks no matter what. In this scramble to evidence progress and achievement it is only natural that teachers develop ways to smooth the process. Unfortunately, such strategies often develop into systems whereby students believe that achievement isn't possible without this kind of support. Take, for example, a conversation that took place between a year 13 student and myself during a revision session a number of years ago:

Student: Sir, can you do us a list of all the studies that we need to know for the exam?
Me: Couldn't you do that yourself as part of your revision?
Student: Oh yes, never thought of that.

In this situation, helplessness had manifested itself in the assumption that learning is something that is 'done to you' rather than something in which you are a partner. Years of over-support has led to behaviour that could only be described as helpless and the feeling that 'I can't do that so someone must do it for me'. After sharing this experience with other teachers over the years, I have realised that this is neither uncommon nor extreme. One teacher recalled the following exchange:

Student: Miss, I've got to the bottom of the page. What do I do now?
Teacher: Turn the page over and continue on the next one.

We might chuckle at such examples, but these exchanges often hide a much deeper and damaging problem, that over-support encourages helplessness and diminishes independent thought and decision-making. We often also end up with students bereft of confidence in their own abilities. Failure becomes a personal indictment of their own stupidity rather than a normative learning process, and teachers become the crutch, the absence of which will only increase the possibility of failure and continue the cycle of helplessness.

Martin Seligman would go on to become the founding father of the Positive Psychology movement and one of the most influential psychologists of the past century, changing the way we view the human condition and reframing psychology in more positive terms. Understanding these processes is essential to understanding just why people give up and, more importantly to us, why students fail to seek help when it's offered and why they give up trying after even the tiniest setback. It also gives us an insight into how we might create helpless students by being over-controlling, stifling their development and independence of thought and action.

Learning orientations and the pursuit of goals

Previously I alluded to the possibility that emotions might be related to perceptions about our ability to achieve goals and our self-assessment of our position between where we are and where we want to be. If learning goals are related to achievement, then we need to ask the question: 'What is it that needs to be achieved?' For many adolescent learners, the answer is simply success in exams, which becomes more crucial as stakes rise (such as needing certain results to move onto A-levels or the right A-level grades to get that place at university). In wider terms, we need to think about how students view themselves as learners – does one student, for example, view exams as the opportunity to stretch themselves academically and to learn new skills, while another student views exam success as a way of looking competent to family and peers and avoiding the possibility of being viewed as incompetent? To some extent goal achievement must be related to effort; however, what happens if continued effort fails to result in the completion of the desired goal?

This area of psychology, often referred to as self-theory, is a complex one. Many areas related to learning remain fairly concrete and easy to measure, such as memory capacity and duration or attention span. Other areas are more subjective and can only really be measured through self-reporting methods, calling into question the validity of individual responses. One of the most well-known self-theories (at least to teachers and others involved in education and training) concerns implicit theories of intelligence (generally referred to as growth and fixed mindset) and is usually associated with the work of Harvard University psychologist Carol Dweck. The theory itself appears simple enough but is, in reality, an intricate and often complex view of the way in which people view intelligence. According to Dweck, most people fall somewhere on a continuum from fixed mindset (those who believe that intelligence is innate and can't be changed) to growth mindset (those who see intelligence as malleable and success down to effort rather than innate ability). Those learners categorised as possessing a growth mindset are more likely to display a *mastery* goal orientation. A mastery goal-orientated student views learning as a personal endeavour based on obtaining a set of skills or knowledge that has benefit for its own sake, rather than a means of confirming their academic prowess and intelligence over others.

Mindset theory has become one of the most popular whole-school interventions of the past few years. However, it is not without its critics. This is perhaps because it is full of potential but often poorly implemented due to its perceived simplicity. Self-theories are complex because people are complex; furthermore, as young people are in the process of self-building, they often behave in unexpected and unpredictable ways. Critics such as psychologist Tim O'Brien (2015) have suggested that the growth-fixed mindset distinction turns education into the pursuit of turning one thing into another rather than concentrating on effective pedagogy. Another point is that mindset theory can be seen as incompatible with our current education system, leading to what psychologists call cognitive dissonance. Put simply, a system whereby students are placed into ability sets and allocated target grades suggests that their intelligence is a fixed entity (a fixed mindset), while at the same time schools are encouraging students to believe that they can achieve through effort (a gross simplification of the original theory). This creates confusion and anxiety because two conflicting ideas can't be held at the same time. Despite such intense fervour, during 2015 and 2016 even Dweck herself was forced to admit that schools had missed the point, and had simplified her research findings so much that the theory had become almost meaningless in practice.[1] Because of this controversy, it's useful to visit Dweck's earlier research that would later inform her current position.

Before mindsets

Dweck's earlier pre-mindset research is perhaps more pertinent to the discussion of emotion because of what it implies about the learner, the development of the self and its relationship to academic attainment. It is also important because so often education concerns itself with mean differences between certain cohorts (such as classes, schools and even countries). Although these statistics might lead to some insightful distinctions, what is perhaps even more important are the variances between groups of learners. Back in the 1980s Dweck, along with Carol Diener, carried out several studies using fifth and sixth grade children in the United States. They divided the children into two groups based on the outcome of a questionnaire, designed to identify those children who displayed helpless characteristics. The aim was to attempt to separate those children who showed persistence in the face of failure (the *mastery-orientated* approach) from those who tended not to persist when presented with the possibility of failing. The children would then be presented with a number of tasks ranging in difficulty in an attempt to see who would persist and who would give up. More importantly perhaps, Dweck and Diener also recorded the flow of the children's thoughts and feelings as well as their performance.

This early research uncovered a number of fascinating behaviours related to learners and the learning process while at the same time highlighting the dangers of helplessness. When children are comfortable with their learning and can complete tasks or problems successfully, they remain quite confident about their ability and intelligence – this is the case regardless of orientation. Setting goals too low may, therefore, create a false sense of success because challenge is negligible; however, increasing the level of challenge will trigger helpless behaviour in certain learners and mastery behaviour in others. Pupils categorised as helpless begin to act in dysfunctional and damaging ways when things start to get harder and success on the task becomes more elusive. One of the first things these students begin to do is denigrate their own abilities and blame their intelligence (or rather, their perceived lack of intelligence) for their inability to succeed. Dweck and Diener found that children made specific verbal attacks on their own ability such as 'I guess I'm not very intelligent' or 'I'm no good at things like this'. In fact, one-third of the helpless group spontaneously denigrated their own intellectual ability while none of the mastery group resorted to such intense self-criticism. The children in the helpless group had already had a string of successes and it was only when they hit problems and began to fail that they began to lose faith in their own ability. Before they hit problems, their performance was indistinguishable from that of the mastery group; they had rapidly discarded these earlier successes and decided that they weren't clever enough even though their earlier success should have made them feel more confident about their ability. When asked how many problems they had solved successfully, the helpless children recalled more unsuccessful attempts – they remembered their performance as poorer than it actually was. In another study, students were presented with difficult problems first and solvable ones later. It was found that the helpless group was less likely to solve the later problems even though they were easier, indicating that the helpless orientation is a reaction to failure that carries negative implications for the self. Furthermore, it works to impair ability and results in less effective cognitive strategies.

We can get a better insight into how helpless-orientated students cope with failure by examining their on-going verbal responses during the task. Dweck and Diener tracked the thoughts and feelings of their participants as they solved the problems in an attempt to gain an insight into their thoughts and feelings. Change in attitude was rapid in the helpless group once the tasks became more difficult and they started to fail. While the problems presented were solvable the children appeared quite pleased with themselves, but when the problems became difficult they lost interest and complained of being bored. The ways in which they coped with the anxiety and self-doubt that arose once they realised they were having difficulties solving the problems often involved drawing attention to other non-task-related successes. In what appeared to be an attempt to counter the failure experienced in the experimental situation, some children would inform the researchers that they had been given an important part in the school play or had succeeded in some other activity unrelated to the task. Others would try to change the rules or give plausible explanations for giving the wrong answer. Even these young children were found to be making desperate attempts to safeguard their self-esteem or self-worth; in other words, they were trying hard not to seem unintelligent. As a result, the helpless group displayed a significant deterioration in the strategies they used to solve the problems as they increased in difficulty. Interestingly, they didn't appear to objectively decide that the task was too hard for them but increasingly condemned their own abilities, leading them to descend into depression and anxiety (see Dweck, 2000 for a more in-depth discussion of these and other studies).

Learned helpless, therefore, encourages a fixed mindset. Dweck and Diener found that those children who displayed helpless characteristics gave up on tasks when they became too difficult and, in certain circumstances, never even attempted easy problems because they had failed at harder ones previously. For some children, the emotional experience of even perceived failure can lead to feelings of helplessness. Of course, experiences affect different people in different ways (psychologists simply call these *individual differences* and they can plague research studies using human participants).

Early negative academic experiences can therefore influence present and future views of ourselves. When I was 11 years old I was living in the small North Yorkshire market town of Skipton. We had moved north from Oxfordshire a few months previously, after my dad was offered work with the BBC in Leeds. I loved Skipton; its open spaces and the bustle of the high street. Back then the high street was lined with market stalls offering everything from fresh local vegetables to walking boots for the brave souls attempting the nearby Pennine Way. Skipton had also, years earlier, decided to retain the system whereby 11-year-old primary school children were required to sit a school selection exam known as the eleven-plus. The exam would decide whether you were clever enough to attend the boys Grammar School (or the selective Girls High School), or the generally considered inferior secondary modern. Needless to say, I failed the exam and spent the next two years at Aireville, the local secondary modern. When I think back to my childhood, my years at Aireville are generally considered to be happy ones, perhaps the happiest I can recall being. My family left Skipton after two years and I was returned to the normality of the comprehensive system, but inevitably my failure at the eleven-plus influenced my attitude towards education for many years to come. It seemed inevitable that I would leave school at 16 with very few qualifications despite my teachers believing that I possessed 'untapped potential'. Even today, with my clutch of qualifications and postgraduate research experience, I still feel like a fraud – how could someone who failed the eleven-plus be doing what I am doing? Surely, I will eventually be found out!

I suspect that many who failed the eleven-plus have had their education shaped by that early setback just as those who passed it were thankful for it. For those fortunate enough not to have sat such a dispassionate exam, there are surely other factors that informed their view of their own learning. Constant high stakes testing provides overwhelming opportunities for failure and the possibility that students who struggle academically will refuse offers of help. While testing itself isn't a bad thing, and I'll explain why later, the high stakes nature of the testing can put some students at a disadvantage. Constant failure gives rise to the feeling that success is far beyond our reach and no amount of cajoling from amazingly dedicated and compassionate teachers is going to change that. Some students have simply learned that nothing they do matters – it will all just end in failure, so why try in the first place? Just like Seligman's dogs, they become despondent and disengaged, habituated to the pain and with no desire to escape it. As educators, these behaviours frustrate us because it makes us believe that these students simply don't care when, often, they don't care simply because they no longer know how to escape the situation in which they have found themselves. Such students become disengaged, find everything boring and often disrupt other students' learning. Eventually they find themselves in lower sets or streams, reinforcing the view that they will never succeed.

As equally important as those students who display a tendency towards learned helplessness are those students who, despite constant setbacks, refuse to give up. I began teaching Laura psychology and sociology in 2014. A moderately able pupil, Laura found it difficult to achieve despite her positive work ethic. She would engage fully in lessons, attempt to answer the questions I posed to the class and didn't care if her responses were lacking. Unfortunately, Laura failed all of her exams at the end of year 12, a result that would have demoralised many students. Laura, however, wasn't deterred by what she considered to be a minor setback, deciding that the best thing for her to do would be to repeat year 12 and learn from the setbacks of the previous year. Others appear less resilient. Rachael was a grade A student who approached A-levels in a very different way. She was quiet and reserved and fearful of answering questions in class in case she gave the wrong answer and looked stupid in front of her peers. Any work that didn't achieve the highest grade was considered a personal failure, and feedback was seen as a personal attack on her ability to achieve. Despite this lack of resilience and low self-esteem, Rachael still succeeded where Laura couldn't, highlighting the differences in both personality and practical strategy. Whereas Laura saw failure as an opportunity to grow, Rachael viewed failure as something from which she could never recover. Ironically (and as we will see), it is possibly the anxiety and fear of failure that drove Rachael to achieve in the end.

I have taught many a Laura and a Rachael; they are the diverse products of our education system and represent its extremes. They also emphasise the diversity amongst learners in that they are both hard workers with admirable work ethics and yet their outcomes are very different; if we widened the spectrum of attitudes and motivations to all learners, it's highly unlikely that we would ever find two who approached learning in exactly the same way. Whereas there appears to be something in some students that inoculates them against learned helplessness, there are others who appear much more prone to it. The polar opposites of optimism and pessimism are perhaps what distinguish

Laura from Rachael; while Laura holds the view that next time she will do better, Rachael expects failure. In the language of Dweck, Laura displayed a mastery orientation while Rachel displayed a helpless orientation. Despite this, it was Rachel who ultimately achieved top grades while Laura just scraped through. The reasons for this are understandably complex. Fear of failure can motivate as well as hold us back because the primary aim becomes one of avoiding the negative emotions experienced when we fail. We also mustn't neglect certain innate, born-with predispositions including the thorny topic of general intelligence and wider issues such as strong support mechanisms including parental support and family influences.

With others, it might be something very different that holds them back, such as levels of motivation, home life, peer-pressure – let's be honest, the list is endless. In his book *The Optimistic Child* (2007) Martin Seligman recounts an influential conversation he had with Jonas Salk, the American virologist who developed the first effective polio vaccine. Salk suggested to Seligman that children shouldn't only be vaccinated physically; they should also be vaccinated psychologically. Laura, you will recall, struggled to do well while Rachael always seemed successful, but while Laura accepted advice and saw failure as a chance to improve, Rachael viewed even the suggestion of failure as the end of her world. Psychologically, Laura seemed immune to learned helplessness, not because she was always successful, but rather because she was rarely successful. It is a similar situation with resilience in that those children who regularly experience adversity are more likely to become more resilient to it. Such anecdotal observations don't add much to our understanding of learned helplessness, but they do force us to ask more interesting questions.

Seligman proposes that the antidote to the 'epidemic of pessimism' is the acquisition of optimism and that optimism can immunise children against learned helplessness. In fact, the most widely trialled resilience intervention in the UK was adapted from the system developed by Seligman and his colleagues in the US. The programme attempted to provide protection against depression and other psychological problems involving learned helplessness with optimism being the key ingredient. Despite disappointing results in the UK, the intervention package continues to be used by many schools. Briefly mentioned in Chapter 1, the Penn Resiliency Project (PRP), so-called because it was developed by researchers at the University of Pennsylvania, is an intervention that attempts to teach children certain cognitive and social skills drawn from cognitive-behavioural therapy (CBT). CBT is perhaps the most widely researched and understood of the psychological therapies and works by re-appraising situations and attempting to frame them in more realistic ways. It has proven successful in the treatment of psychological disorders such as anxiety and depression and is often the preferred choice of many healthcare providers. The PRP does appear to produce positive results and a number of studies, including several randomised controlled trials, have found that the programme can reduce symptoms of anxiety and depression in children. Nevertheless, results are often inconsistent, with some children benefitting more than others. Furthermore, it appears to have little impact on academic achievement.

Threats can feed learned helplessness

Some schools might inadvertently encourage learned helplessness and failure avoidance through the very same teaching strategies that are supposed to help students achieve. An emphasis on success might motivate some learners, but not others. In fact, psychologists Dave Putwain and Richard Remedios found that so-called *fear appeals* (emphasising the consequences of failure, such as 'if you don't get good A-level results you'll never get to university') are much more likely to lead to lower levels of motivation; on the other hand, stressing that the consequences of success can lead to higher levels of motivation (although it doesn't appear to raise academic levels directly) (Putwain & Remedios, 2014).

Carol Dweck's early work investigated the different ways in which helpless and goal-orientated learners approached problems. Other psychologists working in the area of motivation and learning have identified two specific goal orientations (see Table 2.1). These appear to influence the way in which learners approach the goals set for or by them. The first is known as the *performance goal* orientation (similar to the helpless group in the Dweck and Diener study and the orientation displayed by Rachael in the previous example) while the second has been labelled the *mastery goal* orientation (already discussed briefly earlier). The primary aim of the performance goal learner is first and foremost to demonstrate their competence or to avoid looking incompetent. Furthermore, performers tend to select activities that are easier and therefore represent a higher chance of success. For performers, success is everything, even if that success comes about because they have chosen a task that is below their capabilities. Revising and preparing for exams might include constantly going over the same material because they already know it rather than moving onto a topic they don't fully understand. In a similar way, given the choice between a task that requires little cognitive investment and one that takes a great deal of effort and thought, the performer would be more likely to choose the latter. The performer might claim that a particular task is pointless or stupid or say that they just can't be bothered with it. Those displaying a mastery goal orientation, however, are more likely to choose more challenging tasks and persist at them; the primary aim here is to attain a new skill, one that requires dedication and persistence. So the child who constantly complains that it's pointless to become skilled at algebra because he is never going to use it again, is more than likely anxious about others in the class viewing him as unintelligent because he struggles with algebra, whereas another child perseveres because she wishes to master the techniques of algebra regardless of its future utility.

Table 2.1 Summary of learning orientations.

Mastery orientation	*Performance orientation*
• Emphasis on improving skills and developing competencies.	• Emphasis on demonstrating competence.
• Learning for its own sake.	• Avoids situations where failure might arise.
• Doesn't compare ability with others.	
• Displays resilience when tasks become difficult.	• Feels confident when the task is easy.
• Chooses difficult, challenging tasks.	• Gives up when the task becomes more difficult.
	• Chooses easy tasks over difficult ones.

Andrew Elliot, a psychologist at the University of Rochester, further developed the view of mastery and performance orientations, in part due to the inconsistency of the evidence linking performance goals to a number of other motivational constructs (for example, Elliot and McGregor, 1999). Elliot proposes a trichotomous model that further differentiates between *performance approach, performance avoidance* and *mastery goal orientations.* It's important for us to understand that this separating out of the two performance goal orientations grew from the inconsistencies within the research involving the performance-only goal orientation; essentially the original distinctions were unable to be explained in terms of research findings.

Performance approach goal orientations represent the individual's attempts to demonstrate competence (through the strategies already discussed) while performance avoidance orientations represent attempts to avoid being seen as incompetent. Goal orientations fundamentally alter the way learners view achievement situations, having a knock-on effect on the ways in which individuals approach learning situations and, ultimately, achievement outcomes. While those students displaying performance goal orientations will continue to avoid challenging tasks as a means of demonstrating competence, performance avoiders are more likely to disengage and withdraw from the learning process entirely. The performance avoidance orientation has also been linked to a number of other outcomes, including shallow processing, poor retention of information and performance decrements (Table 2.2).

Table 2.2 Two types of performance orientation.

Performance approach	*Performance avoidant*

• Aims to demonstrate competence.
• Avoids challenging tasks in order to appear competent.
• Engages in the learning process but gives up when the level of challenge increases.
	• Aims to avoid failure.
	• Avoids being seen as incompetent.
	• Disengagement and withdrawal from the learning process.
	• Leads to:
	  o Shallow processing.
	  o Poor retention and performance.

Mastery goal learners, on the other hand, are expected to enhance their achievement through placing a greater value on improving their skills and developing competencies. Not only that, but, as Andrew Elliot and Carol Dweck discovered, they are also more likely to display greater levels of persistence and employ more advanced cognitive strategies, leading to the deeper processing of information. Furthermore, empirical evidence has discovered that those students who focus more on trying to develop competence are more resilient in the face of challenge and are more likely to employ higher-level cognitive strategies such as elaboration, critical thinking and self-regulated learning. All this would suggest that a mastery goal orientation is directly related to higher levels of achievement; however, the evidence doesn't necessarily support this view. Lisa Linnenbrink-Garcia, a psychologist at the University of Michigan and one of the foremost researchers into emotions and motivation, analysed seventy-four correlational studies, finding that only about 40 per cent of them showed a positive relationship between mastery orientation and academic achievement, with 5 per cent showing a negative relationship (see Tyson *et al.*, 2009). This would certainly imply that there is some benefit to mastery goal orientation, but in research terms the results are not deemed statistically significant. In other words, the effect is too small, so we can't be sure of any causal relationship. Frustratingly, there is also some concern over the relationship between performance approach goals and academic outcomes, with some studies showing a positive correlation between performance approach goals and cognitive regulation, while other studies have found no significant relationship or even a negative relationship.

It might be prudent here to take a wider look at the research process and discuss why studies investigating the same things are drawing different conclusions. It may surprise you to know that this situation is far from uncommon and that many meta-studies (an analysis of several studies on the same topic) will often highlight conflicting results. The research process is a complex one, and we must take into account that some of the studies that make up the meta-analysis may have been conducted in slightly different ways; they will certainly have been conducted using different samples (that is, people). Furthermore, a meta-analysis often sets out to reveal such inconsistencies in order to move the research forward and advance the theory. Inconsistent findings don't necessarily mean the theory is flawed; it can mean that things are more complex or nuanced than the theory originally proposed. So the research for both mastery goals and performance approach goals is in conflict with academic outcomes; the findings for performance approach goals have also been inconsistent in term of persistence. If you remember, those students displaying a performance approach orientation were less likely to persist with a task once the going got tough and much of the research supports this view. However, while in many studies those performance approach students were more likely to withdraw or opt out of a task and to withdraw their time and energy after experiencing failure, other studies found no significant relationship between performance approach orientation and effort. Just to make things even more complicated, Elliot found a positive relationship between performance approach goals, effort and persistence.

Mediating factors

The main problem we face is that there appears to be no strong relationship between performance approach orientations and achievement. There is certainly an emotional component at play and this could provide us with a way to reconcile these findings. It appears that while some learners are able to successfully regulate possible debilitating emotions, others are unable to do so, leading to less effort and persistence and the feeling that the task is somehow unworthy of their efforts. Mastery goal-orientated learners are less likely to develop debilitating emotions because they view learning as a challenge and something to become skilled at – they view difficulty and challenge as a vital part of the learning process rather than something that exists in order to trick them or to reveal their incompetence to the world. They also see failure as part of the route they must take in order to reach the goals they have set for themselves. In their model of achievement emotions Diana Tyson, Lisa Linnenbrink-Garcia and Nancy Hill proposed that mastery learners are more likely to evoke positive emotions due to the way they view difficult tasks; they don't need to regulate debilitating negative emotions because such emotions are much less likely to arise (Tyson *et al.*, 2009).

However, the assumption here is that all negative emotions are debilitating and those who successfully regulate them are more likely to achieve. As we shall see, the picture is perhaps a little more complicated than this.

The role of self-esteem

It would be difficult to conclude this chapter without a more detailed discussion surrounding the issue of self-esteem, or at least the feeling of self-worth. How students feel about themselves should have an impact on matters related to school and the learning process, yet the reality is more nuanced. There are many definitions of self-esteem dating back to the earliest days of modern psychology, but we can generally think of self-esteem as being related to a person's subjective appraisal of himself or herself as intrinsically positive or negative. William James (one of the founding fathers of what we now call psychology) described self-esteem as being related to our own personal views of success; the more success we achieve, he suggested, and the lower our expectations, the higher our self-esteem. To feel better about ourselves we either have to succeed more in the world or downsize our hopes. This is the view that self-esteem is about both 'doing well' and 'feeling good', further developed by Nathaniel Brandon (Brandon, 1997) as:

- Confidence in our ability to think and to cope with the basic challenges of life (doing well); and
- Confidence in our own right to be happy, the feeling of being worthy, deserving, entitled to assert our needs and wants and entitled to enjoy the fruits of our efforts (feeling good).

Self-esteem can also be seen as a multifaceted construct. Susan Harter (Harter, 1999) has suggested that there exist *domains of self-esteem* consisting of scholastic competence, athletic competence, social acceptance, physical appearance and behavioural conduct. Harter's model is useful because it suggests that self-esteem can differ from situation to situation so that a student might have high scholastic competence but low athletic competence and that this might be influenced by elements related to physical appearance and body image. Psychologist Tim O'Brien (2015) is also mistrustful of the concept of a single global self-esteem, insisting that people don't have a self-esteem that is either high or low, but rather multiple self-esteems (see further reading, p.236). Instinctively, people understand this; it makes sense even though we still cling to the idea of self-esteem as a global construct. This view would also support the notion of a type of self-esteem specific to learning known as *academic self-concept*, which I discuss in more detail later.

If we (reluctantly) view self-esteem as a global construct, how does it impact academic outcomes? The (very) short answer is that it doesn't, at least not directly. Some studies have found a positive correlation, but these tend to be in the minority and have been heavily criticised due to the poor way in which many of the studies were carried out. More generally, however, there appears to be little evidence to suggest that those students with higher levels of self-esteem do any better academically. People with high levels of self-esteem do tend to be happier, but we are yet to fully understand the direction of causation. Certainly, low self-esteem is related to higher levels of depression and there is a relationship with stress and anxiety. Interestingly, high levels of self-esteem in childhood and young adulthood do result in a higher tendency to experiment and therefore doesn't prevent children from drinking alcohol, smoking and taking drugs, but rather increases the chances that young people will engage in these and other risky activities. On a positive note, high levels of self-esteem do appear to reduce the chance of bulimia in females. Some of these might indirectly impact educational outcomes by nurturing positive behaviours towards school and schoolwork, but don't impact directly.

Despite many positives, it would appear more likely that high self-esteem arises from good academic performance rather than high levels of self-esteem being responsible for higher levels of academic success. Furthermore, efforts and interventions designed to help boost self-esteem in underperforming students have sometimes been found to be counterproductive, in that they have lowered academic performance (for an interesting review of the literature on self-esteem and academic achievement, see Baumeister *et al.*, 2003). It's likely that students with very high levels of self-esteem are poor at making realistic judgements regarding their future success and, therefore, overestimate their abilities (so-called defensive optimism which I discuss in detail in Chapter 10). The main problem here is one of causal direction; it is often difficult to establish direction in correlations so we never quite know for sure if high self-esteem is what leads to better academic outcomes, or that better academic outcomes raise levels of self-esteem. What is more important, perhaps, is that some studies have found that high self-esteem can lead to lower academic outcomes and the possibility that many people with higher levels have a dysfunctional view of themselves. This can be seen in research that finds people scoring higher on measures of self-esteem also claim to be more attractive, more likable, to have better relationships and to make a better impression on people than those showing lower level of self-esteem. When these beliefs are challenged using objective measures, however, they are disconfirmed, suggesting that such individuals can appear charming at first but have a tendency to alienate others eventually.

O'Brien (2015) also points to the negative consequences of being told you have low self-esteem. Often such labels are used flippantly and without any thought to their implications. Telling a child they are shy can impact negatively on the way that child sees her or himself, especially considering the negative cultural implications that are attached to being shy. While what we describe as shyness might have multiple causes (including a predisposition towards introversion), there is little reason why it should be imbued with negative connotations. In a similar way, being told that you have low self-esteem can result in anxiety and the reinforcement of limiting behaviours. As we have seen, high self-esteem can be just as damaging as low self-esteem, so it might be wise to reject the idea of self-esteem altogether and adopt a more focused approach.

From self-esteem to self-concept

Viewing self-esteem as a consistent global construct, therefore, provides us with a highly unreliable way to measure the way students feel about themselves and it is much more appropriate to think of self-esteems. A very specific type of self-esteem related to learning is academic self-concept, the view we have of ourselves as learners. Academic self-concept builds up over time and is based around our personal experiences as learners, so favourable experiences of education would lead to higher levels of academic self-concept, more confidence and more adaptive coping strategies. It also appears that academic self-concept is state rather than trait specific (although there is somewhat of a debate surrounding this). In other words, high levels of academic self-concept in one domain (for example, English) won't necessarily mean that levels are high in another domain (maths, for example). This is because our experiences of these subjects might be significantly different and have, therefore, shaped our attitude and ability in diverse ways. I, for example, have always harboured a love of reading and writing. By the time I was 7 years old I was writing my own stories and dabbling in (very bad) poetry. My father was a journalist so he earned a living writing; it's hardly surprising that I grew up with a love of the written word and, for a while at least, thought I would follow in his footsteps. When I began secondary school things changed and, although my early high school days were wonderful, I fell out of love with English for a while.

His name was Mr Hume. I didn't dislike him and I didn't think of him as a bad person, but most of our lessons were spent taking dictation concerning the correct usage of the comma, semi-colon and countless other symbols, many of which I have rarely used since. That said, I probably owe my over-use of the comma to Mr Hume as well as my ability to recite from memory 'I must endeavour to remember to furnish myself in necessary scholastic requisites' (I was required to write it out 100 times on several occasions). Once a week we had an hour of silent reading, a wonderful respite from the hand-numbing note taking that usually took place. I was used to writing stories, not writing notes in record time and in illegible handwriting. My confidence waned and I decided that perhaps a career in writing wasn't for me.

My belief in my abilities in English peaked and troughed over the years, but my academic self-concept remained relatively high. Maths was a different matter altogether. Try as I might I could never excel with numbers and I struggled for most of my teenage years. Later on, I would make a real effort to improve and by the time I was studying for my degree I had managed to handle complex statistics and analysis as well as most of my peers. Nevertheless, my experiences have informed my beliefs and I still view myself as more confident with the arts and humanities than the sciences (despite having a science degree).

Our academic self-concept is personal to us, but feedback from teachers can influence how confident we feel in a particular domain. Being truthful about the ability of a student in a particular subject is vital if we are to avoid building academic self-concept beyond realistic parameters. There has been a great deal written recently about praising effort over ability and I would be the first to support and promote this strategy. Nevertheless, building the belief in ability over and beyond what is realistically achievable lures students into a false sense of security and turns positive emotions in on themselves. If a student is struggling to achieve a grade C in maths, telling them that with more effort they can get an A is pushing expectations beyond reasonable limits. After all, the student might be putting enormous amounts of effort into their work and still only managing to scrape a C on assessments. Confidence is useful and positive; over-confidence or misguided confidence can rapidly turn a positive into a negative.

Emotion as a mediating factor

Educational research is a complex thing, and often what we expect to happen never materialises or doesn't materialise in the precise way we expected it to. There is always a lot of noise in the data when we study people and this is clear when we examine more closely the relationship between mastery and performance orientations. What Tyson and her colleagues have indicated is that there is a mediating role played by another variable and they suggest that this variable is emotional. Essentially, the orientation isn't quite enough to make that causal leap from mastery to achievement, but the way in which learners evoke certain emotions might provide that elusive causation. The danger is that we dehumanise the individuals we are studying, treating them less like people and more like data. Not all learners will behave in the way we expect them to (for example, performers do achieve), but we can attempt to discover some fairly stable predictions. Other groups can also appear equally baffling. The assumption is that people make decisions based on logic, yet it appears that in many circumstances their decisions are based on emotions. Nowhere is this more evident than in voting behaviour, be it general or local elections or national referendums. Why, then, should we assume that students make complex decisions based on the weighing up of evidence? Psychologists often speak of individual differences: they are a nuisance but are also the main reason why psychology as science has many problems that traditional sciences such as physics and chemistry don't experience. There is some predictability about humans (you can see that with street magicians and so-called mentalists), but often, human behaviour is less predictable than we expect, especially when fuelled by emotions. We can identify general rules of behaviour, but, as any teacher will tell you, there is always someone who breaks them.

Throughout this book I will attempt to offer some guidance on how to work with emotions in mind. The strategies suggested all view mastery as desirable and they work towards this goal. Mastery orientation isn't a thing we can give to students, but we can nurture an environment that makes it more likely. In this chapter, I have indicated that the missing link is, indeed, emotion itself and I suggest that it is the emotional experience of learning (and living) that gives rise to success and failure and how these very concepts are viewed.

Chapter summary

- Constant failure can lead to learned helplessness, the feeling that failure is inevitable and nothing the student does will change this. Learned helplessness encourages a performance learning orientation whereby students feel they need to prove their competence (performance approach) and avoid failure (performance avoidant) at all costs.

- A performance learning orientation results in students engaging in easy activities that fail to challenge, so that they can prove to others that they are competent.

- Encouraging a mastery learning orientation places the emphasis on improving skills and developing competencies. Students displaying a mastery orientation view failure as part of the learning process and are more resilient to setbacks.

- Mastery and performance orientations have been reconceptualised as *growth* and *fixed* mindset.

- Students with a fixed mindset view intelligence as innate and unchangeable while students with a growth mindset view intelligence as malleable, placing the emphasis on effort rather than being clever.

- Teachers can encourage a growth mindset through a number of strategies, including praising effort over intelligence. However, praise must be used sparingly and only given when it is deserved.

- Emotions mediate between growth and fixed mindset orientations.

- Strategies and interventions can only be effective when applied at a whole-school level.

- Raising self-esteem in students is rarely an effective strategy; however, nurturing individual academic self-concept can lead to positive outcomes.

Note

1 Dweck wrote a number of articles for the *TES* during 2015 and 2016 clarifying her theory.

References

Baumeister, R.F., Campbell, J.D., Krueger, J.I. & Vohs, K.D. (2003). Does high self-esteem cause better performance, interpersonal success, happiness, or healthier lifestyles? *Psychological Science in the Public Interest* 4(1), pp.1–44.

Brandon, N. (1997). *How to Raise Your Self-Esteem*. London: Random House.

Dweck, C.S. (2000). *Self-Theories: Their Role in Motivation, Personality, and Development*. Hove, UK: Psychology Press.

Elliot, A.J. & McGregor, H.A. (1999). Test anxiety and the hierarchical model of approach and avoidance achievement motivation. *Journal of Personality and Social Psychology* 76(4), pp.628–644.

Harter, S. (1999). *The Construction of the Self: A Developmental Perspective*. New York: Guilford.

O'Brien, T. (2015). *Inner Story: Understand Your Mind. Change Your World*. CreateSpace. Online.

Putwain, D. & Remedios, R. (2014). The scare tactic: Do fear appeals predict motivation and exam scores? *School Psychology Quarterly* 29(4), pp.503–516.

Seligman, M. (2002). *Authentic Happiness*. London: Nicholas Brealey

Seligman M. (2007). *The Optimistic Child*. Boston, MA: Houghton Mifflin.

Tyson, D.F., Linnenbrink-Garcia, L. & Hill, N.E. (2009). Regulating debilitating emotions in the context of performance: Achievement goal orientations, achievement-elicited emotions, and socialization contexts. *Human Development* 52(6), pp.329–356.

Positive and negative emotions

Nothing thicker than a knife's blade separates happiness from melancholy.

(Virginia Woolf, *Orlando*)

I'm about to suggest that positive and negative emotions don't exist and that our subjective experience of all affective states can be thought of as good and bad dependent upon the situations in which they arise. I'm also going to admit that I don't believe happiness exists as a stable consistent affective state and that our pursuit of it can only end in failure. This isn't a particularly popular position to adopt, especially as it means that much of the personal development and self-help industry might actually be wrong. Even our subjective wellbeing shifts across a continuum, as Virginia Woolf suggests, a continuum that sees happiness and misery as only a hair's breadth apart. A slap in the face isn't always negative; after all, the distance between pleasure and pain isn't very far at all.

This view is, of course, in direct opposition to early Positive Psychology. Over recent years a significant shift has taken place in psychology in terms of emphasis. Traditionally, psychology has concerned itself with maladaptation, that is, attempting to identify and classify disorders and then treat people when things go wrong. Clinical psychologists concern themselves with individuals suffering often devastating consequences of mental illness and the impact this has on the sufferer and those around them. However, this began to change in the early part of this century with the advent of Positive Psychology with its emphasis on wellbeing and the unending pursuit of happiness.

There does appear to be a relationship between the prevalence of positive emotions (or the absence of negative ones) and academic achievement. Relationships like this, however, can be misleading and what we need to take into account is that correlations don't necessarily imply causation. What I mean here is that it's one thing to examine correlations and claim the variable A (a positive affect) is related to variable B (academic achievement), but it's quite something else to make the leap from a relationship to a causal factor. There are many spurious correlations floating around out there, for example, piracy on the high seas was common in the sixteenth century but has been in decline ever since. The drop in the number of pirates coincides with the rise in global average temperatures, which has been attributed to global warming. Is it reasonable, therefore, to suggest that the decline in the number of pirates has caused global warming? Hopefully your answer is a resounding no, but if it isn't then I think you need to seriously rethink your understanding of both pirates and global warming. This is a rather silly example but does highlight the danger of accepting correlations in the absence of causation; can we explain why the fall in the number of pirates has led to global warming? Of course we can't. In a similar way, can we explain how positive emotions encourage higher academic achievement?

Psychologist Barbara Fredrickson was one of the first researchers to attempt a theoretical model of how and why positive emotions lead to improved emotional wellbeing and a greater capacity to bounce back from adversity. Drawing on findings from Positive Psychology, Fredrickson explains the relationship within a framework she calls *Broaden and Build* (Fredrickson, 2004). Emotions have an evolutionary function related to survival; our stone-age ancestors lived in dangerous times and needed to constantly adapt to their surroundings. Emotions such as fear acted as a survival mechanism, allowing early humans to escape potentially life-threatening situations, while anxiety kept them alert and constantly on the lookout for danger. When such danger presented itself (such as a wild animal intent on a large portion of human being for dinner), the stress response would activate in order to prevent our ancestor from ending up on the dinner table. Stress activates the fight or flight response, summoning up stores of adrenaline and cortisol, and dampens down unnecessary functions in order to divert resources to those parts of the body needed to attack or (more often) to run as fast as possible in the opposite direction. Emotions such as fear, therefore, narrow our responses in any given situation, essentially providing us with just two options – higher functions are less important in these kinds of situation (you can't reason with a sabre-toothed tiger) while running as fast as the body allows remains a greater priority.

Negative emotions such as fear and anger narrow our choices (what Fredrickson calls our *thought-action repertoire*), while positive emotions like joy, curiosity and interest broaden them. As they broaden, so they build, leading to the accumulation of further psychological repertoires. In other words, positive emotions lead to positive adaptations and the storing of blueprints that can be activated should an appropriate situation arise in the future. We can, therefore, think of these repertoires as a type of psychological capital. In the same way that we can accumulate monetary or cultural capital, so we can also accumulate positive psychological ways to deal with as yet unknown specific situations. Employing positive emotions regularly to cope with different situations allows us to add to the resources available, ready for use in the future when we encounter the same or similar situation. Allowing difficult situations to arise, therefore, encourages people to adapt to these changing situations and ensures that they are better equipped to deal with similar situations in the future. Preventing problematic experiences, on the other hand, stunts personal growth and inevitably backfires when difficulties are eventually encountered.

To illustrate how this might work, let us take a student (let's call her Ellie) who panics when presented with a difficult maths problem. Our prehistoric ancestor detects a threat (a particularly problematic algebraic equation) and immediately activates the stress response. Ellie is now becoming more anxious, adrenaline is rapidly being secreted from the adrenal gland, her hands are shaking and beads of sweat are beginning to form on her forehead. The brain is telling her that higher order functions aren't needed here, so her working memory dampens down and rational decision-making climbs into the back seat. Ellie has become the victim of her anxiety, making it extremely difficult to concentrate on the equation. As we'll see, however, some of this anxiety is useful to Ellie. As it happens, Ellie is rather curious about this particular equation, and although she is still finding it difficult she has activated a number of more positive emotions such as curiosity and interest. These other emotions push her along and keep the anxiety at a much more appropriate level. Eventually, Ellie completes the task and her experience is stored within her toolkit of repertoires for future use.

Children raised in adversity often become more resilient due to their experiences and their adaptive ways of dealing with difficult life experiences, so the more often students hit brick walls and roadblocks, the greater the need for psychological capital and the use of positive emotions. Some students are more resilient than others and can manage setbacks better; however, many struggle and require help every step of the way. Fredrickson would argue that it's our evolutionary right to be happy (a suggestion that we might have to argue against a little later). Positive emotions, therefore, serve a number of interconnected functions to do with personal growth and development and general wellbeing. Fredrickson also suggests that positive emotions can undo negative ones, due to our inability to experience two conflicting emotions simultaneously. A student who, for example, is particularly interested in a subject and finds the experience of learning joyful, cannot experience fear, stress or anxiety over his or her studies. Furthermore, a student who is plagued by anxiety and fear is less likely to view setbacks as productive and much more likely to see them as a direct attack on self-esteem and self-worth. Consequently, positive emotions feed resilience and the determination to overcome obstacles that ultimately increase the chances of success.

There's a very strong argument here suggesting that positive emotions aid learning and negative emotions hinder it. Fredrickson's model appears sensible and somehow fits comfortably with what we understand about our own emotions; after all, emotions like anger and anxiety are destructive, aren't they? Making distinctions between positive and negative emotions can be useful; the problem is that emotions are far too complex to be thought of in such a dichotomous way. Many negative emotions are far from maladaptive. Fear, for example, doesn't always lead to the dark side. In fact, without fear our ancestors would have been sabre-toothed tiger fodder pretty much every day. Emotions like anxiety and fear exist for our survival, raising our levels of adrenaline and transporting essential sugars to the muscles that are used for a quick getaway. Sure, chronic anxiety becomes debilitating and humans can become ill if levels of adrenaline and cortisol remain high for too long. Nevertheless, an optimum amount of anxiety quickens our responses, heightens our awareness and fuels our cognitive processes. But when anxiety levels pass that optimum threshold, our cognitive functions become impaired. I discuss anxiety in more detail in Chapter 6. The problem is that behaviour and affective states really don't work this way.

Perhaps it's not a matter of positive or negative affect, but rather the ratio of one to the other? It has been claimed that a healthy ratio between positive and negative affect is around 3:1, while anything below this ratio represents languishing rather than flourishing. This would mean that you can do pretty well so long as you experience more positive emotions than negative ones, and if you adopt this view then we can assume that the same would be applicable to the pursuit of goals – you have your anxiety, just so long as you have joy and curiosity as well. This was the suggestion posited by Fredrickson and Chilean psychologist Marcel Losada in what became known as the *critical positivity ratio* or *Losada Line*. The problem is that it's simply not supported by the data.

This view did hold steady for a number of years before Nick Brown, a graduate student in Applied Positive Psychology, thought that the mathematics of the theory seemed a little dodgy. Along with Alan Sokal, a professor of mathematics at University College London, and psychologist Harris Friedman, Brown re-examined the data presented by Fredrickson and Losado as well as previous papers by Losada that also referred to the critical positivity ratio (Brown *et al.*, 2013). Their findings disputed the mathematical method adopted by Losada, rendering the theory invalid. While Losada remained silent, Fredrickson responded to the criticisms, claiming that she didn't have the necessary expertise to defend the findings and accepted the theory was flawed. The Losada Line controversy casts further doubt on the reliability of the Broaden and Build theory despite Fredrickson standing by the general idea. Like much of Positive Psychology, the view that positive emotions are somehow superior to negative ones simply doesn't stand up to scrutiny.

The happiness fallacy

Happiness is preferable to being miserable, right? This was the assumption in the early days of Positive Psychology, as well as suggestions that happy people are more successful, have more fulfilling relationships and live longer. While some of these suggestions might be supported by rigorous longitudinal studies, many more are based on erroneous correlations. It might be hard to accept but happiness isn't always a good thing, and this suggestion might seem counterintuitive seeing as we all want to be happy and engage in behaviours that will (to a certain degree) lead us in the right direction. One of the problems with such an endeavour brings us back to the idea that emotions are based on the pursuit of goals, the assumption being that positive affect is in some way preferable in this pursuit. The problem arises when we realise that positive emotions can actually interfere with long-term success because the emphasis is often placed on short-term goals.

Another problem is that happy people display a tendency towards lazy thinking. This revelation runs somewhat counter to some of our earlier discussions and causes problems with reconciling the view that happy people are lazy thinkers, which doesn't fit well with Fredrickson's view that positive emotions broaden and build psychological capacity. According to this alternative view, happy people tend to rely on superficial strategies in order to collect information from the outside world and are more likely to employ stereotypes than their unhappy counterparts. In fact, some negative emotions may actually enhance certain types of learning as Sandi Mann of the University of Central Lancashire discovered when she found that boring activities could enhance creativity (see

Chapter 7). Furthermore, research conducted by Elizabeth Kensinger, a psychology professor at Boston College, discovered that negative life events are remembered better than positive ones; negative affect actually enhances memory (Kensinger & Corkin, 2003). Laboratory studies have also found that items thought to be negative (for example, a poisonous snake) are more likely to be remembered than neutral items (like a picture of a door) or positive items (like an ice cream) as well as negative emotions leading to fewer errors in recall (I'll discuss this in more detail in Chapter 4).

Studies have also found that happy people are much more likely to resort to stereotypes when evaluating some situations. Christian Unkelbach conducted an experiment using a *shoot 'em up* computer game where participants were told to shoot characters carrying guns (Unkelbach *et al.*, 2008). The interesting part of the experiment was that some of the characters were wearing turbans (displaying the stereotypical image of Muslims). Happy people were more likely to shoot the characters wearing turbans (even if they were unarmed) than less happy individuals. Apart from revealing some very sad truths about the destructive nature of stereotyping, the so-called *Turban Effect* also suggests that people who display higher levels of positive affect are less likely to judge the situation in any real depth, unconsciously choosing instead to activate stereotypes stored in long-term memory and fuelled by current events and media representations.

If happiness can interfere with cognition and learning, can sadness enhance it? By sadness we don't mean the debilitating depression that ruins the lives of so many people each year. Depression, as we have seen in a discussion on learned helplessness, impairs cognitive function, reduces motivation and leaves us feeling drained. Sadness, on the other hand, is a mood state that fluctuates quite rapidly, often within the same day. I'm going to use the term *negative affect* here just so we can be sure about what we mean. Negative affect is rarely thought of in favourable terms and often we wish to snap out of those inexplicable bouts of low mood. We often attempt to help our friends and loved ones to raise their spirits if they seem down because we rarely view such a state as adaptive or useful. In classrooms we quite rightly identify pupils who might be upset or showing signs of low mood, the symptoms of which could suggest a deeper psychological problem (although only in rare cases). Most bouts of low affect lift rapidly and the child who seems sad in the morning will be laughing and joking with her friends by lunchtime. But could these occasional episodes of negative affect actually enhance learning?

As it turns out, low affect can lead to positive consequences, certainly in terms of cognitive processes. Joseph Forgas, a psychologist at the University of New South Wales, has conducted a number of fascinating studies into the impact of negative affect on a number of cognitive and social psychological behaviours. In one study, Forgas asked people to recall items they had seen in a shop. In the first condition, the task was carried out on one of those grey rainy days when most of us feel a little down and perhaps even in a bit of a bad mood. In the second condition, and in an identical situation, the task was carried out on a bright day. Forgas found that the rainy day condition resulted in a larger recall tally and that memories for items were in much greater detail than the same task carried out on a sunny day (see Forgas, 2013 for a number of interesting studies). The suggestion is that while positive mood impairs memory, negative affect somehow enhances it. Convinced? Perhaps the participants in the second condition were just eager to get out into the sun and enjoy the good weather, impairing their attention and making them impatient?

In a second study, participants were shown a photograph of either a car crash or a wedding. Later on, the same participants were asked to recall either a happy memory or a sad memory from their past in order to shift their mood into either negative or positive affect. They were then asked a series of questions about the photographs including some misleading information (for example, asking about an object that didn't appear in the photograph). The use of misleading information is common in studies that test the accuracy of eyewitness testimony, and research conducted over the past 30 years or so has found that many people are highly susceptible to such information. Whereas studies of this kind tend to focus on interview techniques, Forgas was interested in how negative or positive mood would impact on recall. It was discovered that those participants who had recalled a negative memory from their past (the negative-affect group) were better able to recall the original details and were much less likely to be influenced by the misleading information. Participants in the positive-affect group, on the other hand, were much more likely to recall details that had been contaminated with the false information. Psychologists have known for some time that our memory of the past can be altered by false information given later on (and it's surprisingly worrying how the human brain effortlessly slots these details in, forever altering our memories of these events). However, Forgas managed to prove that our mood can either make us more or less susceptible and that negative mood appears to protect against the formation of false memories. Studies like this would also support the view that happy people are lazy thinkers because the susceptibility to false information indicates that happy people are paying less attention and are less focussed when processing information.

It turns out that it's not just memory that is influenced by emotion; negative affect can also make us better at judging other people's motives and also turns us into more efficient lie detectors. In another study, participants were asked to detect deception in videotaped accounts of people accused of theft. Those participants displaying negative affect were not only more likely to reach a guilty judgement, they were also better at detecting lies and other deceptions than those in a more positive mood. In yet another study, participants were given 25 true and 25 false trivia statements and asked to rate the likely authenticity of each statement. After they had made their judgements all participants were given the right answers. Two weeks later only those participants with low mood were able to distinguish between the previously seen true-false statements. Positive mood participants displayed a greater tendency to rate all their previously seen statements as true. The study indicates that negative affect decreases the tendency to believe that what is familiar is also true, while positive affect appears to increase it.

Negative affect also makes people less susceptible to certain judgemental or cognitive biases such as the fundamental attribution error (the tendency to attribute behaviour to an individual rather than to circumstances). It also makes us less likely to relate certain positive attributes (such as being smartly dressed) with other factors (being intelligent). The so-called *halo effect* can certainly have detrimental consequences in the classroom, such as associating the scruffy boy at the back of the class with low levels of achievement. Finally, negative affect can reduce primary effects caused when people place too much emphasis on early information and ignore later details.

Negative affect also leads to a more detailed and attentive thinking style. Not only is low mood better for memory processing and recall, and protecting us from stereotyping and bias – it also appears to make people more motivated. This perhaps makes more intuitive sense than some of the other research I've discussed. After all, if we are motivated by the pursuit of happiness, what happens when we achieve it? The problem with happiness is that it makes us too comfortable; we strive for it, and if we eventually reach our destination, the likelihood is that we will find that it's so damn good that we will want things to stay exactly how they are. Becoming settled in the status quo means that there is little motivation to move on, in fact, moving on might lead to less happiness. Sad people, on the other hand, have something to strive for and aim towards: that small but personally significant achievement that lifts the spirit for a moment, filling us with good vibes and a more acute feeling of self-worth. Happy people (if they really exist at all) have no real need to deal with challenge in their environment, while those with a more negative mood are more motivated to challenge them-selves and push for change in order to lift their mood.

In another study conducted by Joseph Forgas, participants watched either a happy film or a sad film and were then given a demanding cognitive task to complete. The task included a number of questions that had no time limit, so participants could spend as long on them as they wished; this would measure their perseverance levels. They were then assessed on total time spent on the questions, the number of correct answers and the number of questions attempted. I suspect that by now you can pretty accurately guess the results. Those participants who watched the happy film (let's call them the *happy group*) spent less time on the questions, attempted fewer questions and received a lower score than the *sad group*. It seems that people are less motivated to exert effort if they are already experiencing a positive mood; those with a more negative mood, however, have more to gain from persevering in terms of elevating their negative affect.

There are many other instances where seemingly negative emotions produce positive and adaptive behaviour. For example, pessimism better prepares you for major setbacks and failures while jealousy can motivate you to achieve because, for example, you can't handle the fact that someone else is doing a better job than you. A student might witness a classmate obtaining high marks on a test and work harder in order to obtain a better grade than them next time. This particular kind of jealousy (known to psychologists as *benign jealousy*) can often lead to positive consequences due to the motivation it instils in other people.

It's clear that emotions impact behaviour in more complex ways than first envisaged. In fact, it appears that the only thing we can be clear about is the lack of clarity. Emotions do impact learning and behaviour, but it is perhaps fruitless to attempt to classify emotions as either positive or negative. If emotions are related to the pursuit of goals, then we must consider the possibility that some negative emotions are more suited to certain situations than positive ones. Certainly, when preparing for confrontation, negative emotions are more suited to resolving some issues and positive emotions are perhaps less useful when we want to persuade someone to change their opinion. In fact, anger can be a useful emotion in conflict resolution, especially when we note that anger rarely leads to aggression. Studies have found that positive outcomes tend to arise from anger and allows for the separation between the person to whom the anger is directed and the behaviour that has prompted the anger.

It is less likely that we can guarantee a positive outcome when complaining to a company about poor customer service if we insist on being bright and bubbly; showing our frustration and disappointment at the service we have received seems more appropriate in this situation. Similarly, displaying anger when discussing pupil progress with a parent is unlikely to lead to a fruitful meeting. Anger, therefore, might be useful in confrontational situations; anxiety, on the other hand, might allow us to take precautions against looming danger, giving us time to prepare for a difficult meeting or other potentially problematic situations. As we have seen, even sadness can prove functional either by activating important higher-level cognitive functions or by eliciting help when faced with difficulties.

Katie was perhaps one of the most able and motivated students I have ever had the pleasure of teaching. She was dedicated and hard working, curious and questioning. There were also two sides to Katie. One side I saw most often, the friendly, chatty Katie who loved her friends dearly and helped them out when they struggled. The other side of Katie was very different and ruled by her anxiety. You could almost feel the tension rising inside her as she became irritable, short with her friends and withdrawn. This wouldn't last for long but would always culminate in Katie bursting into tears and running from the classroom. Her friend would give me *that* look, I would usually nod and she would follow Katie to the toilets or the sixth form common room. The Katie who returned was happier, more motivated and contented than the one who had run from the classroom, and her progress would jump up a notch. Those staff who had taught Katie since year 7 would tell me that this was the way she coped; it was also the way she achieved. Her anxiety motivated her to a point, but when it passed that magical optimum she would wobble and break down before balancing out again. This was the strategy that worked for Katie and, although it can be thought of as maladaptive, it does illustrate how some people use negative emotions to push themselves forward.

The reality is that positive emotions don't always motivate and they certainly don't always lead to higher levels of academic achievement. Sometimes we have to rely on negative emotions to do this. In some respects, the emotions we usually think of as adaptive mechanisms can actually turn out to be maladaptive. Confidence can be very positive in learning environments and we often praise students for it, but when that confidence leads to the framing of situations within unrealistic parameters it can lead to disappointing outcomes. Some years ago I taught a young man called Josh. He was a very capable student and had chosen A-level psychology as a fourth subject (one that he intended to drop after year 12). He was also studying maths, physics and chemistry and was progressing very well in these subjects. Psychology was going to be his least demanding lesson, he assured me, because all of his other subjects were highly challenging. But his confidence in his ability to succeed in them was very high, so much so that he felt that real effort was unnecessary when it came to psychology (which wasn't a *real* science anyway). In terms of his three main subjects, his confidence was a positive attribute; he knew he could succeed because he was realistic about the challenges involved, but he assumed he would do well in psychology and simply didn't do the work he needed to obtain a good grade. Although Josh passed psychology, his grade was lower than for his other subjects because of his unrealistic framing of the situation. A few years later I received an email from Josh telling me that he was studying for an MSc in cognitive neuroscience. He admitted to me that he didn't work as hard in psychology as he should have done; his confidence had turned to over-confidence and this negatively impacted on his level of motivation and engagement.

Beyond positive versus negative

Feeling good and happy is certainly a desirable state in which to find ourselves, but being aware of their capacity to restrict certain outcomes is a useful strategy. This poses a huge dilemma for parents and teachers because neither would wish children to be unhappy and I'm in no way suggesting this. However, I would advise against assuming that by raising levels of positive affect in children we can ensure that they perform better academically. There is a strong relationship between wellbeing and academic success, but that doesn't necessarily mean happy children get better grades; things are always much more complicated.

You might be wondering why we took the time to look in-depth at the Broaden and Build theory and then insist that is was flawed. Emotions are complex (as you are probably beginning to realise) and pinning down their influence on behaviour is fraught with problems, especially when linking them to learning and young people. Keeping a critical and open mind prevents us from falling into the trap oft seen in education where theories are accepted out of hand with no real evidence to support them. Most school teachers aren't researchers and have to rely on others to guide them towards what works and what doesn't. Unfortunately, many of the teaching strategies employed in schools for decades have been bereft of any solid evidence. At least now if someone attempts to convince you that you need a healthy ratio of negative to positive emotions, you are well equipped to send them packing.

At the beginning of this chapter I presented the hypothesis that positive emotions help towards the achievement of academic goals by expanding our thought processes and allowing us to invest in psychological capital. Negative emotions, on the other hand, restrict these options, leading us into either–or situations (Broaden and Build). However, there is a problem with this suggestion because positive emotions don't always help and negative emotions don't always hinder. Could it be that the usefulness of emotions changes in response to the situational conditions? This is an interesting proposition and one that brings us back to the suggestion that classifying emotions as either positive or negative represents an error in our understanding of their complex nature.

Reinhard Pekrun has spent much of his academic career investigating the tangled web of emotions and motivation. While emotions influence motivation, these effects might be different for different types of positive and negative affect, suggests Pekrun (Pekrun *et al.*, 2007). What he means by this is that in certain circumstances both negative and positive emotion can either activate or deactivate our motivational responses. On the other hand, deactivating negative emotions such as hopelessness and boredom can undermine motivation. So far so good – this appeals to our common sense and current understanding. For some emotions, however, the interaction is more complex. Pekrun suggests that positive emotions such as relief and relaxation deactivate motivational responses and that these responses have both long-term and short-term consequences (Pekrun *et al.*, 2007). For example, a student might experience relaxed contentment after having taken an important test, reducing immediate short-term motivation and a reluctance to re-engage with schoolwork. However, this same emotion may well motivate the student to engage at a later time. Remember Josh? His confidence activated his motivation for maths, physics and chemistry because he viewed those as challenging subjects, but he didn't see psychology as particularly challenging so his confidence became a deactivating positive emotion.

Pekrun describes such emotions as *achievement emotions* due to their emphasis on academic goals (Pekrun *et al.*, 2007). These emotions can arise during both activities and outcome. An activity, therefore, might result in curiosity if the students find the task interesting, or boredom if the demands of the task are mismatched (too easy or too difficult). Outcome-related achievement emotions arise when an activity (for example, a test) has been completed and the outcome known. This might include joy or pride at the favourable result or anger at the seemingly insurmountable task demands. As well as achievement emotions differing in terms of activity and outcome, they also differ in terms of valence and activation. Valence refers to the extent to which an emotion is seen as positive or negative, pleasant or unpleasant. Activation refers to the extent to which the emotion was activating or deactivating (see Table 3.1).

In the same way that positive-deactivating emotions can hamper motivation, some negative emotions can strengthen extrinsic motivation. Anxiety, as we have seen, can negatively impact on academic achievement; however, it can also motivate if the expectation of the

Table 3.1 Positive and negative emotions.

Object focus	Positive		Negative	
	Activating	*Deactivating*	*Activating*	*Deactivating*
Activity focus	Enjoyment	Relaxation	Anger Frustration	Boredom
Outcome focus	Joy Hope Pride Gratitude	Contentment Relief	Anxiety Shame Anger	Sadness Disappointment Hopelessness

outcome is likely to be a positive one. In these circumstances, fear of failure motivates because there is a very real chance of success and not achieving the anticipated success would be viewed as a personal attack on intelligence and self-worth. This is interesting because this view argues that emotions react in different ways in regard to different types of motivation. Intrinsic motivators in learning (a personal desire to engage with activities because of individual interest or the joy it brings) tend to be preferable due to their resilience and long-term sustainability, while extrinsic motivators (the desire to succeed based on a reward for doing so) are often short-lived and can backfire when incentives are withdrawn. The research underpinning the view that anxiety can enhance extrinsic motivation has produced variable results, perhaps due to the subjectivity of the evaluation of possible success. Of course, if the student feels that success is less likely, then anxiety is assumed to lead to lower level of activation or, worse still, deactivation because of the feeling that failure is inevitable (I'll look at motivation in more depth in Chapter 5).

We began this chapter with a simple hypothesis: positive emotions lead to higher levels of academic achievement. What started out as a fairly straightforward suggestion proved to be more complicated than anticipated because the idea of positive and negative emotions being separate from each other turned out to be an unhelpful distinction. Emotions are more accurately described as affective states and the dichotomy of positive and negative emotions turns out to be false when we take the evidence into account. Positive Psychology was certainly founded upon laudable principles, but its foundations are weak and unable to support many of its ideas. When we delve deep enough we discover a highly complex yet fascinating situation where positive emotions sometimes hinder and negative ones often help, amounting to a direct attack on the view that happier learners are more successful. We do, however, need to stress the view that severe negative emotions such as chronic anxiety and depression do negatively impact on both wellbeing and academic achievement (and while I do discuss these in more detail later, the impact of severe psychological problems is beyond the limitations of this book). Emotions, as I have already stated, are slippery characters and should be treated with a degree of respect; negative mood is not a bad thing but when an individual spends the majority of their time in this state then problems can ensue – I'm not advocating that teachers should induce negative states just to raise levels of achievement, but neither should teachers fall into the trap that all positive emotions are useful in all circumstances.

The theory proposed by Pekrun is perhaps the most useful for our purpose (Pekrun *et al.*, 2007). Learning is without doubt influenced by emotions just as all human behaviour is influenced by our emotional states. These states fluctuate wildly and are involved in an intricate interplay of biology and environment that will impact on the pupils in a classroom in highly diverse ways. Furthermore, the complex brain and self-building during the teenage years can make these emotional states more volatile, but this isn't inevitable, so teenagers deserve special consideration (see Chapter 9 for a more in-depth discussion of teenagers). The view is that emotion has activating and deactivating qualities (regardless of their positive or negative nature). Recognising and working with these states is part and parcel of the teacher–learner relationship, and encouraging emotional awareness in both teachers and learners allows us to better utilise states that we seemingly have little control over. Eradicating certain emotional states is unhelpful and will often backfire; removing components from the curriculum because they are too sensitive or anxiety-provoking is also unhelpful, yet deliberately placing young people into anxiety-provoking situations to make them more resilient is equally erroneous.

Chapter summary

- Emotions can be seen as positive and negative, but it is more useful to view them as activating and deactivating.
- Happy classrooms don't necessarily result in better academic outcomes.
- Emotions such as anxiety can both activate and deactivate and recognising both the negative and positive consequences of these emotions can enhance learning in the long term.

References

Brown, N.J.T., Sokal, A.D. & Friedman, H.L. (2013). The complex dynamic of wishful thinking: The critical positivity ratio. *American Psychologist* 68(9), pp.801–813.

Forgas, J.P. (2013). Don't worry, be sad! On the cognitive, motivational, and interpersonal benefits of negative mood. *Current Directions in Psychological Science* 22, pp.225–232.

Fredrickson, B.L. (2004). The broaden-and-build theory of positive emotions. *Philosophical Transactions of the Royal Society of London. Series B, Biological Sciences* 359(1449), pp.1367–1378.

Kensinger, E.A. & Corkin, S. (2003). Effect of negative emotional content on working memory and long-term memory. *Emotion* 3(4), pp.378–393.

Pekrun, R., Frenzel, A.C., Goetz, T. & Perry, R.P. (2007). The control-value theory of achievement emotions: An integrative approach to emotions in education. In P.A. Schutz & R. Pekrun (eds) *Emotion in Education* (pp.13–36). San Diego, CA: Academic Press.

Unkelbach, C., Forgas, J.P. & Denson, T.F. (2008) The Turban Effect: The influence of Muslim headgear and the induced affect of aggressive responses in the shooter bias paradigm. *Journal of Experimental and Social Psychology* 44(5), pp.1409–1413.

What we think and what we feel

The complex relationship between cognition and emotion

As heady as our progress has been, we need to stay completely honest with ourselves and acknowledge that we have only discovered a tiny fraction of what there is to know about the human brain.

(V.S. Ramachandran, *The Tell-Tale Brain*)

It's around 4:30pm on Wednesday 13th September 1848 and 25-year-old Phineas Gage is with his railway construction gang building the bed for the Rutland to Burlington railroad in Vermont, USA. The gang are preparing to blast a cutting through the large rocky outcrop and Gage, the foreman, is deciding where to drill the holes in the rock and how much gunpowder will be needed in each one. He'll place the powder and the fuse into each hole and very gently *tamp* it down using a tamping iron before sand is added. He'll then give it a more vigorous tamping. The tamping iron is three feet seven inches long and weighs 13-and-a-half pounds. It's tapered at one end and Gage uses the larger end to gently compact the powder. Gage is momently distracted and he begins to tamp the powder and fuse before the sand has been poured; the tamping iron strikes a rock that in turn causes a spark to ignite the powder. The resulting explosion propels the tamping iron out of the hole through the unsuspecting

Gage's head, entering just under the cheekbone and exiting through the top of his skull. The tamping iron continues its journey, landing about twenty-five feet behind its victim.

The punch line, if it can indeed be described as a punch line, is that Gage survives. He loses consciousness momentarily, but his gang carry him to an ox-cart before transporting him to a nearby inn where he soon begins to regale onlookers with the story of his accident. But Gage is no longer Gage. The man once described as 'strong' and 'active'; a man with an 'iron will' (unfortunate term under the circumstances), a 'capable foreman' with a 'well-balanced mind' has changed. Gage is now 'fitful', 'irreverent' and 'grossly profane'. He is 'impatient' and given to abandoning future plans. That part of the brain that made Gage, well, Gage, has been damaged beyond repair. The story of Phineas Gage highlights the complexities of the human brain and where that vital component resides that makes us who we are. Gage's motor functions remained largely unaffected, but his personality took a distinct turn for the worst. Unable to regulate his emotions and prone to fits of anger and violence, Gage never returned to his job on the railroad and, instead, bounced from one job to another.

The story of Gage illustrates some important points. First is that brain structure is, to a certain extent, one of localisation, that is, specific parts of the brain are responsible for certain functions; damage incurred through injury or infection can effectively knock out certain functions. Second, it highlights that who we are is an interaction between all parts of the brain, not just those related exclusively to memory and learning – learners aren't cognitive machines any more than they are stimulus-response machines; they are so much more than that.

Cognition is perhaps what we tend to think of when we discuss learning. Certainly, there has been a growth of interest from teachers over the past few years with regard to processes such as memory, attention and problem solving. Cognitive psychology concerns itself with thought processes and how these manifest themselves in certain behaviours. A variety of these processes is linked to specific regions of the brain in a concept known as functional localisation. For example, Broca's area is a region located in the frontal lobe of the dominant hemisphere and is said to be responsible for speech production (although, once again, it's much more complicated than that). Damage to certain regions of the brain, therefore, can cause impairment of one function but not another, so a person could lose the ability to create new memories if that specific region of the brain is damaged but maintain the ability to access previously stored long-term memories. Traditionally, there has been a tendency to think of the brain as either *affective* or *cognitive*, and the general view has been that these functions reside in different regions. For example, the pre-frontal cortex is associated with cognitive functions while the amygdala has been associated with emotion (including the fear response and emotional memory). Brain structures related to emotions are subcortical and often described as primitive, having responsibility for many of the automatic responses that we are often unaware of. But it's not as simple as all that either. The amygdala is the emotional centre linked to fear processing (it's the part that decides what is a threat and prepares the body for action); the complicated part is that the amygdala is also linked to attention and learning. Similarly, regions of the brain once thought to deal only with cognition have recently been found to play a role in emotion as well. Rather than thinking of the brain as either cognitive or emotional, it's far more likely that complex cognitive-emotional behaviour emerges from the dynamic interactions between the two networks, specifically at areas with a high degree of connectivity (areas known as *hubs*).

This view of the brain has important implications for learning by emphasising the relationship between how we learn and how we feel. If we return to the role of the amygdala, for example, this particular brain architecture suggests that fear will also impact on our attention and learning processes. Similarly, attention is linked to memory, so this is why high levels of anxiety can impair the functioning of working memory.

When thought and feeling part company

David was a student of the highly celebrated neuroscientist V.S. Ramachandran who spent two weeks in a coma following a car crash. As Ramachandran explains in his book *The Tell-Tale Brain* (2012), once David came out of his coma he appeared to display few of the cognitive impairments common to injuries of this kind. David could think clearly, was alert and attentive, he could understand what was said to him, recognise objects and people, and could read and write. The only visible deficit was slightly slurred speech. That was, however, until David met his mother. 'Doctor', he would say to Ramachandran, 'this women looks exactly like my mother but she isn't – she is an imposter pretending to be my mother'.

David displayed similar behaviour towards his father, but nobody else. He suffered from a curious disorder called Capgras syndrome, first described by French psychiatrist Joseph Capgras in 1923. Early explanations of the disorder included one drawn from Freudian psychodynamic theory suggesting that it represented the repression of a man's sexual desires towards his mother (the Oedipus complex) but, as Ramachandran points out, this didn't explain why another patient of his suffered from the same delusion towards his pet poodle *Fifi*. As it turns out, there is a more sensible anatomical explanation for David's condition that involves neural pathways and the way in which memory and the associated emotional responses interact (or don't in the case of David). When visual information enters the brain via the optic nerve, it is first sent to a region known as the fusiform gyrus; this is where the brain processes objects, including faces. The output from the fusiform gyrus is then sent to the amygdala (the emotional centre of the brain) where the information is processed and the appropriate emotional response attached. In David's case, part of the pathway connecting the fusiform gyrus to the amygdala had been damaged in the accident and while the part connecting meaning and language had remained intact, the connection between perception and emotion had been severed. This damage resulted in David being able to recognise his mother but without the emotional connection. David's brain then had to somehow reconcile this mismatch between what he was seeing and what he was feeling; the only logical and rational explanation for David was that an imposter had replaced her.

Knowing a person is so much more than just recognising them, so much more than simply retrieving their trace from long-term memory. When we see someone we have some kind of emotional reaction because we have some kind of emotional connection; we might feel delight at seeing them or despair when we spy them walking down the corridor towards us but, no matter what our reaction, there is always emotion attached. If the emotion is taken away, we recognise the person but fail to *know* them – recognition isn't necessarily the same as knowing – it goes much deeper than that (and this has wider implications for classroom strategies such as rote learning). Memory, therefore, is as much about emotion as it is about cognition, and how or if we recall something accurately is, in part, an emotional response. Emotion is also about knowing ourselves; being able to look in the mirror and for the sight of the figure staring back at us to evoke the mental response, 'That is me'. For many of us such a sight evokes lots of different emotions and thoughts: 'Am I looking old?' 'Am I looking tired?' For young people, the sight of themselves in the mirror can often cause anxiety about being too fat, too thin or not being pretty enough to be considered worthy. When I was a teenager I had the most terrible acne and would stare into the mirror as the spotty youth stared back at me and think, 'What girl could ever fancy a boy with a face like a pizza?' Whatever we think when we see ourselves, we know who that person is because we possess an emotional connection to that person just as we do to our family, friends and all the people we know. What if we looked in the mirror and didn't feel that emotional connection? Ramachandran once met a man named Ali at a hospital in Chennai in India with a similar condition to David; only Ali was convinced the he was, in fact, dead. Ali was suffering from a condition known as Cotard syndrome, sometimes macabrely called *walking corpse syndrome*, that appears to share many of its characteristics with Capgras syndrome, only this time not even the feeling of *being* elicits any emotional response. In fact, people suffering from Cotard syndrome pretty much lose interest in everything; viewing art, listening to music and reading literature fails to evoke any emotional response at all; looking in the mirror only results in the feeling of a stranger staring back.

Throughout this book there is an assumption that cognitive and emotional brain networks are intricately linked. Additionally, the term *non-cognitive skills* is used more for the sake of convenience, as we can quite convincingly argue that all skills have a cognitive as well as an emotional component. It's therefore highly problematic if we assume that cognition and emotion are completely separate entities; it's also highly irresponsible to neglect the role of social interaction and elements related to social psychology, seeing as learning rarely takes place in isolation. There is a disturbing tendency growing in some sections of education that emphasises the role of cognition above and beyond all other social and psychological influences. Certainly, the role of cognition constitutes the largest proportion of the learning process, but in order to complete this highly complex tapestry it needs to be recognised that other factors also play an important part.

Memory and emotion

The cognitive function most relevant to learning has to be memory (although others such as attention and perception are also important). For this reason, this chapter will concentrate on the ways in which emotions can enhance and limit our ability to process, retain and access information. I don't intend to describe theories of memory here or explain the different models that exist in cognitive psychology – there are other education books that do justice to these topics (for example, Smith and Firth, 2018). This chapter is intended to offer some explanations of the way internal states (that is, emotions) affect our memory, and I'll introduce some of the research related to it. This chapter also comes with a warning attached, one that you might not come across very often, especially if you glean much of your knowledge about memory and learning from online sources like blogs. The warning is this: the majority of research studies into memory are conducted in laboratory-type situations and are therefore highly controlled and artificial environments. There is also a tendency for researchers to draw their participants from their own student population (usually, but not exclusively, psychology undergraduates). Very few studies are carried out in real-world environments (like schools, for example) so we can't always assume that research findings will translate directly into the real world. In research terminology, such studies lack *ecological validity*. Many of the studies conducted into explicit memory for emotional experiences have been conducted in this way, often by asking participants to recall previously presented negative, positive and neutral stimuli; however, there have been several studies that have asked people to recount real events. Despite such weaknesses, research can certainly provide some indication as to the power of emotions to enhance or diminish our ability to recall information, more specifically, in the quantity, the quality (or vividness) and the amount of accurate detail remembered about a prior event.

Memory doesn't live in a specific spot in our brain, we can't crack open the skull, point and say 'Ah, that's where my memories are'. The *things* that make up our memories are distributed throughout the brain; however, one of the most important areas is a region known as the hippocampus. Apparently, the hippocampus looks like a seahorse (hence the name), although I've never really been able to see the likeness. It forms part of the limbic system and is said to build and store cognitive maps. Eleanor Maguire, a cognitive neuroscientist at University College London, conducted a four-year study on London taxi drivers to examine areas of the brain related to mental mapping. Maguire and her team scanned the brains of taxi drivers during the time in which they studied for *The Knowledge*, a test all trainee London taxi drivers must pass, involving the memorisation of tens of thousands of streets in the capital. The researchers found that the hippocampal region of the brains displayed significant differences by the end of the training period in terms of grey matter volume – the hippocampus was actually bigger and this was attributed to the information they were required to learn (Maguire *et al.*, 2000). The hippocampus, therefore, is pretty important and we know that damage to it can lead to anterograde amnesia (the inability to make new memories). It's also vital to what is known as *memory consolidation*, which is the process by which memories are converted from short-term memory to long-term memory. Although it's possible to form new semantic memories (memories related to meaning) without the hippocampus, we can't form episodic (autobiographical) memories without it, that is, those memories related to the events of our lives.

Another important component (certainly for us) is the amygdala – the so-called emotional centre of the brain (although this is a gross oversimplification) that is also associated with emotional learning and memory. The amygdala responds strongly to fear so it's also important for other aspects of learning such as anxiety and the fear of failure. It's also involved in the encoding and enhancement of emotional memories, leading to the deeper and more accurate processing of emotional events, although (as we'll see later) they aren't always as accurate as we think they are. The fragile nature of emotional experiences and events means that they take longer to fully set into memory so the consolidation process is much slower, allowing our emotions to influence the way in which the memories are stored. The amygdala, therefore, encodes recent emotional information into memory, enhancing the emotional aspects of it during the process.

It might surprise you to know that, in general, our memories aren't as good as we like to think they are. While there are some people with exceptionally good memories (for example, super-recognisers have the astonishing ability to remember faces), most of us have to cope with a fairly average ability to remember things. We can practice strategies and tricks that might win us a prize at the World Memory Championships (yes, there really is such a thing) but being able to recall thousands of random digits or memorise a dozen decks of playing cards won't turn you into a genius. Strategies, however, don't always work – I recall being quizzed as a child on the geographical term for a piece of land jutting out into a river or stream; I confidently insisted that it was called a stirrup because I had associated the word with horse riding (it is, of course *spur*; perhaps my love of old westerns helped to contaminate my memory). Cognitive psychologist George Miller found that most of us are capable of holding around seven chunks of information (seven plus or minus two, to be precise) in our short-term memory at any one time, but that was back in 1956; Nelson Cowan more recently suggested that it's more like four (Cowan, 2000). Memories are not snapshots and our brains don't act like cameras; they take new information, assimilate it with already stored information, plug gaps, reconstruct events and spit them back out with emotional baggage attached. Our working memory (the short-term dynamic store we use to manipulate information in real time) can easily become overloaded; we can become distracted, lose attention, allow our minds to wonder or simply zone out from time to time. When we're anxious our memory works better, but when we're too anxious it doesn't work so well. Our brain also processes positive, negative and neutral events differently but recalls them differently as well – sometimes more and sometimes less accurately.

All memories are not created equal

Research has found that recall rates tend to be higher for both positive and negative stimuli than for neutral stimuli, indicating that emotions are playing some role in the accuracy of memory. This also seems to be the case using a variety of stimuli including words, sentences, pictures and narrated slideshows. Many such studies also investigate the use of autobiographical memory – essentially the memory of the events of our lives, where similar effects to the ones for other stimuli have been found. For example, when people are asked to generate memories in response to cue words, retrieved memories are often rated as personally significant and emotional. Emotion, therefore, can impact on what we remember because of the boost our feelings give to our ability to recall. This is why we are much more likely to remember positive and negative events and much less likely to recall neutral ones. Not only is this supported by research, it also makes a great deal of intuitive sense – happy events and sad events have greater meaning for us while a boring meeting or a lesson about a topic that holds little interest fail to produce that emotional hook that can suspend the moment in time and space.

It would appear that the *valence* of an event influences the likelihood that the event will be remembered and operates like a boost to our ability to recall. Valence is concerned with the extent to which an event elicits a positive or negative response or the extent to which we consider something to be pleasant or unpleasant. If, for example, I showed you a photograph of some puppies and asked you to rate your immediate emotional response to it on a scale of, say, one to ten, I would expect you to rate it quite high (even if you were fearful of dogs). If, on the other hand, I were to show you a photo of a door, it's unlikely that the image would elicit a particularly high emotional response. I could also ask pupils about the extent to which a recent lesson (or, more likely, a learning episode) elicited an emotional response. Pupils might have found that they experienced no emotional response (apart from, perhaps, when Danny was leaning back on his chair and ended up on the floor), or they might have experienced extreme excitement, interest or even mind-numbing boredom.

In laboratory studies that assess memory for verbal and pictorial stimuli, negative items are more likely to be recalled than positive ones, but in studies assessing memory for real-life autobiographical events there is a greater tendency to recall positive events. This contradiction highlights some of the complexities of memory research and the problems that can occur when different methodologies are used to assess similar tasks. One possible explanation for these conflicting findings is that our memory mechanisms have evolved to encode and retrieve information that is most relevant to our goals. Remembering negative events might actually aid our survival and wellbeing by helping us to plan for the future and avoid similar events from occurring. However, sometimes positive events might be more relevant to the pursuit of goals than negative ones, and research has found that when positive and negative stimuli are equally related to current concerns they appear to be equally attended to. Furthermore, if people are seeking a positive goal state (success, for example), it appears that they are more likely to show better memory for positive events in comparison to negative events. In fact, this would be consistent with our current understanding of depression, in that depressed people dwell on the negative events in the past and project that negativity into the future. You may recall that this is a state recognisable in people with learned helplessness – positive goal states aren't seen as either realistic or achievable because past events are viewed in such a negative light.

Results from studies can also be supported (to an extent) through neuroimaging, and although the use of brain scans to support explanations of behaviour remains fraught with problems and inconsistencies, there are certain *knowns* that can help us to understand what is going on in the brain when we process emotive events. To explain this, we have to briefly return to that magical seat of emotional processing, the amygdala. The amygdala, it would appear, is specifically related to memory for emotional but not neutral information and damage to this region leads to no boost for emotional information. In other words, while healthy people derive an enhancement in their recall abilities via the amygdala, this effect disappears in those people who have suffered damage to it. People with such damage are no more likely to remember positive and negative events than they are to remember neutral ones. This absence of emotional memory enhancement has also been found in patients with focal amygdala damage and in those with amygdala atrophy (essentially the wasting away of the amygdala) caused by Alzheimer's disease. From these observations, it would appear that the amygdala plays an important role during the encoding stages of emotional information, that is, when the memory is converted into a form that can then be laid down as a concrete memory trace. This is consistent with studies that have found greater amygdala activity during the viewing of emotional items that in turn leads to greater emotional memory enhancement. Emotional items that also elicit the greatest amygdala activity during the encoding stage are much more likely to be remembered, and the amygdala appears equally active during the successful encoding of both positive and negative information.

As we have seen with disorders such the Capgras delusion, brain regions don't work in isolation, neither do regions of the brain only deal with cognitive processing and others with emotional processing. The amygdala, for example, also deals with rewards-related information and with threat-related information (so it also plays a role in the perception of fear of failure). The amygdala's interaction with other parts of the brain allows it to modulate both sensory and mnemonic functions. This in turn increases the likelihood that emotional information is perceived and retained as a stable memory trace. Our brains, it would seem, are designed to utilise emotional reactions to enhance other functions such as memory and attention and allow us to recall more information when it has been attached to an emotional reaction.

Interestingly, this would also suggest that negative memories are rarely, if ever, repressed in the way described by some psychology traditions and used liberally by the entertainment industry as a backdrop to many a thriller and murder mystery – traumatic events are more likely (not less likely) to be remembered. Emotions, therefore, allow us to recall more, but do they also increase the quantitative nature of those memories, that is, do we remember emotional events more vividly and are they more accurate as a result?

So how accurate are our memories for events? I'm sure that I recall the birth of my son in perfect detail while at the same time remaining fully aware that my memories are also reconstructed. I recall a tiny human looking up at me, frowning and letting out a single and seemingly very violent hiccup. Some of the moments are incredibly vivid, while others are hazier. Ethan was born just shy of a month early, much to the dismay of his Mum who was hoping for at least a couple of weeks maternity leave to rest up and prepare for the impending chaos. In the end he couldn't wait, and arrived shortly after 7 a.m. on 8th September 2001. He was born a little bit jaundiced with a very faint yellow tinge to his skin, so mother and baby remained in hospital for a couple of days before finally being discharged on the evening of the 10th. This meant that 11th September 2001 was our first full day at home with our new baby. You might have already realised where I'm heading with this anecdote, because for the vast majority of the world's population this is a date that will forever be etched into their memories. I was in the kitchen making a cup of tea when Vanessa called from the living room (where she was sat with Ethan) watching the television. She was a little confused; they were saying that a plane had crashed into one of the towers of the World Trade Center in New York. The events that followed have become part of the history of the early twenty-first century, events whose repercussions echo through time. We sat and watched the events unfold, wondering what kind of world we had brought our son into. This kind of memory elicits a strong emotional change, seemingly creating a memory that is both highly accurate and long lasting. Known as *flashbulb memories*, such events might not be as accurate as the name suggest.

The problem with flashbulbs

Are these my real memories of that day or are they an amalgamation of different sources and the result of the constant retelling of the story? Did subsequent news footage through the years taint and contaminate my memory of the day? Vanessa would succumb to a brain tumour four years later, so there remains no independent corroboration of events. Nevertheless, my memories of that day appear so clear and vivid to me, as if they were literally branded onto my brain. In 1977, Roger Brown and James Kulik coined the term flashbulb memory to describe the vivid recollection of a surprising and consequential event. Some events, they argue, are so colossal and evoke such a strong emotional response that they somehow become etched into our memories in vivid and exceptional detail. As it turns out, however, these so-called flashbulb memories are just as prone to the same distortions as other memories. Ulric Neisser, the father of cognitive psychology, described how he recalled listening to a baseball game on the radio when he first heard about the Japanese attack on Pearl Harbor in December 1941; the problem for Neisser, however, was that December was outside the baseball season so his memory of the event must have been inaccurate (it has been suggested that he was actually listening to a football game). The point is that quantitative assessments might underestimate the influence of emotions because they don't take into account the qualitative influence of emotion on memory. What I mean here is that emotion might have a greater impact on the vividness of our memories rather than on the number of things we remember, even though such memories would still be prone to distortions. Of course, we all remember things in a slightly different way and recollections of the same event will differ from person to person.

I remain quite confident that my recollection of those few days in September 2001 are reasonably accurate, despite a lack of independent corroboration. Nevertheless, these so-called flashbulb memories are curious things. In studies where people have been tested for both their confidence in accurately remembering a momentous event and their ability to be consistent in their recollections, one thing doesn't always lead to another. If I were to have been tested on my recall over the past 14 years or so, would my memories have been consistent – would I have told the same story each time? The answer is *probably not*. In fact, the more confident I am that my memories are accurate, the less likely they are to be. Over the years I have retold that story hundreds of times (if not more) and each time I tell it, the greater the likelihood that it is slightly different to the telling that preceded it. Not only that, but our brains abhor a vacuum and will insist on plugging gaps with likely scenarios. This is why eyewitness testimony has been found to be consistently inaccurate – if we didn't get a good look at the bank robber, our brain will anxiously scroll through all the likely suspects and stick their face onto the head of the criminal we didn't even see. This is what Jennifer Talarico and David Rubin found when they interviewed 54 students from Duke University in the United States about their memories of first hearing about the 9/11 terrorist attacks. They had them record both their memories of the specific event plus an everyday memory (one with no particular emotional whack). They were then tested again up to 32 weeks later. Both memories declined over time but ratings for vividness, recollection and accuracy of memory declined only for the everyday memories; importantly, confidence in their ability to be accurate over time failed to match consistency. Despite these inconsistencies there is certainly an enhancement to be obtained if the event is attached to an emotional reaction. British cognitive psychologist Martin Conway asked people to recall their memories of when they heard about the resignation of UK Prime Minister Margaret Thatcher. UK citizens displayed a greater emotional response to the news than non-UK citizens and also showed greater consistency over time, suggesting that the emotional component was important for the vivid recall of the memory (see Talarico and Rubin, 2003).

Successful recognition, of course, doesn't require a vivid memory of the event and most of the time we rely on the gist of it rather than an accurate memory. However, we can recognise an item because we vividly remember the situation in which it was presented to us. In fact, simply knowing that we've seen something before is sufficient.

In research studies where people are asked if they both recognise an item and vividly remember the time when the item was presented to them, rates of remembering tend to be much higher for emotional pictures or words than for non-emotional ones. There is, therefore, a relationship between the emotional aspects of the item or event and the vividness of the memory. This goes some way to explaining why we are often drawn to people who remind us of pleasurable events or even because they perhaps wear the same aftershave or perfume as someone to whom we are already close. My father, for example, used to smoke a pipe (yes, people really did do that once) and even today, the smell of pipe tobacco has the magical effect of making me feel calm because it reminds me of a time that was more relaxed and carefree. The smell also prompts me to recall pictures of my dad sitting in his armchair, smoke bellowing around him. Of course, it also works in the opposite way; aspects of a person might trigger negative memories, prompting us to stay clear of them.

In common with many of the topics covered in this book, we appear to be faced with as many questions as we have answers. Does the arousal (the degree to which we feel aware, alert and attentive) or valence (the emotional value) elicited by the event influence how vividly we remember the experience? To test the influence of arousal on the vividness of memories, Elizabeth Kensinger and Suzanne Corkin of the Massachusetts Institute of Technology used MRI scanners to investigate the brain functions of volunteers while they carried out a number of tasks (Kensinger & Corkin, 2003). Participants were scanned while they memorised words that were neutral, negative and non-arousing (such as *sorrow* and *mourning*) or words that were negative and arousing (such as *rape* and *slaughter*). At the same time participants were asked to perform a hard auditory discrimination task, perform an easy discrimination task or perform no secondary task. They found that the secondary tasks impaired the vividness with which the non-arousing words were remembered. Conversely, the secondary task did not have a large effect on the vividness of memories for the arousing words. This would indicate that the memory enhancement for arousing words takes place automatically, even when attentional resources are diverted towards a secondary task. On the other hand, the mnemonic boost for non-arousing stimuli requires controlled and elaborated processing. Divided attention studies have found a detrimental effect on the vividness of negative non-arousing items that essentially lead to the disappearance of any mnemonic enhancement. Arousal might be important for memory vividness but it doesn't appear to be essential. Studies into valence, however, suggest that negative events are remembered with a greater sense of vividness than positive events and that positive events are often only remembered with a general feeling of familiarity. In the previous chapter we posited the suggestion that happy people are lazy thinkers and this would appear to be one explanation why negative events are remembered better than positive ones, at least in laboratory studies. Certainly, a positive mood is associated with more memory reconstruction errors, perhaps because happy people rely more on stereotypes and *gist-based* information. Nevertheless, this isn't always the case in real-life situations where the reverse applies (that is, positive events are more likely to be remembered).

Implication for classroom practice

The big question, of course, is what exactly does this mean in terms of classroom practice? The main point perhaps is that separating the cognitive processes involved in the encoding of information from the emotional states elicited by the to-be-remembered information neglects an important part of the process. With the growing interest in rote learning and memorisation, we perhaps begin to neglect the evidence that says our memories are far from infallible and instead (and armed with only partial information) overlook the context in which the information is memorised (or encoded). Emotions can affect both the likelihood of remembering an event and also how vividly the event is remembered. It also impacts on items (such as single words) and how likely we are to remember these. Certain items are more likely to be remembered because of their valence, so any item that evokes a strong emotional reaction, whether it be positive or negative, has a greater chance of being recalled in the future. As we have also seen, certain emotional states such as severe anxiety impair the ability to encode, process and recall information.

One seemingly unusual way to encourage memory consolidation might be to show students emotion-laden images immediately following a test. This might sound like a highly dubious suggestion; after all, what could possibly be the point of getting students to do a test and then displaying emotional pictures? To understand why this might be effective, we first need to understand that mental retrieval of an item enhances the memory trace for that item. Henry Roediger has consistently shown that retrieval has the ability to modify memory and promote long-term learning; in fact, the so-called *testing effect* has found that tests enhance later retention more than additional study of the material. Despite this being known for some time now, schools still often rely on revision techniques that involve re-reading, taking notes and highlighting (or, as I like to call it, *colouring in*). One of the most effective ways to remember material, however, is to recall it again and again and again. In a 2011 study, Bridgid Finn and Henry Roediger found that when negative emotional pictures were presented immediately after success on a retrieval test, later test performance was enhanced. But there was no enhancement for those who were shown neutral pictures or a blank screen. It would therefore appear that the period immediately following retrieval plays an important role in determining later retention (Finn & Roediger, 2011).

This is all very interesting, but in the 2011 study recall was enhanced for material that the participants had already got right. What would the same procedure do for those participants who had originally been unsuccessful? A year later Finn and Roediger, along with graduate student Emily Rosenweig, set out to discover if the effect would still work when the answer given by the participants was wrong (Finn *et al.*, 2012). The 2012 study also leads into an interesting discussion about the nature of getting things wrong and the value (or otherwise) of having a guess if we're not sure of the answer. While a fear of failure can often prevent students from *having a go*, the possible merits of such a strategy are less than fully understood. Many researchers insist that making errors can hinder later test performance due to the complex nature of memory mechanisms. We can learn a great deal about the negative consequences of guessing through research conducted to investigate the accuracy of eyewitness testimony, especially when witnesses are required to offer an answer even if they aren't 100 per cent sure that their answer is correct (so-called *forced-response* questions). Reid Hastie, Robert Lamdsman and Elizabeth Loftus found that individuals who were encouraged to guess the answer on a test would then go on to use the same incorrect answer on subsequent tests, even when they knew the answer to be wrong (Hastie *et al.*, 1978). Elizabeth Marsh and Henry Roediger (along with Robert and Elizabeth Bjork) also reached similar conclusions in their 2007 study, concluding that when people make errors on multiple choice tests the errors can persist on later cued-recall tests (when participants are given cues to help them recall previously seen material) (Marsh *et al.*, 2007). These and other research studies have led leading cognitive psychologist and expert on eyewitness testimony Elizabeth Loftus to suggest that guessing can be dangerous because when people guess, they might later recall their incorrect guesses as being correct. The problem, then, is one of memory; when people are forced to guess the answer on a test they often remember their guesses as being part of the original to-be-learned material, which perhaps explains why teachers continue to receive incorrect answers from students even when they have stressed that the answer they have given is wrong.

The problem with this, however, is that results can often be inconsistent. Other studies have identified the benefits of unsuccessful retrieval to learning. As long as the correct answer is in the end generated by the participant or provided by the experimenter then the error shouldn't carry over to subsequent tests. Bridgid Finn found that when unsuccessful retrieval attempts were followed by feedback, long-term retention was better than when the correct answer was just given. This shows that not only is the testing effect replicated, but also that feedback is vital in order to correct any errors or misconceptions.

We left our original question somewhat hanging in the air: does presenting a negative picture presented in the interval following an unsuccessful retrieval attempt lead to greater long-term retention of the correct answer? The short answer is yes. It would appear that even when the original answer is wrong elaborate processing still takes place following feedback and the presentation of the negative image. Later recall of the correct answer is enhanced (supporting the test effect). As long as the retrieval attempt is effortful enough to trigger necessary reconsolidation, the picture then activates the emotional regions of the brain which enhance the testing effect and aids later recall. Roediger has also suggested that the emotion-eliciting picture need not be presented externally and that simply bringing to mind an emotional image should impact memory enhancement in the same way.

The role of working memory

The impact of emotions on our memory of events or on our ability to recall and recognise positive, negative or neutral words flashed up on a screen in front of our eyes is one thing, but what about the memory processes we use to learn things? Working memory is the short-term store that allows us to manipulate information in the present moment; it allows us to count the windows in our house without being anywhere near our house or to tot up the price of a basket of shopping to make sure we've brought enough money (for those of us who still insist on using cash). Working memory also has a major impact on the lives of students, anything from mental arithmetic to following a sequence of instructions. Children with working memory deficits find it difficult to follow instructions unless those instructions are broken down for them into different parts. This would mean that asking a student to 'finish the sentence you're on, put down your pen and bring your book to the front of the class' could essentially overload a system that already suffers from limits in capacity. According to one of the major models of working memory, developed over several decades by British psychologists Alan Baddeley and Graham Hitch, short-term dynamic memory uses different systems in the maintenance of verbal, spatial and visual information. These systems are pretty limited in their ability to handle multiple inputs simultaneously and can become overloaded even if the person doesn't suffer from a specific memory deficit.

To demonstrate this, I would ask my students to silently read a page from a textbook while reciting 'lalala . . .' out loud. They would then have to describe to the person sitting next to them what they had just read. Now and again I would discover a student who was particularly skilled at this, but generally few students had the faintest clue of what they had just read. This is because the system that deals with acoustic information (known as the phonological loop) can't cope with carrying out multiple tasks at the same time; it becomes overloaded (it's also why teachers should never allow students to listen to music while working). Working memory requires the use of long-term memory to give meaning and relevance to the information being manipulated – you can't count the windows in your house if the meaning of the word *window* hasn't been accessed and neither can you if the image of your house is still stuck deep down in your long-term memory. You can overload the system in other ways too. If you think of a neutral word such as *table* and repeat it out loud over and over again, it remains familiar but begins to eerily lose its meaning – a phenomenon known as jamais vu (literally, *never seen*). One possible explanation for this curious phenomenon is that the word is being vocalised before the long-term memory has had time to access its meaning; however, it is often brought on by fatigue and is also seen as a component of epileptic seizures.

Working memory certainly has its limitations and many factors can overload its capacity. Anxiety is one way that capacity can become impaired because the worry can lead to mindwandering, daydreaming and general distraction – all activities that can take the capacity beyond workable limits. Joseph Mikels and colleagues have suggested that working memory might process emotional material differently and that there exists the possibility that an affective store should be added to the model, that is, a component that specifically processes emotional information (Mikels *et al.*, 2008). While it's probably too early to tell if working memory really does deal with emotional information differently, we do know that emotional stimuli can impact on the ability of working memory to function adequately.

Many of the ideas discussed in this chapter are speculative and it might be difficult to see how they can be applied to the classroom.

Perhaps the main take home point is that emotion does impact memory, often through the complex interaction between cognition and emotion and through the power of emotional stimuli to strengthen memory traces. The influence of emotions on memory processes also highlights, once again, that when we speak of emotions and learning we aren't only concerned with emotional reactions to learning, but rather with how these biological and psychological reactions influence learning from within; from a cognitive position.

We are yet to fully understand the relationship between emotions, cognition and academic achievement; we do, however, know a great deal about emotions and wellbeing and cognition and learning. We also understand pretty well the link between wellbeing and academic achievement and how higher levels of wellbeing in school, work or life generally are a good indicator of success later on in life (however we decide to measure success). Success is an important factor here because the term means different things to different people – while some crave fame and fortune, others measure success through less tangible means such as family, friends or through work that is personally fulfilling rather than financially rewarding.

Chapter summary

- While learning is certainly cognitive, emotions are intricately linked with other brain functions that assist in the learning process.

- Memories are fallible and often highly inaccurate. Emotional states during processing of the original memory and during recall can have both positive and negative effects on how well information is remembered.

- Both positive and negative emotional states affect memory processes, but negative states appear to enhance memory better than positive or neutral states.

- Anxiety can reduce the ability to accurately process and recall learned information in some circumstances.

References

Brown, R. & Kulik, J. (1977). Flashbulb memories. *Cognition* 5(1), pp.73–99.

Cowan, N. (2000). The magical number 4 in short-term memory: A reconsideration of mental storage capacity. *Behavioral and Brain Sciences* 24(1), pp.87–185.

Finn, B. & Roediger, H. (2011). Enhancing retention through reconsolidation. *Psychological Science* 22(6), pp.781–786.

Finn, B., Roediger, H. & Rosenzweig, E. (2012). Reconsolidation from negative emotional pictures: Is successful retrieval required? *Memory & Cognition* 40(7), pp.1031–1045.

Hastie, R., Landsman, R. & Loftus, E.L. (1978). Eyewitness testimony: The danger of guessing. *Jurimetrics Journal* (Fall), pp.1–8.

Kensinger, E. & Corkin, S. (2003). Effect of negative emotional content on working memory and long-term memory. *Emotion* 3(4), pp.378–393.

Maguire, E.A., Gadian, D.G., Johnsrude, I.S., Good, C.D., Ashburner, J., Frackowiak, R.S.J. & Frith, C.D. (2000). Navigation-related structural change in the hippocampi of taxi drivers. *Proceedings of the National Academy of Sciences* 97(8), pp.4398–4403.

Marsh, E.J., Roediger, H.L., Bjork, R.A. & Bjork, E.L. (2007). The memorial consequences of multiple-choice testing. *Psychonomic Bulletin & Review* 14(2), pp.194–199.

Mikels, J.A., Reuter-Lorenz, P.A., Beyer, J.A. & Fredrickson, B.L. (2008). Emotion and working memory: Evidence for domain-specific processes for affective maintenance. *Emotion* 8(2), pp.256–266.

Ramachandran, V.S. (2012). *The Tell-Tale Brain*. Oxford, UK: Windmill.

Smith, M. & Firth, J. (2018). *Psychology in the Classroom: A Teacher's Guide to What Works*. London: Routledge.

Talarico, J.M. & Rubin, D.C. (2003). Confidence, not consistency, characterizes flashbulb memories. *Psychological Science: A Journal of the American Psychological Society* 14(5), pp.455–461.

5 | Personality, motivation and emotion

> . . . people are innately curious, interested creatures who possess a natural love of learning and who desire to internalize the knowledge, customs and values that surround them.
>
> (Christopher Niemiec and Richard Ryan)

Motivation can be a highly personal behaviour even though many aspects of it are predictable. This might sound like a contradictory statement but appears less so when we consider the role of personality. Whether we view personality as a distinct set of traits or see it more as simply what separates me from you doesn't really matter, even though I will dedicate a few pages to personality theory. The important point is that we are all individuals with both predictable and unpredictable behaviours. Classrooms are rarely (if ever) filled with clones who all behave in exactly the same way, no matter how hard some schools might try and make it so. It the same way, I would argue, the search for a universal and all-encompassing teaching strategy is also erroneous; not only does it not match our own experience of the world, it's not strongly supported by the evidence either.

Personality, it can be argued, is what makes us who we are; it represents our traits, behaviours and dispositions and these might be fixed or flexible depending on the position we adopt. We might describe someone as an introvert or an extrovert, conscientious or resilient, open to new experiences or perhaps less adventurous. Teachers will see different personalities in their classroom and parents will detect the differences between their own children. I have three brothers (yes, I know, my poor mum) and while we are similar in many ways, in others we are completely different. I'm the introvert of the family (I'll explain a little bit about what that means in the classroom later) so I'm quieter and more contemplative than my older brother who thrives on social interaction and adventure. He spent 13 years in the army and that shaped his personality to some extent; however, I suspect his personality traits led him in that direction. As for me, I was a little bit confused. My more contemplative nature and love of books and writing created in me a desire to involve myself in these activities and for a few years as a child I thought I wanted to be a journalist. However, at 16 I left school and followed my older brother into the army. Four months later I had seen the error of my ways, realising that my personality (who I am) wasn't suited to the same career in which my brother thrived. My two younger brothers are different still, but they do share some of my personality traits. We all have very different jobs and have done very different things with our lives; I am the only one with a university degree, perhaps because academic study suited my personality. This is the same in the classroom; some students will be *live wires* while others will be content to introspect; some will want to go on and study at university, but others won't be suited or display any desire to remain in education longer than they have to.

Psychologists interested in personality don't always agree on what constitutes a trait, or if traits are universal constructs that can be measured using psychometric tools, or if traits are unique to individuals. In fact, personality theory is a highly contested area of psychology, with many voices in disagreement and some even suggesting that the personality *types* don't exist at all. It's tempting to engage in this wider debate but perhaps more prudent to concentrate on the theories that exist and present them with a health warning, as is often the case with many areas of psychology. Certainly, the idea of personality types and traits is one area of psychology that captures the imagination; people enjoy completing personality tests and reading about psychopaths. Books like Susan Cain's *Quiet* encourage us to examine our own personalities in terms of being contemplative (the introvert) or more outgoing (the extrovert). The idea of personality permeates our wider world and colours our perceptions of ourselves. Personality, therefore, represents a perfectly valid topic for discussion.

Personality: a contentious construct

One of the early pioneers of personality theory, Gordon Allport, believed that we can divide traits into two distinct groups: common traits such as aggression are universal (although will exist somewhere along a scale) while others are individual traits that cannot be applied to all people and cannot be measured using standardised tests. These distinctions represent an idiographic and nomothetic difference – the discussion over whether every person is unique or whether we are all basically the same. Whether the ideographic–nomothetic dichotomy is useful or even real is a topic best left to those who care about such things, but it's worth mentioning in order to further emphasise that disagreements exist. Generally speaking, a trait is a habitual pattern of thought, behaviour and emotion that remains relatively stable over time. This suggests that the behaviour you see in a toddler will be equally visible in later life, although research is beginning to find that certain traits can change with growing age and maturity. Brent Roberts and Wendy Delvecchio of the University of Tulsa found that the consistency of personality increases up to the age of about 30 then stabilises between 50 and 70 (Roberts & DelVecchio, 2000). Research conducted by Avshalom Caspi found similar results (Caspi, 2000). Caspi followed a group of children from age 3 up to the age of 21 and found that 3-year-olds who were viewed as uncontrollable grew up to be impulsive, unreliable and antisocial, and that those children viewed as inhibited displayed higher levels of depression, were more likely to be unassertive and had fewer sources of social support later on in life.

Decades of research have narrowed the number of traits down to five broad dimensions known as the Big 5 (or the Five Factor Model). These five factors consist of extroversion, agreeableness, conscientiousness, emotional stability (or neuroticism) and intellect/openness to experience (see Table 5.1). The factor represents the desirable trait and its opposite the undesirable trait, so extroversion is desirable and introversion is undesirable (I'll discuss this particular suggestion later). Table 5.1 outlines the characteristics associated with each trait. Notice that some of these characteristics can also be thought of as emotions; emotion and personality, therefore, play an important part in the ongoing task of self-building. Twin studies suggest that the Big 5 factors are highly heritable (anywhere between 40 and 60 per cent) but that the environment also plays a major role in the development of personality. It's worth emphasising that traits appear on a continuum, so few people are wholly introvert or wholly extrovert and tools used to measure the Big 5 will place the individual somewhere on the continuum. Furthermore, some of these traits might be more stable than others.

Robert McCrae, along with a team of international researchers found that some traits appear less fluid than others. They examined the Big 5 traits in a sample of people aged between 14 and 30 from Germany, the UK, Spain, Turkey and the Czech Republic and found that some (such as openness to experience) decreased over time while others (agreeableness and conscientiousness) increased (McCrae *et al.*, 2000). Also, some traits might be displayed in some situations and not others; for example, a student might appear reserved and introverted in the classroom but excitable and sociable when amongst close friends. In a more recent study, researchers at the University of Edinburgh and Liverpool John Moores University found no correlation between measures of personality in the same group of participants taken when they were 14 and again when they were 77 (Harris *et al.*, 2016). Of course, a study conducted over such a long time is highly problematic, the most obvious drawback being the developments and changes in personality classifications that have taken place since the 14 year olds were tested back in 1950 (there was no Big 5 back then, for example). The upside of this study is that it indicates our capacity for change.

Do your students appear to display certain characteristics that help or hinder their achievement? Do you think they would fall into one of the Big 5 groupings?

Table 5.1 The Big 5 personality traits.

Trait	Characteristics
Extroversion	Outgoing Sociable Assertive
Agreeableness	Kind Trusting Warm
Conscientiousness	Organised Thorough Tidy
Neuroticism/emotional stability	Calm Even-tempered Imperturbable
Openness to experience	Imaginative Intelligent Creative

Some traits might be more useful than others

We need to think about why some traits might be more useful than others and in what specific contexts. Certainly, traits such as conscientiousness and emotional stability are positive attributes to possess, especially in the classroom. Indeed, emotion is what this whole book is about, but as we will see emotions come in many colours and flavours and some thought to be undesirable might actually work in our favour. The odd suggestion is that there is a right type of personality and that society should strive to ensure that the most useful traits are nurtured while the less useful (invariably the undesirable traits) are somehow squeezed out or prevented from developing. This might seem like a view adopted by some future dystopian society bent on creating the perfect workforce but, in fact, this suggestion has already been proposed. Researchers recently discovered that extrovert traits are more likely to produce successful individuals – at least in terms of earning capacity. This in turn led to the suggestion that schools should teach extrovert traits as part of a programme of *character education*.[1] It would appear that extroversion is a highly prized trait in (mainly western) society and that introverted children are in someway suffering from an affliction that should be cured. In recent years there has been a backlash to this view, partly due to Cain's international bestseller. Introverts, claims Cain, have much to offer society and rather than being marginalised, their particular skills should be celebrated. Of course I'm biased here; I have always thought of myself as an introvert and my results have always been consistently introverted on a number of psychological personality measures (for example, the most widely used yet equally controversial Myers-Briggs Type Indicator, or MBTI). As a child I was generally thought of as shy (a word I learned to despise) and, although I had lots of childhood friends and spent a great deal of time with them, I was equally (if not more) comfortable in my own company and with my own thoughts. Personality may, therefore, play a role in what motivates us.

Introverts: a special case?

Rather than attempting to turn introverts into extroverts, long-term benefits are more likely to be seen by accepting that introverts simply behave in a different way. In some circumstances they can be seen as more emotionally vulnerable than their more extrovert counterparts, but in other ways they are more emotionally resilient. For example, in 2015 Matt Hilton, a PhD student at Lancaster University, found that those students considered as shy suffered from greater problems with learning new words than their less shy classmates (Hilton & Westermann, 2015). However, their contemplative nature does suggest that introverts spend more time thinking through problem-solving strategies in their own minds. We must also be careful not to equate shyness with introversion, because they are not necessarily the same thing. Furthermore, introversion is certainly more prevalent than you might think, with some estimates suggesting that up to 40 per cent of students fall into this bracket.

The sensitive nature of introverts often means that their self-esteem is more fragile; unfortunately, they are also better skilled at picking up cues related to disapproval, such as a frustrated sigh, an angry facial expression or subtle criticism. This enhanced awareness can often make them withdraw even more and make them less likely to engage in classroom activities. Certain classroom techniques that involve children working in groups can be a nightmare for introverted children; furthermore, they gain less from such strategies than more extroverted pupils. Introverts prefer to be one of the early guests at any party and become anxious when forced to join a pre-existing group. Pair work is therefore preferable in the early stages; pairs can be joined later to form larger groups, so that less dominant voices can get a chance to be heard and grow in confidence.

Helping introverted children to cope with novel situations will eventually lead to fewer anxious reactions to new environments. Children new to your class or school will want to understand the rules as well as the practical elements of their surroundings, such as where the toilets are; they will try and work these things out for themselves (because that's what introverts do) but by making them explicitly clear there's less for them to worry about.

Motivation

Of more interest to teachers than personality is the role of motivation. Just like personality, we all hold some common-sense ideas about what we mean by motivation without being able to explicitly describe what it is. One definition, 'the biological, emotional, cognitive or social forces that activate and direct behaviour', seems too technical. An alternative definition, 'the process that initiates, guides, and maintains goal-orientated behaviours' works well for us due to its emphasis on the pursuit of goals. Both definitions can also be appropriately applied to teaching and learning, although more specifically student motivation is also about the desire to engage in the learning process. Like many processes in learning, detecting motivation in students isn't always easy; some students might appear motivated but be disengaged while others might seem unmotivated but be deeply engaged in a more introverted way (they might, actually, be introverts). Definitions, models and theories aren't always useful and often they will confuse rather than simplify. Nevertheless, as I'll be using terms related to motivational theory at several points throughout the following chapter, a brief trip into the world of motivational theory will prove useful.

We can think of motivation as being comprised of three basic characteristics:

- *Activation* – The initiation or trigger of a specific behaviour. So we might feel hungry and go to the kitchen to make ourselves a sandwich.
- *Persistence* – The continued effort we put into the task or how long we persevere with it. Some students might give up on a task quickly while others keep going. Over the past few years certain terms such as resilience, grit and mental toughness have been associated with persistence.
- *Intensity* – The strength of the response to the activity.

Theories of motivation

A number of psychological theories have been proposed as way of explaining motivation, the most useful of which are instinct theory, drive theory and incentive theory.

Instinct theory

Instinct theory sees people as motivated to engage in certain behaviours due to evolutionary mechanisms. William James, the American psychologist and philosopher and one of the greatest thinkers of the late nineteenth century, proposed a number of instincts that he believed were vital for survival, including attachment, disgust and shyness. These instincts compel us to behave in certain ways in order to survive. For example, ethnologist Konrad Lorenz was able to use a concept known as *imprinting* on goslings to trick them into thinking he was their mother. The gosling would attach to the first living thing they came into contact with after hatching to ensure safety and protection. Normally the mother would be the source of such imprinting, but Lorenz ensured that the goslings imprinted on him instead. The goslings would follow Lorenz wherever he went, just as they would have done their mother (Lorenz, 1935). Psychologist William McDougall (1871–1938) became one of the first to develop an instinct theory of motivation, outlining 18 different instincts, including curiosity, laughter, comfort, sex and hunger.

Unfortunately, instinct theory provides a less than adequate explanation of motivation although more recent researchers have tried to incorporate environmental components into the biological model. There are a number of important problems with the theory including its inability to explain all human behaviours and the unobservable nature of instincts themselves. Some instincts, however, can be thought of as emotion-based, such as curiosity. But applying such a theory to student motivation and learning dynamics would prove problematic because instincts can't really be measured objectively.

Drive (and arousal) theory

Drive theory represents another biologically based motivational theory, viewing behaviour as motivated by the desire to reduce internal tension caused by unmet biological needs such as hunger or thirst. These unmet biological needs drive us to behave in certain ways to ensure our survival. For example, our need for food or water make us hungry or thirsty (the drive) and compels us towards drive-reducing behaviours, in this case to eat or drink something. The behaviour that reduced the drive is then reinforced and the cycle begins again. Drive theory operates in this way because our bodies are biological systems that are delicately balanced to ensure survival. Our bodies strive for a state of homeostasis (the physiological equilibrium that the body strives to maintain), so, for example, when we are hot our body will attempt to cool down by sweating and when our body is cold it will attempt to warm up by shivering. Motivation occurs, therefore, because disruptions in homeostasis produce states of internal tension that result in behaviour to reduce the tension. Unlike drive theory, arousal theory is based on the assumption that people find very high and very low states of arousal unpleasant. I'll discuss this in more detail when I look at boredom and interest (Chapters 7 and 8). When arousal is too low people become motivated to increase the level by seeking out more stimulating experiences; for example, when students are bored they might misbehave in order to alleviate the unpleasant feeling that boredom produces. If arousal is too high, people are motivated to reduce it by seeking out less stimulating environments.

Incentive theories and token economies

We can also explain motivation in terms of incentives – a reward or a punishment. Incentive theories are much more appropriate to schools than either instinct or drive theories. Many, if not all, schools already apply incentive theories to behaviour management. Behaviour is seen as motivated by certain *pull* factors such as money, recognition or other such rewards. Based on the principles of operant conditioning, incentive theories view behaviour as based on the expectation of consequences that reinforce certain types of behaviour. If we think we are going to be rewarded for certain behaviours, we are then motivated to engage in those behaviours, while we will avoid behaviours that we know will result in punishment. Such strategies are effective to an extent and can work very well with younger children. Sticker charts and naughty steps are bread and butter to super-nannies in the same way that detentions and merit points are to schools. Unfortunately, they don't work for all children and less often for older teenagers (and I'll discuss why later) and in some circumstances, they actually encourage the wrong type of motivation.

Motivation beyond survival

So far, I have discussed motivation in terms of survival, the reduction of uncomfortable feelings and the desire to be rewarded (and the desire to avert punishment). Often, we are motivated to engage in activities for their own sake. Perhaps you have a personal desire to learn a new language or a musical instrument; perhaps you want to complete an evening class on classical civilisation because you're interested in the ancient world of Greeks and Romans. How does this fit in? Humanistic psychology might have the answer (and I stress *might*) because its principle aim is the pursuit of *self-actualisation* – the process by which people reach the pinnacle of their own capabilities and creativity. Arising as a reaction against the narrowness of behaviourism and the pessimism of Freudian psychodynamics, humanistic psychology has its roots more in existential thought and Eastern philosophy than in traditional psychology. One of the most influential models of personality and motivation based on humanistic principles was Abraham Maslow's hierarchy of needs, familiar to many people from different disciplines (see Figure 5.1). Maslow first proposed his model in *Motivation and Personality* published in 1954 and, although it's gone through a few revisions and adaptations, the basic premise remains the same.

According to Maslow, there are two sets of motivational forces: those that ensure survival by satisfying basic physical and psychological needs (for example, safety, love and belongingness) and those that promote self-actualisation; the realising of one's full potential, or as Maslow put it, 'becoming everything that one is capable of becoming', especially in the intellectual and creative domains. As the name suggests, the hierarchy of needs states that lower levels require satisfying before higher order needs, so those behaviours related to survival (deficiency needs or D-needs) need to be engaged first because they satisfy our basic survival needs and without them we could potentially die. Those behaviours that relate to self-actualisation (B-needs) are engaged for their own sake (they have no survival advantage) and are intrinsically satisfying. B-needs represent the fulfilment of ambitions, the acquisition of admired skills, the steady increase in understanding about people and oneself and the development of creativeness. Most importantly, perhaps, B-needs represent the desire to be a good human being. These higher level needs are thought to be a later evolutionary development in human beings simply due to survival being the vital component in the lives of our ancestors. In a similar way, higher level

Figure 5.1 The hierarchy of needs

needs develop through the life span, and self-actualisation becomes possible only as we mature – babies, after all, are more concerned with the basics (such as keeping their bellies full) rather than the development of their higher intellect. As we move up the hierarchy, more of our needs become linked to life experience than to biology, and when self-actualisation occurs it will be different for all of us.

In educational settings, we can think of basic needs as having to be satisfied before intellectual endeavours begin. Students who are hungry or thirsty won't learn as well as those who have consumed a healthy breakfast, just as those who haven't had enough sleep will find it equally difficult to concentrate. This tends to make intuitive sense; students who have satisfied basic needs, feel safe and who have feelings of higher self-worth will work and learn better. Unfortunately, Maslow's theory (in common with much humanistic psychology) lacks the empirical evidence to support it. There's little evidence to suggest that a hierarchy exists at all, or that all lower order needs require satisfying before the task of self-actualisation can begin. Furthermore, the higher order behaviours seem more appropriate to individualistic societies than collectivist societies, raising the problem of ethnocentricity or the universality of the theory.

Intrinsic and extrinsic motivators

What Maslow's theory does highlight, however, is the suggestion that some forms of motivation are intrinsic, that is, activities and tasks are carried out without the need for external reward. Much of the early research into motivation examined the impact of intrinsic and extrinsic motivation and their relationship to each other. Intrinsic motivation is about doing activities because they are personally interesting to us and spontaneously satisfying. The reward for carrying out the activity is the pleasure and positive feelings we experience when we are doing it. Compare this with extrinsic motivation – engaging in an activity because it will lead to a separate consequence, such as some kind of material reward or feeling that we are more intelligent or more worthy than those around (students who adopt a mastery orientation are more likely to be motivated intrinsically). The promotion of extrinsic motivation has become commonplace in our schools despite the negative consequences being understood for decades. The basic premise is that hard work is rewarded externally and the assumption is that the work is so boring or so unwanted that students are unable to develop a true passion or interest for it.

Studies over several years have consistently discovered that extrinsic rewards undermine intrinsic motivation (although, as I will discuss later, there are ways around this). Rewards also appear to result in a fall in interest and produce work of a lower quality. Edward Deci suggested that when a person expects a reward for carrying out an activity, they attribute their behaviour to the reward and not the activity itself. This might not matter that much, just so long as the activity is completed (after all, who really cares about the motivation behind it?). However, once the activity has been associated with a particular reward the person becomes less inclined to participate in the future if the reward is no longer present. To illustrate this point, Deci asked students to solve a puzzle; in one group they were told that they would be paid to partici-pate while a second group would receive no reward. Once the payment stopped, the group who had previously been paid became less moti-vated and less inclined to participate in the activity (Deci, 1972).

In one of the most cited studies into the impact of extrinsic rewards, Mark Lepper, David Greene and Richard Nisbett studied the con-sequences of offering external rewards to a group of children at the Stanford University nursery school. Lepper and his colleagues first spent some time observing the children and identifying those who chose to spend their free time on a drawing activity. After selecting participants from their original observations, children were placed into one of the experimental groups: the expected award group were asked to engage in a drawing activity and told that they would receive a certificate with a gold seal and a ribbon for doing so; the unexpected award group carried out the same activity but were presented with the certificate without being told that they would receive it beforehand; the third group neither expected nor received an award for taking part in the activity. The three researchers then repeated the activity a couple of weeks later with the same children but without the reward. They used covert observation (they stood behind a one-way mirror) and collected measures of intrinsic motivation. It was found that those children who had previously received the award after being told that they would be rewarded for the activity, spend less time drawing and were less interested in the drawing materials; however, the children from the other two groups were still fully engaged in the activity. The children in the no award group had never been given the opportu-nity to make any extrinsic link between the activity and any external reward, but even the unexpected award group appeared not to associ-ate the activity with the award because it came as a surprise the first time around (Lepper *et al.*, 1973).

Studies such as the ones described imply that the implementation of external reward systems to promote motivation might have nasty long-term effects. The expectation of the reward does motivate but when the rewards are withdrawn motivation can dip lower than before the rewards were offered. This would also indicate that implementing such strategies as a way of improving behaviour could result in worse behaviour once the rewards are withdrawn – a clear example of making a rod for your own back.

Other factors also play a role in reducing intrinsic motivation. Research has found that threats of punishment and deadlines also reduce intrinsic motivation, while choice increases it. Intrinsic motivation, therefore, is linked to autonomy and this results in outcomes of a much higher quality, while the prospect of being evaluated adds to pressure, makes us feel as if we are being controlled and diminishes satisfaction in what we do. Feedback also plays a role in enhancing intrinsic motivation. Good feedback represents the cornerstone of education (and much more besides) and can make the difference between a student who views it as an opportunity and the student who sees it only as a confirmation of their shortcomings. Positive performance feedback is viewed as informative rather than controlling (it praises when necessary and offers advice on how to improve), and helps to boost levels of intrinsic motivation. Negative feedback, on the other hand, undermines intrinsic motivation and results in an amotivated student; one that lacks both extrinsic and intrinsic motivation.

The role of self-determination

Edward Deci and Richard Ryan view motivation in terms of different types, and like earlier researchers stress the importance of intrinsic motivators over extrinsic ones. They suggest that people have three basic psychological needs: the need for competence, the need for relatedness and the need for autonomy.

- *The need for competence* – Our desire to control or master the environment and its outcomes. People want to know how things are going to turn out and they want to know the results or consequences of their own actions.
- *The need for relatedness* – Our desire to interact with, be connected to and experience caring for other people. Everything we do in some way concerns others and our actions impact on those

around us. Through this need to build up a sense of belonging develops the feeling that we are part of a wider world beyond the limits of ourselves.

- *The need for autonomy* – The urge to be causal agents and have full volition and choice over what we do. If autonomous motivation concerns choice, then controlled motivation relates to the lack of choice. Ryan and Deci describe it as 'behaving with the experience of pressure or demand towards specific outcomes that come from forces perceived to be external to the self'. Autonomy, however, does not necessarily mean acting independently; it merely means acting with choice, so it can mean acting alone but also acting interdependently with others.

The main premise of Ryan and Deci's theory involves the role of self-determining factors, and hence is known as *self-determination theory* or SDT (see, for example, Ryan & Deci, 2000). SDT is a theory of human motivation, emotion and development concerned with factors related to assimilative and growth-orientated processes in people. The theory's primary concern is with the factors that promote or prevent people from intrinsically engaging in positive behaviours. In order to be intrinsically engaged we need to feel that our actions are based on choice and free will, even if such feelings are illusionary. People's motivation can be effected in many different ways and we all often feel unmotivated towards tasks we view as less rewarding. Procrastination often overwhelms us and we put off things until tomorrow. This book, for example, has been two years in the making but only really began to take shape when I set myself daily goals, resulting in the first full draft in a little less than six weeks (although many more drafts were written later). Motivation ebbs and flows but is often at its highest point when we feel that the activity we are engaged in is being done because we want to do it, rather than us being told to or coerced into doing it.

Motivation, therefore, becomes intricately entwined with emotional states such as interest, curiosity and boredom. How motivated we are is often related to how we feel – whether a task bores us, excites us or sends us into a state of anxiety or helplessness. Yet, motivation isn't just about internal states – environments play a major role as well. The interpersonal climate of the classroom, for example, can have a major impact on motivation, especially motivation of the intrinsic kind. Teachers, classrooms and schools all differ in terms of the control they use. Some might be highly controlling, relying heavily on the absolute authority of teachers over pupils, strictly adhered-to rules of behaviour, and consistent in and heavily reliant on extrinsic reward and punishment procedures. Others might be more liberal in their approach towards control, allowing students a greater say in how and what they learn, implementing more restorative behaviour management policies and more flexible classroom rules. Schools represent complex systems and some might require more stringent behaviour management policies than others. I have taught in many schools during my career, from large inner city comprehensives to small rural community high schools, and what works in one doesn't necessarily work in another. Furthermore, a greater emphasis on rules doesn't always have to mean a more controlling environment.

The nature of control

Highly controlled classroom environments undermine intrinsic motivation while autonomy-supportive classrooms nurture it. This doesn't mean that extrinsic reward systems don't work in the classroom – they often do, so long as the interpersonal classroom context remains informational and supportive rather than critical and authoritarian. Conversely, positive feedback given in a controlling context will also tend to decrease intrinsic motivation. Classroom environments that encourage autonomy (autonomy-supportive) lead to greater learning and performance outcomes than controlling styles, and there is ample evidence indicating that practices and policies that rely on motivating pupils through sanctions, rewards and evaluations (and other forms of coercion and manipulation) undermine quality student engagement. I use the term *quality student engagement* here simply because engagement doesn't always lead to enhanced learning. Furthermore, a great deal of what we mean by engagement isn't visible (in the same way that learning itself isn't always visible). While controlling environments often stifle motivation, autonomy-supportive classrooms that foster interest, value and volition encourage greater persistence and better quality engagement and learning. Autonomy and competence are essential to the maintenance of intrinsic motivation – it's difficult to find an activity either exciting or enjoyable if we feel we have little control over what we are doing. In his 1968 book *Personal Causation*, educational psychologist Richard deCharms described this as our *internal perceived locus of causality*, meaning an experience that emanates from within ourselves rather than from any external source (our perceived locus of causality can be both internal and external). Intrinsic motivation, therefore, represents a locus of causality that is internal, although there it often occurs on a continuum. Students must feel both autonomous and confident if they are to sustain intrinsic motivation, so that a student who feels competent but feels that they have little or no autonomy will be unable to maintain intrinsic motivation.

Teacher and classroom style is often a prickly subject and is often dictated by personal ideology. Authoritarian teachers maintain that an approach that insists on things being done correctly, students being told what to do and using a number of controlling strategies, leads to more manageable classrooms and more positive outcomes in terms of exam results. Others emphasise the importance of allowing students to be more self-directed, to learn from their own successes and failures, and to solve problems for themselves, and, although I have known teachers at both extremes, the majority of teachers fall somewhere between them. There is a growing view in education that there exists a uniform way of teaching and that as long as these skills can be taught to teachers, outcomes will improve. However, many of these skills appear authoritarian in nature (even going as far as punishing students for failing to maintain eye contact with the teacher when the teacher is addressing the class). Unfortunately for us, authoritarian teaching styles appear to do little in terms of intrinsic motivation and related educational outcomes. Early research conducted by Edward Deci found that in classrooms where teachers were more autonomy-supportive, students tended to be more intrinsically motivated, displaying behaviours such as curiosity, a preference towards challenge and greater mastery orientations. They also felt more competent in their schoolwork and had higher levels of self-esteem. Cross-cultural evaluations appear to support this. Wendy Grolnick and Richard Ryan found that evaluative pressure undermined students' intrinsic motivation and their school performance in the USA, while Kage and Namiki obtained similar results with Japanese students. Additional cross-cultural studies have found that interest is enhanced for lessons where the teacher is autonomy-supportive but diminished when the teacher is more controlling. The hypothesis has also been tested in various subject domains. Martyn Standage of the University of Bath compared student and teacher ratings of autonomy, autonomy-support, confidence, relatedness and self-determined motivation in physical education. Standage found that perceived autonomy-support was associated with higher levels of autonomous self-regulation, including intrinsic motivation and these, in turn, were associated with greater effort and persistence (Niemiec and Ryan, 2009 provide a comprehensive discussion of these and other studies).

Such studies are indicative of a number of important points. First of all, teacher orientation and certain aspects of the learning task play a role in the development of intrinsic motivation. Teachers perceived as autonomous-supportive nurture students higher in intrinsic motivation than those teachers with more authoritarian styles – and this remains consistent across cultures. Second, where children are high in intrinsic motivation and are taught in environments that support autonomy, they display a tendency towards better learning, especially on tasks requiring conceptual understanding. Finally, the way in which teachers introduce learning tasks is important in that when tasks promote the basic psychological needs of autonomy and competence, they allow for greater intrinsic motivation and deeper learning. If these basic psychological needs are not met, intrinsic motivation and achievement suffer.

Sometimes learning just isn't that interesting

Intrinsic motivation might positively impact learning but much of the time learning just isn't that interesting. Learning doesn't have to be fun, although it can be, and I would argue against the view that teachers have to make their lessons fun and exciting (terms not necessarily synonymous with achievement). Some subjects or topics will simply never turn some students on (I recall, as a teenager, sleeping my way through a geography lesson on hydroelectric power) and teachers can find boring topics equally painful. Rote learning serves a useful purpose and the memorisation of facts can lay the foundations on which deeper learning is built, but reciting the eight-times-table over and over again could never be thought of as exciting. In such cases the only thing teachers can realistically do is to fall back on extrinsic rewards. Carrot and stick approaches are far from ideal, despite their prevalence in many schools, but their failings can be mediated by examining different types of extrinsic motivation and their position on an autonomous scale (from least to most). While we can't magically transform extrinsic motivation into intrinsic motivation, we can internalise it, that is, make it feel as if it originates internally, but it depends on the type of extrinsic motivator.

There are essentially four types of extrinsic motivators: external regulation, introjected regulation, identified regulation and integrated regulation, all of which are associated with classroom practices (for example, autonomy-supportive vs. controlling instruction) and learning outcomes (such as conceptual understanding vs. rote memorisation).

External regulation

This represents the least autonomous form of extrinsic motivation and is based firmly within the incentives camp. The main problem with this kind of extrinsic-based motivation is that it represents short-term rather than long-term achievement. When I first began teaching A-level psychology, we would enter students for the first module exam in the January. Because the module was pretty much self-contained, once the exam was over we would move onto the next module and the students would forget about the content they had just been examined on (a shock to many who found themselves resitting it in the summer). The reward became the feeling experienced once the exam was over;

motivation was shallow and unsatisfactory. Similarly, punishments for failing to complete homework increase the number of students completing it, yet do little to increase the quality of the homework – especially if it's copied from your mate on the bus to school. Once the work is handed in, the motivation dissolves until the same time next week. The importance of the task is solely influenced by the reward or the punishment rather than the task itself. Additionally, motivation is prompted by external factors rather than internal ones and there is very little in the way of feelings of autonomy (or, it seems, competence).

Introjected regulation

Like external regulation, introjected regulation is on the lower end of the autonomy scale. Here, behaviours are enacted in order to satisfy some internal contingency, that is, to protect self-worth or self-esteem. A student might work hard in order to give the impression of dedication or to look intelligent. The student might also be thinking less about gaining knowledge and understanding and be more concerned with protecting him or herself from looking unintelligent or avoiding the feelings of guilt for not working hard enough. This kind of motivation is about the protection of the ego and can easily result in strategies related to the fear of failure, discussed later in Chapter 10. Locus of causality is still external, but we are moving towards internal.

Identified regulation

We're now moving into the internal perceived locus of control and greater autonomy. Tasks, activities and subjects are now seen to have some kind of value and importance, rather than being based on reward or ego protection. A student might, therefore, work hard in a biology lesson because of a desire to become a doctor or show motivation and dedication in order to get accepted into a specific university. Motivation is still extrinsic because there is an ultimate external reward available (studying for a medical degree) rather than an internal desire for knowledge.

Integrated regulation

The most autonomous kind of extrinsic motivation is integrated regulation, which also represents internal locus of causation. Here, behaviours are integrated or synthesised with other aspects of our self, such as our desires, wishes and hopes; behaviour becomes consistent with our values and interests. For example, our student doctor is motivated to work hard in biology in order to train as a doctor so that she can help people.

The internalisation of extrinsic motivation is, therefore, important for both educational outcomes and psychological functioning. Several studies support these conclusions. Wendy Grolnick found that students who scored higher on measures of self-regulation for learning were also rated by teachers as higher on measures of academic achievement and adjustment to the classroom, while Niemiec found that high school students who reported higher autonomous self-regulation for attending college reported high wellbeing (in terms of vitality and life-satisfaction) and lower levels of depression and externalising of problems (Niemiec & Ryan, 2009).

Promoting internalisation

If internalisation is so important, there needs to be a way for teachers to facilitate it in their learners. If teachers can help students to satisfy their basic psychological needs for autonomy, competence and relatedness through support in the classroom, students are then better equipped and more likely to internalise their motivation to learn and be more autonomously engaged in their own learning. Teachers can support autonomy by minimising the salience of evaluative pressure, reducing coercion in the classroom and maximising students' perceptions of choice in the activities in which they are engaged. This is perhaps easier said than done when we consider the emphasis of high stakes testing in many educational systems. However, providing autonomous support can also help students to cope better with the pressures of exams and reduce test anxiety.

Activity importance

Motivation for a task is often difficult if we don't understand the reasoning behind it or its importance. Research has found that if teachers explain the importance of an activity, students are more likely to internalise their motivation for that activity which leads to a greater effort to learn. Teachers who are able to provide students with this kind of meaningful rationale are more likely to promote such internalisation.

Challenge

By introducing learning activities that are optimally challenging, teachers allow students to test and expand on their own academic capabilities. Furthermore, teachers who provide the appropriate tools and informational feedback are able to promote success and feelings of efficacy in their students. This allows students to fully engage in an activity with high personal value that they can understand and master. Feedback should downplay evaluation but provide relevant advice and guidance on how to master the task.

Relatedness

Relatedness refers to our desire to feel connected to others, and studies have found that people are more likely to internalise and accept as their own practices and values when helped by those they either feel more connected to or want to be more connected to. Such feelings increase our sense of belonging (a basic psychological need). Classrooms are full of people we are or would like to be connected to; teachers and other students are the obvious inhabitants of such environments and those inhabitants we like, respect and value create greater opportunities for internalisation. For example, a student might have little intrinsic motivations towards history and might find the content uninteresting or difficult. This student will lack intrinsic motivation and will have to rely on extrinsic behaviours in order to engage in lessons. However, the teacher is passionate about history, is highly skilled, supportive and nurtures positive relationships with students. While our unmotivated student will never have a true passion for the subject, they are able to internalise extrinsic components as a result of the teacher–student relationship. Students who report such relatedness are more likely to work harder on more difficult tasks while being disconnected or feeling rejected by teachers who encourage students to rely more heavily on external contingencies such as rewards and punishments.

Autonomous teachers

Even when teachers are mindful of the need to encourage autonomy in their students, they still often fall back on strategies that are controlling. In his study of Israeli teachers, Guy Roth found that those teachers who felt more controlled were themselves more controlling and less autonomy-supportive (Roth *et al.*, 2007). Similarly, Luc Pelletier of the University of Ottawa found that the more Canadian teachers felt pressure from above, the less autonomous they were towards teaching and the less autonomy-supportive and more controlling they were towards their students (Pelletier *et al.*, 2002). This kind of research suggests that, while the need to nurture autonomy and self-directed learning in students is vital, if teachers feel that they themselves are being controlled, the more controlling they will be in the classroom. When perceived autonomy is undermined, teachers become less enthusiastic about their teaching, and that pressure towards specified outcomes promotes a reliance on extrinsically focussed strategies; teaching becomes less effective, less interesting and less inspiring, impacting not only on the quality of learning but also on the quality of teaching.

Motivation, schools and 'the real world'

Theories are great, especially when they are supported by evidence, but schools don't exist as theories and research environments. One of the themes running through this book (and that I will repeat on a number of occasions) is that evidence should be used to inform and not be used as a straitjacket to bind teachers to strict and inflexible policies and strategies. Promoting and nurturing intrinsic motivation is much harder and much more time consuming than adopting extrinsic reward systems. There is also the problem of ideology and teacher orientation with some saying that students need more autonomy and others claiming that they need less. Both camps take their evidence from alternative sources and our inherent bias often prevents us from accepting the findings of research that don't support our ideology. Realistically, however, these kinds of debate rarely take place in the school staffroom and are usually confined to the small cliquey corners of social media. At the heart of teaching lies relationships, and teachers are fully capable of using their own professional judgement to gauge the extent to which certain groups of students would benefit from more or less autonomy.

Many of the topics introduced in this chapter will resurface elsewhere, albeit in a slightly different context. Emotions fuel motivation and motivation impacts emotion. Anxiety, fear, interest and curiosity can enhance and undermine motivation and engagement in the classroom, and an awareness of these factors can provide yet another tool in that vital teacher toolkit. Thinking about our own autonomy is also important here; if we feel controlled we will in turn be controlling, yet, at the same time, we can become too fearful when we are given too much autonomy; just like students, teachers need to be guided and developed, not pushed and prodded. By recognising our own passions, we become better equipped to pass these onto others, which is, in essence, the very nature of teaching.

Chapter summary

- Personality traits appear to affect how individual students learn in specific situations.

- Introverted students, for example, might benefit from different teaching strategies.

- Intrinsic motivation is more effective than extrinsic motivation, but, if used carefully, extrinsic motivators can enhance learning.

- Extrinsic reward systems can produce short-term benefits, but are rarely effective long term. If discontinued, extrinsic reward systems can negatively affect behaviour and learning.

- Creating the feeling of autonomy in students can help to nurture intrinsic motivation and improve learning outcomes.

- Autonomous teachers are better equipped to nurture autonomous classrooms.

Note

1 In January 2016, The Sutton Trust published their report *A Winning Personality* indicating that extrovert traits result in higher earnings. This led to the suggestion that character education programmes should include the teaching of such traits.

References

Caspi, A. (2000). The child is father of the man: Personality continuities from childhood to adulthood. *Journal of Personality and Social Psychology* 78(1), pp.158–172.

DeCharms, R. (1968). *Personal Causation: The Internal Affective Determinants of Behavior.* New York: Academic Press.

Deci, E.L. (1972). The effects of contingent and noncontingent rewards and controls on intrinsic motivation. *Organizational Behavior and Human Performance* 8(2), pp.217–229.

Harris, M.A., Brett, C.E., Johnson, W. & Deary, I.J. (2016). Personality stability from age 14 to 77 years. *Psychology and Aging* 31(8), pp.862–874.

Hilton, M. & Westermann, G. (2015). Shyness affects word learning: Evidence from eye-tracking. Poster presented at the Society for Research in Child Development (SRCD), Philadelphia, PA. 19–21 March 2015.

Lepper, M.R., Greene, D. & Nisbett, R.E. (1973). Undermining children's intrinsic interest with extrinsic reward: A test of the 'overjustification' hypothesis. *Journal of Personality and Social Psychology* 28, pp.129–137.

Lorenz, K. (1935). Der Kumpan in der Umwelt des Vogels. Der Artgenosse als auslösendes Moment sozialer Verhaltensweisen. *Journal für Ornithologie* 83, pp.137–215, 289–413.

Maslow, A.H. (1954). *Motivation and Personality*. New York: Harper.

McCrae, R.R., Costa, P.T., Hrebickova, M., Avia, M.D., Sanz, J., Sanchez-Bernardos, M.L., Kusdil, M.E., Woodfield, R., Saunders, P.R. & Smith, P.B. (2000). Nature over nurture: Temperament, personality, and life span development. *Journal of Personality and Social Psychology* 78(1), pp.173–186.

Niemiec, C.P. & Ryan, R.M. (2009). Autonomy, competence, and relatedness in the classroom: Applying self-determination theory to educational practice. *Theory and Research in Education* 7(2), pp.133–144.

Pelletier, L.G., Séguin-Lévesque, C. & Legault, L. (2002). Pressure from above and pressure from below as determinants of teachers' motivation and teaching behaviors. *Journal of Educational Psychology* 94(1), pp.186–196.

Roberts, B.W. & DelVecchio, W.F. (2000). The rank-order consistency of personality traits from childhood to old age: A quantitative review of longitudinal studies. *Psychological Bulletin* 126(1), pp.3–25.

Roth, G., Assor, A., Kanat-Maymon, Y. & Kaplan, H. (2007). Autonomous motivation for teaching: How self-determined teaching may lead to self-determined learning. *Journal of Educational Psychology* 99(4), pp.761–774.

Ryan, R. & Deci, E. (2000). Intrinsic and extrinsic motivations: Classic definitions and new directions. *Contemporary Educational Psychology* 25, pp.54–67.

6 | Anxiety

Anxiety can just as well express itself by muteness as by a scream.

(Søren Kierkegaard)

It's like my head is full of cotton wool. I can't concentrate on anything and sometimes I can't even work out what the teacher is asking me to do. I know I should ask for help but instead I just sit and stare at the page or look at the thing I need to do but the words don't make any sense.

(Ella, 14)

I get angry. In my head I just say **** it, I can't be arsed with this anymore.

(Josh, 17)

Sometimes I can't sleep because I'm thinking about all the bad things that might happen at school.

(Harry, 10)

We all suffer from anxiety to some extent; anxiety is actually an evolutionary adaptation designed to help us survive. However, anxiety can have a major impact on our lives, preventing us from pursuing our dreams and reducing our quality of life. For students of all ages, anxiety can have a devastating impact on their academic lives, often leading to disengagement and a feeling of helplessness. Anxiety also affects students of all abilities, from those struggling at the bottom end of the scale to the most able.

Alice was a very competent student who had a very clear sense of purpose and direction. In many ways, she was very mature for her age; she planned well and usually handed in homework early, acted on feedback and honed her essay writing skills. The problem was that when it came to any kind of test situation, Alice would fall apart. Even low stakes tests filled her with dread and negatively impacted on her ability to concentrate and focus on her studies. I first met Alice when she entered sixth form, but her problems with anxiety predated her A-level studies. Her doctor had prescribed a number of medications including beta-blockers and anti-depressants and she had seen a counsellor on several occasions. The solution provided by the school was to allow Alice to take her exams in a separate room so that she wasn't overwhelmed by the experience of the exam hall; however, this just seemed to make her even more anxious.

Like many anxious students, Alice was destined to underachieve. She did obtain a place at a good university, but her options had been limited by her anxiety and her resultant lower than expected exam results. Socially, Alice was confident, even though she chose her friends carefully. At times, her social confidence appeared strained and it sometimes felt that she was trying hard to appear confident. Despite these specific behaviours (common amongst teenagers), Alice wasn't a generally anxious person; her anxiety was confined to certain situations that she found personally threatening in a number of ways. These certain situations were confined to those in which her ability and intelligence were measured in some formal way.

How might the school's response lead to Alice feeling more anxious?

Does your own school have a policy for dealing with test-anxious students and, if so, is it better than the approach used with Alice?

What kind of things might test-anxious students worry about?

Why the school's approach was wrong

The school may have had the best intentions and listened carefully to Alice when she explained what it was that made her anxious. In all probability, however, it's unlikely that Alice would have known the triggers or would have been able to describe them in any objective way. I've stood outside exam halls for many years, chatting to students and attempting to calm their fears and one thing is clear: all students are anxious before an exam (even the ones who tell you they are not). There is often something about the environment, as well as the exam itself, that is anxiety-provoking. Chatting to students about their exam fears can be enlightening and doesn't always involve the exam itself. In fact, their anxieties will include a number of general worries that indirectly raise levels of exam specific anxiety. For example:

> *'What if I can't find my seat?'*
>
> *'What if all of my five/six/seven . . . pens run out of ink?'*
>
> *'What if they give me the wrong exam paper?'*
>
> *'If I ask for extra paper will people think I'm cleverer than I am?'*
>
> *'If I don't ask for extra paper will people think I'm stupid?'*
>
> *'Are you absolutely sure I don't need a calculator for the English exam?'*
>
> *'What if I need a wee?'*

These questions might sound illogical, but anxiety often is. My own anxiety results in a need to know what I have to do in particular circumstances. For example, I had to know the procedure for asking for more paper in exams and knowing what to do if I needed to go to the toilet. Oddly, I was less anxious about the formal exam itself. Allowing a student to sit the exam alone rarely deals with any of these anxiety-promoting circumstances and the alternative environment can often lead to greater levels of anxiety. The strategy attempts to deal with the symptoms of the anxiety rather than helping the student to overcome his or her fears. We can attempt to deal with a fear of dogs by avoiding all dogs or a fear of social situations by ensuring that we never find ourselves in the company of strangers, but these measures represent weak short-term solutions that ultimately fail.

What we know about anxiety

According to the Office for National Statistics, around one-fifth of children in the UK suffer with anxiety. The anxiety they experience might not necessarily be related to test-taking or even education, so it remains difficult for us to estimate the number of young people experiencing this kind of anxiety. One of the first things we need to establish is that we all suffer from a degree of anxiety. Anxiety, worry and fear are evolutionary adaptations that help humans to survive and the species to flourish. Anxiety is seen in all animals, especially those at the lower end of the food chain due to the increased number of predators. Furthermore, a degree of anxiety is beneficial even in exam situations as it acts as an activating emotion, motivating us and forcing the body to pump oxygen to the brain. Too much anxiety, however, has a debilitating effect, impairing concentration and reducing working memory capacity. Prolonged or chronic anxiety can put a strain on our organs, cause physical and behavioural changes, cause depression and generally limit quality of life and overall wellbeing. Anxiety can also cause us to withdraw, thereby limiting those all-important social relationships, leading to the neglect of beneficial support networks.

Anxiety and the brain

I mentioned in Chapter 4 that specific regions of the brain are responsible for specific functions (known as localisation or localisation of function), but stressed that regions can also be responsible for a number of functions. In terms of anxiety, the brain areas of particular interest are the hippocampus and the amygdala. The amygdala is the almond-shaped structure nestled deep within the brain and often thought of as our emotional centre. However, it also acts as a communication hub between parts of the brain used to process incoming sensory signals and the parts of the brain that interpret these signals. The amygdala alerts the rest of the brain that a threat is present and triggers the fear or anxiety response (often described as 'fight or flight'). Emotional memories stored in the central part of the amygdala play an important role in anxiety related to specific fears such as phobias, so this is where the emotional component of that early encounter with an aggressive dog is to be found, leading to a lifelong fear of all dogs. More specifically, this is where those feelings related to the fear of exam situations reside. Recent studies have discovered that the right amygdala is smaller in Post-traumatic Stress Disorder (PTSD) patients with a history of childhood trauma (Veer *et al.*, 2015). The hippocampus is responsible for consolidating short-term memories into long-term memories, including threatening events. Some studies have shown that the hippocampus is smaller in some people who were victims of abuse or experienced military combat, although studies are often inconclusive. This indicates a link between emotional experiences and brain structure and the likelihood of a reciprocal relationship between the two.

During the fight or flight response, the brain triggers the secretion of noradrenaline and cortisol that gives us a boost by enhancing our powers of perception, our reflexes and our speed. Our heart rate also increases in order to get more blood to the muscles and air into the lungs. All this is vital to our survival, certainly way back in the days when early humans would have needed to hunt and escape dangerous wild animals. Under normal circumstances, once the danger has passed, the stress response subsides and returns the body to its default setting.

Anxiety, therefore, is not in itself our enemy; on the contrary, it exists to protect us from danger. Not only is anxiety a protective mechanism, it also helps us complete tasks including high stakes examinations. In 1908, psychologists Robert Yerkes and John Dillingham Dodson found that animals trained to perform a task were more successful when made moderately anxious beforehand. Similar studies over the decades with humans have reached the same conclusions. However, too much anxiety will impair performance; just enough psychological arousal is good, but once we pass the optimal point, the anxiety has a negative impact. This phenomenon has become known as the Yerkes-Dodson law (see Figure 6.1).

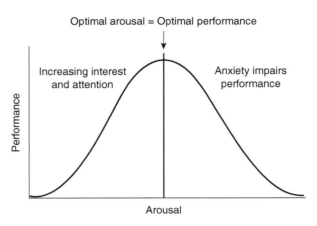

Figure 6.1 Yerkes-Dodson law

Types of anxiety

Anxiety manifests itself in many ways and appears in many guises. PTSD, Separation Anxiety Disorder, specific and social phobias, and Obsessive Compulsive Disorder are just a few specific anxiety disorders recognised by the psychiatric and psychological community. Generalised Anxiety Disorder (GAD) is, as the name suggests, a condition leading to chronic, excessive worry about a number of different things (anything from meeting new people to answering the telephone). Although GAD tends to affect older people, it can often be seen in children and adolescents. Children with GAD often display perfectionist traits, nervous habits, concentration problems, sleep issues and a decrease in self-confidence. They might also display more physical symptoms including headaches, other bodily aches such as stomach aches and shortness of breath. Another, more specific, disorder would be social phobia, the symptoms of which include a fear of public speaking, a fear of embarrassing oneself in public and the avoidance of social situations. Teachers and parents might be able to identify some of these symptoms in young people (although a visit to the GP is the only way to confirm these suspicions) and students might display some or all of these behaviours.

One extreme, and thankfully relatively rare, response to anxiety is selective mutism. I have only come across one selective mute in my teaching career; a year 7 pupil whom I only taught for a few months but who was unable to speak while at school (let's call him Nathan). At other times (outside school) Nathan spoke like any other 11-year-old and had lots of friends and a stable, supportive home life. Nathan's anxiety was very specific and related entirely to the school environment. I remember a member of senior management being perplexed by the idea of a student who 'refused to talk' and suggested several sanctions (punishments) that would *make* him speak. The problem was that Nathan wasn't refusing to speak; he couldn't speak. The fear of the school environment led to Nathan feeling frozen, a state specific petrification caused by his anticipation of anxiety-provoking situations. Nathan needed support, not punishment and in time (with help of a psychological services and amazing and sympathetic teaching assistants) he was able to manage his anxiety and play a greater role in the classroom.

Responses to anxiety can be highly complex; Nathan coped with his anxiety by retreating into a self-imposed silence, while others might become verbally aggressive or painfully withdrawn. Little humans are just like big humans; they adapt their behaviour in ways that make unbearable situations that little bit more bearable.

Psychological explanations

Biological models of anxiety are particularly advanced so we already know a great deal about how the body responds to stressful situations. However, anxiety has a psychological element and many anxieties have formed as a result of learned responses. People often develop phobias because something in their past has created a connection between a specific event and an emotional reaction. For example, as a child you might have been walking down the street when a large ferocious dog leaps out of a doorway, bears its teeth and barks and growls loudly. The fight or flight response kicks in and, with it, feelings of fear, dread and threat to personal safety.

Psychologically, these emotions are then attached not only to the specific dog that scared us, but also to all dogs.

A classic study from psychology demonstrates clearly how anxious responses to specific situations or things can be learned. In a now notorious and ethically questionable study conducted in 1919, pioneering behavioural psychologist John B. Watson and his assistant Rosalie Rayner attempted to produce an extreme conditioned response in a human subject. The human subject they selected was a 9-month-old infant known only as Albert B., or little Albert, and the feared stimulus a white rat. Prior to the experiment, Albert displayed no fear response at the presentation of the rat, but after several instances where the rat was paired with a load noise (Watson would hit an iron bar with a hammer until Albert showed signs of distress, including crying and attempting to crawl away), Albert began to associate the anxiety caused by the loud noise with the rat. After several trials, Albert developed an extreme phobia not only to the rat but also to a rabbit, a dog and even a fur coat. There is no indication that Watson ever intended to reverse the conditioning and, in fact, the first ever deconditioning of fear was only performed four years later by Mary Cover Jones. Fear and anxiety, therefore, are both an evolutionary adaptation and a learned response.

Not only can we explain anxiety in terms of a learned response, we can also explain it in terms of distorted thought processes. People might also develop anxiety over specific things or situations due to what are known as *cognitive distortions*. These are irrational thought patterns that make us view things as a physical threat even though no threat exists. People might, for example, avoid certain situations for fear of being seen as foolish or perhaps less intelligent than those around, even though the evidence fails to support this. Cognitive distortions are often seen in students with test anxiety and those who perhaps are less likely to engage in classroom activities. The reasons for such distortions are multifaceted, involving a number of processes including previous experience, peer relations and self-esteem. Such distortions then impact on the behaviour of young people in classroom situations and the wider educational environment.

Anxiety in the classroom

Although anxiety tends to be higher in test or exam situations, the classroom itself can become quite anxiety-provoking for some students. While test anxiety (discussed in the following section) remains an important concern, many individuals also suffer from anxiety in social situations, including the classroom. Studies have found that socially anxious people are often faster and better at picking up on behavioural cues from other people. Not only are they more skilled at this, they are also more likely to interpret these cues as negative (as opposed to positive or neutral). So not only are socially anxious children more likely to notice that yawn or tick of frustration from the teacher, they are also more likely to interpret it as negatively directed towards them. Brain imaging studies have discovered that people suffering from acute social anxiety react more powerfully to negative comments than do controls, suggesting that the brains of socially anxious children may be wired to respond to negative comments with hypersensitivity.

Such negative reactions are particularly evident in instances of *status-based anxiety*, where children measure themselves against peers in terms of their ranking. Groups tend to form a natural hierarchy (essentially, a pecking order) and classrooms are no different. Higher status students are thought to be more intelligent and popular than lower status students and this often causes a reluctance to engage from some lower status students. This is magnified in socially anxious students who fear being seen as unintelligent in front of their higher order peers. This would explain why some students are often *struck dumb* when challenged directly – it's best to say nothing than to be seen as unintelligent. This is similar to behaviour often seen in students displaying higher levels of introversion. So-called introverts tend towards hyper-vigilance and require longer thinking time to reduce their anxieties. While the extroverted students will often revel in being fully involved, introverts think deeply before committing themselves. Like introverts, socially anxious students prefer to work on their own or in small familiar groups and often recoil when challenged publicly. Working in unfamiliar groups can negatively impact progress in socially anxious students, particularly when placed within a pre-existing group.

Test anxiety

At the beginning of this chapter I introduced you to Alice and described the symptoms of her anxiety and how they were directly related to tests and exams. Alice might display some symptoms of GAD but her anxiety is much more specific and directed towards particular situations. What we are dealing with here is *test anxiety*, an extreme anxiety that occurs when faced with performance on an academic test; it is therefore the source of the anxiety that is at issue here and the reasons why this particular source results in such extreme psychological discomfort. Educational and developmental psychologist Moshe Zeidner describes test anxiety in terms of a combination of physiological over-arousal, tension and somatic symptoms, along with worry, dread, fear of failure and catastrophising that occur before or during test situations (Zeidner, 1998).

Catastrophising is another cognitive distortion, a symptom often seen in depression. It involves an irrational thought process that views all possible outcomes as negative. A student, therefore, might see the only possible result of an exam as failure or at least disappointment and this might have little to do with past experience (even if these experiences have been positive). On the other hand, past failure might lead to an expectation of future failure, with all the negative baggage that comes with it. Test anxiety is, therefore, real and specific. Not only that, but research consistently concludes that highly test-anxious students score around 12 percentile points below their low anxiety peers. There is also no upside to test anxiety – it will always remain a negative deactivating emotion because it takes sufferers over the threshold and away from any motivating qualities anxiety and fear may possess: test anxiety will invariably lead to lower academic achievement. This decreased academic achievement is multifaceted and includes many of the topics covered in this book; however, we know from studies that high levels of test anxiety are also associated with lower levels of resilience, specifically lower levels of academic buoyancy (the ability to bounce back from daily, low level adversity).

Some students are more prone to test anxiety

Some people are simply more anxious and this could be down to personality and genetics. It could also be the result of the way in which students respond to outside pressures, and while we don't wish to apportion blame, there does appear to be a role played here by influential others. Psychologist David Putwain and his colleagues, for example, found an association between parental pressure and higher levels of worry, test irrelevant thoughts and stronger bodily symptoms (Putwain *et al.*, 2010). Parents, of course, want the best for their children and have to walk a thin line between encouragement and pressure. Studies do find that those countries with systems that place greater emphasis on academic achievement also have lower levels of child wellbeing and higher levels of adolescent mental health problems (although these results aren't always consistent).

Blaming parents is certainly unhelpful, but it does provide us with an interesting insight into the mechanisms that can lead to higher levels of anxiety. This would also suggest that schools might also be inadvertently raising levels of test anxiety and reducing levels of achievement by placing too much pressure on individual students. You will have noticed that there are many components at play here and that different students act in a wide variety of ways to identical situations. While some students might act negatively to increased parental pressure, others will be thankful for it; some might even become anxious due to a lack of parental involvement. Parenting styles differ and young people react in diverse ways to these styles.

Test anxiety in younger children

While older children (specifically, those in the test intensive final years of secondary school) are perhaps under the greatest pressure, primary school children are increasingly required to undergo standardised tests in order to measure progress. Many argue that such testing is unnecessary and places undue pressure on young minds at a time when they should be enjoying their education. Research has found that children are more than aware that performance on such tests is important to their teachers and their parents and that anxieties are often transferred onto the child by outside players. In other words, the children themselves only become anxious when they detect the anxieties of others. Parents want their children to succeed primarily because of the implications they believe are attached to the test, but also, in some cases, in order to rank their children against others in the class. Teachers also want the best for their pupils but are still aware that bad performance on the test could reflect badly on them as professionals charged with the education of children. Young children are much more likely to pick up on these attitudes and associated behaviours and feel under pressure to make their parents and teachers proud of them.

Younger children who display more resilient characteristics are better equipped to combat the problems associated with test anxiety. In particular, children who believe they can succeed, trust and seek comfort from others and aren't overly sensitive tend to cope better with the pressures of testing. This view is not only supported by recent research, but also by longitudinal studies conducted over the past 30 years or so that have found that support mechanisms from within and outside the school setting help to build resilience and the ability to cope under pressure (as well as the ability to bounce back when things go wrong).

Even though parental pressure does play a role, it's certainly not the only cause of test anxiety. Other causes include fear of failure, procrastination, previous poor test performance and the test environment itself. Some of these topics are included elsewhere in this book, but it's worth taking some time to discuss them briefly in relation to test anxiety.

Fear of failure

This is covered in much greater detail later, along with the strategies learners might employ to avoid failure. Fear of failure can be thought of as a symptom of a society based on success or a natural desire to do well. The truth is that failure is something distinct and concrete and has a major impact on the way we view ourselves. In relation to education and learning, failure is a natural part of the learning process but is often thought of in a more negative way than it perhaps should be. Just like fluffing your lines in a school play or having your marriage proposal rejected, we all fear the possibility that we will potentially look less worthy, successful or intelligent than the people we judge our own standards by. Fear of failure can, therefore, drive test anxiety by making us fearful of negative consequences, be they looking less intelligent or losing out on that place at university. Young people especially are in the business of safeguarding their self-esteem and any situation that can potentially damage that is seen as threatening.

Procrastination

Procrastination is a highly complex phenomenon in itself and can be fuelled by a number of things, including fear and an erroneous perception of time. Test anxiety and procrastination are closely related in that test-anxious individuals are more likely to put off important tasks and decisions. For example, Norman Milgram and Yosef Toubiana found that those students who were more worried about an exam or the completion of a paper were more likely to delay preparation for the activity (Milgram & Toubiana, 1999).

Previous poor test performance

Under normal circumstances we base future success on past success so it would seem rational and logical to have higher anxiety levels when presented with an assessment that we did badly at previously. Past experience informs our feelings of the type of learner we are – this is known as *academic self-concept*. Just as experience informs our view of ourselves generally, academic self-concept works in unison with global self-esteem to produce a feeling of confidence or lack of confidence in specific academic areas. Previous poor test performance might indicate poor future performance, reducing confidence and increasing anxiety. This could also lead to a vicious cycle whereby poor performance on one test increases feelings of anxiety on the next. This anxiety and fear of failure then snowballs and performance is impaired.

Test environments

There is much more to sitting an exam than, well, sitting and doing the exam. Certain elements of the assessment might be more anxiety-provoking than others, as might the difficulty level. A multiple-choice test is less likely to provoke high levels of anxiety than, say, one based on extended essay writing. Remember Alice? She found the scientific nature of the psychology exam problematic and was put off by the lack of flexibility in the questions. Alice much preferred (or feared less) her English literature and philosophy exams because they allowed her to engage in extended writing and, to an extent, explore a range of ideas. The environment always plays a role – many students are made anxious by the formal nature of exam halls. Time constraints mean that students must organise their time to ensure that all test questions can be answered, meaning that there is little time for mind blanks (which can exacerbate the anxiety).

Some groups are more vulnerable to test anxiety

Research in Israel, the US and the UK have identified certain groups that appear to suffer more from anxiety related to test-taking (Putwain, 2007). Putwain and his team in the UK found that the most vulnerable groups tended to be females, those from lower socio-economic backgrounds and those with an ethnic origin other than white British. Learners with English as an additional language do score higher on levels of test anxiety, but the data suggests a much lower significance level. These results are very similar to those found in US and Israeli studies. Interestingly, Black and Asian groups both appear to score high on levels of test anxiety even though these groups differ significantly in terms of educational outcomes. While specific British-Asian groups (most notably British-Chinese and British-Indian) outperform all other ethnic groups, learners from the Black community have been identified as underachieving. This seemingly contradictory pattern perhaps highlights the cultural differences between the groups and the value different cultures place on success. It's possible that the high value placed on success by some cultures leads to higher levels of anxiety in these groups of learners while other groups have become tainted by the seemingly inevitable negative consequences of test-taking.

Another interesting group are those from low socio-economic families. These results are also consistent with the US and Israeli studies; however, different ways of measuring socio-economic status could reduce the validity of these comparisons. For example, the Israeli study relied on social class while in the UK there has been a move away from this towards a system based on labour relations. It would be interesting to discover if other measures led to similar results, such as free school meals or the pupil premium. Of course, the mechanisms involved are highly complex; why should students from poorer families be more anxious about taking exams than those students from better off backgrounds? Similarly, middle-class parents have a tendency to be more *pushy* when it comes to academic success, suggesting that the children of wealthier families should be more (not less) anxious about success. This further complicates our understanding of activating-deactivating positive and negative emotions. You will recall that some emotions might be useful even if they are negative, and you will also recall my suggestion that test anxiety can never be viewed as activating negative emotions because of the harmful behavioural and cognitive outcomes. Furthermore, Putwain found only a small (and statistically insignificant) increase in levels of test anxiety in year 11 pupils, suggesting that levels of anxiety don't rise as high stakes exams draw nearer. This would further suggest that test anxiety is a relatively stable and trait-like disposition or that individuals have developed stable ways of dealing with the pressure.

Stress contagion

Stress contagion refers to the transmission of anxiety from one individual to another. More broadly, *affect* contagion is the transmission of any emotion to other people. The suggestion here is that some students aren't necessarily anxious in themselves but have picked up the anxieties of others, primarily teachers but also parents.

The evidence supporting the existence of affect contagion is strong. A 2014 study looked at how stress experienced by mothers can be transferred to their young children, discovering that mothers' stressful experiences are contagious to their infants and that the anxiety caused by such experiences can reciprocally influence both mother and infant (Waters *et al.*, 2014).

Research is now beginning to reveal a complex reciprocal relationship between teacher stress and rising levels of stress amongst students. A study conducted in Canada found that teachers suffering from occupational burnout tend to have students who suffer from high levels of anxiety, indicating that teacher and student stress are linked (Oberle & Schonert-Reichl, 2016). This study is particularly interesting because instead of using self-completion questionnaires to measure levels of anxiety in students, it used biological markers, namely the levels of the stress hormone cortisol.

In previous studies of pre-school children, high levels of cortisol have been found during increased levels of teacher–pupil conflict, while lower levels of conflict predict a decrease in cortisol levels. Similarly, less academically successful teenagers who displayed poor behaviour have been found to have higher concentrations of the hormone. Higher levels of the stress hormone have also been found in children excluded from their friendship groups and teenage boys who have been victims of bullying. Cortisol, therefore, is an excellent objective way of measuring student stress, one that bypasses the potential bias of self-completion questionnaires.

In the Canadian study, those teachers who scored high on measures of burnout tended to have students with higher levels of cortisol in their saliva. Eva Oberle and Kimberly Schonert-Reichl who carried out the study, suggest that stressful classroom climate could be the result of inadequate support for teachers. Lack of support then impacts on the ability of teachers to manage student behaviour, which in turn results in poorly managed classrooms where the needs of the student aren't being met. This increases levels of stress and consequently levels of cortisol secretion. There is, of course, an alternative explanation, whereby stress originates from the students rather than from the teacher. Issues such as student anxiety and behaviour problems result in teachers feeling overwhelmed, ultimately leading to higher levels of burnout. Either way, if teachers don't feel as if they are adequately supported, students become collateral damage.

Certainly, teachers who score higher on dimensions related to burnout also report other negative symptoms, including higher stress levels, less effective classroom management, less satisfaction in the workplace and less efficacy in teaching. Burnout itself is often the result of time pressure, lack of support and resources, and challenging relationships with pupils. Teachers perhaps rarely consider that their own anxieties could be feeding those of their students, and although this book isn't about the impact of emotions on teaching, there does seem to be a strong link between the emotional learner and the emotional teacher. It's therefore worth keeping in mind that ensuring our own anxieties are managed effectively and that management structures ensure that teachers are supported will ultimately reap benefits for pupils. It's also worth noting that reducing student anxiety could have a positive impact on teacher anxiety and burn out.

Reducing anxiety

Students will experience chronic anxiety over exams for many different reasons, and targeting those learners will not only increase their own wellbeing but also increase the chances of academic success. Researchers have known for some time that so-called *fear appeals* can backfire dramatically. For example, telling students that if they don't revise they will fail and never get a good job only increases anxiety and reduces performance. It's also clear that few schools understand the mechanisms or the consequences of anxiety and are therefore ill-equipped to help those students who suffer from it. Teachers aren't mental health professionals and shouldn't be relied upon to intervene in issues relating to anxiety; however, many teachers will instinctively offer advice and support to those students who become overwhelmed by the pressures of high stakes testing. Anyone can pass on simple relaxation techniques that help to reduce some of the symptoms of chronic anxiety. General practitioners might prescribe medication such as beta-blockers and anti-depressants, but these treat the symptoms rather than the cause and can result in uncomfortable side effects. Interventions often centre upon reducing the symptoms of anxiety, because such interventions are relatively simple and generally effective. Several small-scale studies have identified a number of strategies that appear to alleviate some of the more damaging symptoms of test anxiety.

Mindfulness

Mindfulness techniques have proved effective in a number of studies targeting general anxiety and emotional regulation. *The Learning to BREATHE* programme is one such intervention that has seen positive results, albeit using rather limited sample sizes (Metz *et al.*, 2013). Mindfulness works by self-regulating attention and the non-judgemental awareness of experience, which in turn impacts on cognitive processes and physiological symptoms. Concentrating on the breath and being mindful of our own bodily symptoms helps to slow the heart rate and quieten the mind. It doesn't work for every-one, however, and there have been instances where mindfulness has increased rather than decreased the level of anxiety. Furthermore, there is so far little evidence from randomised controlled trials that mindfulness has any long-lasting benefit in terms of academic achievement. In the end, only time will tell.

Simple behavioural strategies for test anxiety

This technique is based on the premise that test anxiety is the result of an association between an event (the test) and the emotional experi-ences (anxiety). Because tests are associated with anxiety, we need to be able to help the student re-learn and associate test-taking with less stressful emotions.

- Go through some simple relaxation techniques such as breath counting or guided meditation. I have found that allowing the stu-dent to monitor their heart rate while doing this is useful, either through specific heart rate monitors or fitness trackers with a heart rate function. Actually seeing your heart rate fall reinforces the belief that the technique is working.

- After around four to six relaxation sessions (some students will become skilled at this faster than others, especially if they practice at home), begin to introduce elements that they associate with test-taking. Exam papers or photographs of students in an exam hall are useful to begin with. While the student examines the exam paper or looks at the photograph, ask them to practise their breathing or other relaxation techniques at the same time. The aim here is to associate the exam with a feeling of relaxation rather than one of anxiety.

- Over the next few weeks, gradually increase the level of stimulus, for example, ask the student to answer some of the easier questions from the paper and work up to the more difficult ones. If possible, allow them to sit at a desk in the exam hall during the later stages, practise the relaxation technique and work through the exam paper. Discuss with them any outstanding anxieties and incorporate these into the schedule.

This technique (known as systematic desensitisation) has proved highly successful with people suffering from often extreme phobias. The stages can be extended or reduced depending on progress.

Familiarisation with the exam environment

This can be used with whole groups and helps to deal with anxieties directly related to place and procedure. Students' anxiety is often irrational (such as not having enough pens or not being able to find their seat in the exam hall). Visiting the exam hall and describing the procedure can often help with these anxieties, as can filling out the front sheet of an exam paper. If possible, allow them to stand or sit in the place where they will be on the day of the exam and take note of the students around them.

Defeating anxiety with FEAR

FEAR – Face Everything And Recover – is one of the cornerstones of Cognitive Behavioural Therapy. When we first dive into a swimming pool, the water feels cold, but the longer we remain, the warmer it seems. The same is true with anxiety; if we regularly remain in the stressful situation until the anxiety subsides, we experience less anxiety when we next find ourselves in that situation – this is called *habituation*. A friend of mine had an irrational fear of answering the phone until she spent several months working in a call centre (she needed the money). Within a couple of days she was feeling less and less anxious when a phone rang because she was having to do it all day. Exposure to the anxiety-provoking event should be challenging but not over-whelming, as the exposure gradually desensitises the student to the exam situation and can be used with whole classes (not just those with specific anxiety issues).

At the beginning of the year explain to students that they will be tested regularly (this reduces the possibility of nasty surprises that can shut down the more anxious individuals). Emphasise the *low stakes* nature of these tests and perhaps begin with multiple-choice questions that tend to result in lower levels of anxiety. Raise the stakes as you go, with more difficult tests that gradually begin to more closely resemble an exam paper.

FEAR normalises exam-taking. Instead of it being an unusual event that happens at the end of the year, tests and exams become part of every-day lessons. We are far less likely to become anxious about everyday events, especially if they are expected and continually repeated.

With younger children

Keeping standardised testing low key can often reduce test anxiety in the more fearful pupils. Often, pupils are made anxious by the build up of such tests and practice sessions that take place in the weeks preceding them.

Reducing the transfer of anxieties from parents and teachers onto children can make a big difference in terms of how the children view their own anxieties. Adults might understandably feel anxious for the children who are required to sit the tests, but this anxiety might not be present in the children themselves. Ensuring that good support systems are in place is vital in order to reduce anxiety. When a child understands that there are others they can go to and discuss any fears they have, they are more able to face those fears successfully. Understanding that such tests aren't a judgement on the child's ability or intelligence helps them to cope with any pressure they might experience.

Dealing with social anxiety

In many ways helping students cope in social situations is much more problematic than helping them to cope with test anxiety. It's tempting to try and *bring them out of their shells*, but this strategy often backfires because fears are often deep-seated and arise when the student feels threatened.

Be strategic with groupwork

Groupwork can prove arduous at the best of times and its efficacy is difficult to gauge. Socially anxious children become more anxious when having to work with people they don't know very well, so friendship groups are better than random groupings. Pair-work, often more effective anyway, is an ideal strategy for the socially anxious, and pairs can be joined together later in the activity to discuss what they have done.

Other ways to challenge

Directly challenging anxious children rarely achieves results. Younger anxious children often become emotional when singled out, while with older ones it can become a battle of wills. Generally, the socially anxious children will be the ones who rarely raise their hands in class and while *no-hands* policies can be successful, they still tend to favour the more confident. Mini-whiteboards are wonderful for calming the fears of anxious children and ensuring that all in the class are making progress. Students write their answer on their whiteboard and everyone raises them high in the air when prompted by the teacher. This technique is successful for two reasons. First, the social anxious children (as well as the introverts) gain extra thinking time while they are writing their answers; they have time to consider their response and correct any error that they recognise. Second, it reduces any status-based anxiety by allowing students to realise that even the most favourable students (the ones at the top of the social hierarchy) aren't invulnerable to failure.

Don't just avoid: embed coping strategies

These strategies might suggest that the best way to deal with anxiety is to avoid anxiety-provoking situations. Avoidance, however, is far from a long-term solution. With test anxiety, we can employ strategies that gradually help reduce the fear. With social anxiety, we can attempt a similar strategy by gradually increasing the level of interaction. Teachers can advance the whiteboard technique by gradually introducing discussion and clarification around some of the answers such as 'Can you explain why you chose that answer?' or 'Could you have chosen a different answer? What might that have been?'

Some final thoughts

Anxiety is a part of everyday life, and some people are naturally more anxious than others. Learners aren't all the same and they will approach their studies and their exams in different ways. I don't believe that young people can be or should be trained to behave in identical ways and fear that such an approach will inevitably lead to lower levels of wellbeing and greater mental health problems. Identifying those at risk of failure because of anxiety is crucial and complex, and providing appropriate help can be problematic. Nevertheless, debilitating emotional states can be relieved even in cultures where high stakes testing places enormous strain on our young people. I have not attempted to debate the role of high stakes testing here; I have taken a pragmatic position rather than a confrontational one. Anxiety can be positive and negative as well as activating and deactivating; however, test anxiety and social anxiety are always debilitating. One emotion that spans the divide between positive and negative is boredom, and it's to this surprisingly interesting topic we now turn.

Chapter summary

- Anxiety can impact learning in both positive and negative ways.
- Some students will suffer more with anxiety than others and will require greater support.
- Understanding the cause of the anxiety is the first step to developing effective interventions.
- Students prone to severe anxiety are more likely to underperform.
- Coping strategies should be embedded in all students.
- For test-anxious students, normalising test environments and situations can help them to cope more effectively.
- Anxious teachers and parents can pass these anxieties onto students through stress contagion.
- Strategies such as mindfulness can help calm anxious students, while regular low stakes testing can acclimatise them to the test-taking environment.

References

Metz, S.M., Frank, J.L., Reibel, D., Cantrell, T., Sanders, R. & Broderick, P.C. (2013). The effectiveness of the Learning to BREATHE Program on adolescent emotion regulation. *Research in Human Development* 10(3), pp.252–272.

Milgram, N. & Toubiana, Y. (1999). Academic anxiety, academic procrastination, and parental involvement in students and their parents. *The British Journal of Educational Psychology* 69(3), pp.345–361.

Oberle, E. & Schonert-Reichl, K.A. (2016). Stress contagion in the classroom? The link between classroom teacher burnout and morning cortisol in elementary school students. *Social Science & Medicine* 159(April), pp.30–37.

Putwain, D.W. (2007). Test anxiety in UK schoolchildren: Prevalence and demographic patterns. *The British Journal of Educational Psychology* 77(3), pp.579–593.

Putwain, D.W., Woods, K. & Symes, W. (2010). Personal and situational predictors of test anxiety of students in post-compulsory education. *The British Journal of Educational Psychology* 80(1), pp.137–160.

Veer, I.M., Oei, N.Y.L., Van Buchem, M.A., Spinhoven, P., Elzinga, B.M. & Rombouts, S.A.R.B. (2015). Evidence for smaller right amygdala volumes in posttraumatic stress disorder following childhood trauma. *Psychiatry Research: Neuroimaging* 233(3), pp.436–442.

Waters, S.F., West, T.V. & Mendes, W.B. (2014). Stress contagion: Physiological covariation between mothers and infants. *Psychological Science* 25(4), pp.934–942.

Zeidner, M. (1998). *Test Anxiety: The State of the Art*. New York: Springer.

7 Boredom

Boredom is the root of all evil – the despairing refusal to be oneself.

(Søren Kierkegaard)

Kids get bored because sometimes the material they have to learn is quite dull.

(Andy, Secondary School teacher)

Often they [the children] simply don't have the attention spans necessary for good quality learning.

(Helen, Primary Head)

Some of the teachers are just so boring. They have no idea how to make the subject interesting. They just drone on in this boring voice then tell us to answer the questions in the textbook.

(Rachael, 17)

I like fun things. I like it when we can have fun and learn at the same time.

(Oliver, 8)

Why do you think students get bored?

Do you think that your explanations match those of the students themselves?

We all experience boredom in different ways, but we also attribute boredom differently. Students often identify the teacher as the source of their boredom, while teachers themselves attribute student boredom to other factors (such as the curriculum or some characteristic of the student). Regardless of the source, boredom can scupper the best planned lesson if it results in student disengagement.

Ironically, boredom is a quite interesting academic emotion; indeed, it's also an interesting emotion outside the learning environment. Some philosophers have much to say about boredom. The German philosopher Arthur Schopenhauer didn't really think much of it: 'for every human life', he wrote in 1818, 'is tossed backwards and forwards between pain and boredom'. Schopenhauer saw boredom as suffering, a reminder of the ultimate meaningless of human existence. To be fair to the gloomy Arthur, I have spent many hours of my life sitting in meetings, pondering the meaning of life and reminding myself that with every tick of the clock I am one second closer to death. I think I have a propensity towards boredom, or at least a malfunctioning attention system (having checked my emails once and Twitter twice since I began writing this paragraph). Perhaps, as Kierkegaard suggests, I'm just refusing to be myself; sitting in a mind-numbing meeting rather than getting up and leaving (which is usually what I really want to do). Many of us find boredom almost physically painful, and even when we are engaged in an activity our minds begin to wander. We daydream; we *zone out* and we flit from one activity to another. If, as adults, we find it painful to sit through meaningless meetings and as teachers we begin to nod off during a presentation on training day, then how can we be critical of our pupils when they behave in a similar way? Should we make lessons lively and entertaining in order to engage (whatever that means)? Furthermore, do we really understand the reasons why pupils get bored in the first place?

Organisational psychologist Cynthia Fisher describes boredom as 'an unpleasant, transient affective state in which the individual feels a persuasive lack of interest and difficulty concentrating on the current activity' (Fisher, 1993), while psychologist Mark Leary offers a more concise definition: 'an affective experience associated with cognitive attentional processes'. Both these definitions adequately describe my feelings of being bored, but suggest little about the motivational aspects of boredom – in that when I'm bored I feel a desire to escape the boredom by doing something (even if I don't do anything) and the near tangible pain it appears to cause me. I recall sitting in a meeting that was scheduled to last one hour even though there wasn't enough content to keep anyone there for that long (in fact I recall sitting in a great many meetings like this). As the seconds ticked by, my mind began to wander, resting upon all the work I had to do and becoming more and more anxious at the realisation that I was wasting valuable time. I doodled in my planner, checked my phone several times, closed my eyes for a few moments, and looked at my watch, the clock on the wall and the watch on the wrist of the person seated next to me. I could feel my heart rate quickening and palms becoming clammy as the stress response began to kick in – my pain was real; I was bored to the point of anxiety, I wanted to escape but protocol decreed that the meeting must last one hour, no more and no less.

In fact, boredom can even cause us to inflict pain on ourselves. In a recent study, Chantal Nederkoorn and her colleagues actually found that people would inflict painful electric shocks on themselves in order to relieve the symptoms of boredom (Nederkoorn *et al.*, 2016). While I don't believe I've ever been in a meeting that has inflicted so much psychological pain upon me that I would want to inflict physical pain upon myself, I've never had the equipment to do so. Perhaps I would given the opportunity.

Reinhard Pekrun feels my pain. The University of Munich psychologist defines boredom as 'an affective state composed of unpleasant feelings, lack of stimulation and low physiological arousal'. This pretty much sums up my experience although I would suggest that, at times, my arousal is high (I want to get out of that meeting!). Pekrun's interest in boredom is also a little different from Fisher and Leary in that Pekrun is specifically interested in how boredom manifests itself in classroom settings.

Boredom, and people's propensity towards it, has been linked to academic underachievement. Boredom also appears to be associated with other non-academic behaviours such as depression, anger, impulsivity and even pathological gambling and bad driving. While gambling and bad driving are unlikely to impact academic achievement, depression, anger and impulsivity might (Pekrun *et al.*, 2014). According to Eric Dahlen of the University of Mississippi, boredom predicts a propensity to experience anger and also to display maladaptive anger expression, aggression and deficits in anger control (see Goetz *et al.*, 2013 for a more detailed discussion). This suggests that boredom could lead to some behaviours teachers witness in the classroom, especially from those students who display higher levels of aggression and poor emotional regulation. So are bored students simply not interested? Thomas Goetz of the University of Konstanz, Germany thinks not. A lack of interest is neutral in that it doesn't cause any emotional pain or discomfort, whereas boredom can be emotionally distressing. They also have different motivational consequences; a student who lacks interest neither wishes to engage in an activity nor do they wish to avoid it, whereas, a bored student will feel compelled to escape the situation. Such behaviour led the late Daniel Berlyne to suggest that boredom results from high (not low) arousal (Berlyne, 1960). The behaviours arising from boredom, such as restlessness, agitation and emotional upset, motivate the individual to escape, perhaps by misbehaving, falling asleep, daydreaming or simply letting the mind wander. The classroom represents a closed system (there is no physical escape) whereas if you or I are at home and bored we could go for a walk or a drive or engage in other activities beyond our four walls. So in some students the tension builds and behaviour can turn maladaptive.

Boredom, therefore, represents an academic emotion; an emotion that is tied to learning situations and achievement-related activities. Common sense suggests that bored students aren't learning efficiently because they aren't fully engaged with the activities related to the subject or content. However, there might be many reasons why pupils become bored and these reasons often differ between student and teacher. If you are a teacher you might have specific ideas about what creates boredom in your classroom; perhaps it's certain topics within the subject that are boring or perhaps the delivery. My students always found research methods the most boring part of the A-level psychology specification. I suspect this was in part to do with their expectations of the subject, even though we tried hard to emphasise that A-level psychology was very little to do with reading people's minds and catching serial killers. Research methods represented a detour that they didn't want to take and this was perhaps one reason why they found it less than stimulating. In other words, the content failed to meet the expectation. It's a bit like waiting for that new superhero movie to come out, watching all the fantastic trailers and immersing yourself in all the hype, only to find that, on viewing, it fails to live up to the hype and your high expectations of it. You feel bored, disappointed and a little bit let down.

Teachers and students differ in their views about what makes us bored

I've spoken to many teachers about this, both in the staffroom and when I deliver talks and workshops. These chats seem to support the research that reveals that often the reason students are bored isn't the same as why teachers think they are bored. Teachers have a tendency to blame either the content or the individual characteristics of the students, while students point to content and delivery, that is, the teacher. Elena Daschmann along with Thomas Goetz and Robert Stupinsky were also interested in this (Daschmann et al., 2014). They administered open-ended questionnaires to 111 grade nine students and conducted semi-structured interviews with 117 grade nine teachers in German schools about what led to students' boredom. Results overlapped somewhat, for example the relevance of the subject or the content of the specific topic. Some students directed the cause of their boredom to other students (others in the class being 'too loud', for example), while teachers suggested the size of the class had an impact. Some were unrelated to school ('I was in a bad mood because of a boy', was one response), so perhaps we need to acknowledge that students bring their own baggage with them and that this can impact behaviour inside the classroom.

The main reason for boredom cited by students was the continual monotony of the scheme, the going over of the same content every day. Teachers, however, thought that boredom arose when pupils were over-challenged with 'a nut that they can't crack' or under-challenged because the teacher was going over material the students felt they already knew. However, the most startling difference was that while students identified the teacher as a source of boredom, the teachers themselves never did – 'When the teacher is as boring as a sleeping pill', was one comment. Teachers therefore might have a reasonably good idea of the specific things that make their students bored, even though they don't appear to see themselves as a source of the boredom. With such a small sample, it's difficult to see if these results are universal, but they do provide some indication about the disparity of boredom beliefs and the way in which multiple personal and public elements can feed it.

The results from this study are quite detailed and specific, suggesting that there are many reasons why students become bored. More general models have also been proposed, often related to a number of factors both internal and external.

Internal and external antecedents of boredom

Cynthia Fisher (1993) has proposed a three-pronged model based on aspects outside and within the individual and the fit between the two. Certain antecedents of boredom, suggests Fisher, lie outside the person, for example the task or the environmental conditions, while others inhabit the person. Aspects within the person are perhaps more complex and could certainly include personality. Genetic components unrelated to personality also play a role, specifically those related to academic achievement such as intelligence (as measured by IQ). The third antecedent involves the fit between the external component and internal component. The fit is important because you need to gauge the complexity of the task with the ability of the individual to complete it; if the task is too hard then the student will feel overwhelmed, too easy and they will feel under-challenged.

Pekrun's Control Value Theory also relates to both subjective and environmental factors. Boredom arises through the interplay between certain external determinants (such as quality of teaching) and individual internal appraisals (Pekrun *et al.*, 2007). Learning environments are approached through aspects of personal control and subjective evaluation. For example, if teaching quality is poor and the students feel that they have little personal control over the situation, plus the student feels the task has little value, is meaningless or irrelevant to their needs, the likelihood that they will be bored is increased. On the other hand, if the quality of teaching is high and the instructions are clear (the students have some kind of control) then whether or not the students become bored will be the result of perceived value and meaning of the task. In the aforementioned study one comment from a student was 'I think German is the most pointless subject in general', meaning that even if instruction and teaching were excellent, the perceived value of the subject was low and this was the antecedent of the boredom the student experienced. Unfortunately, this would imply that some subjects, or topics within subjects, would always be boring to some students, no matter how much of a cabaret teachers try to stage. That said, teachers exist to educate and not to entertain and the idea that teachers should always aspire to make learning fun can be as equally damaging to the learning process as Mr or Mrs Boring. Often, the objective of the learning episode is lost in the desire to make the task fun and exciting.

All boredom is not the same

You would think that all boredom was the same, but actually when we look more closely we discover subtle and not-so-subtle differences. Researchers have actually identified five types of boredom: indifferent, calibrating, reactant, searching and apathetic.

Indifferent boredom

Indifferent boredom is associated with a relaxed, calm yet withdrawn demeanour. There appears to be little emotional discomfort and it's likely you'll never even notice students suffering from it. You'll struggle to recall their name and face at parents' evening. It's the boy at the back of the class who never disrupts the lesson and rarely makes any impression or significant progress.

Calibrating boredom

Calibrating boredom is the type associated with mindwandering and daydreaming. People with this type of boredom know that they need to do something different but aren't sure of what to do or how to do it if they did know. It often occurs when people do repetitive tasks and need to reduce the boredom but don't know how.

Reactant boredom

Reactant boredom is considered the worst. Reactant bored individuals have high levels of arousal and display lots of negative emotions. They are often restless and aggressive and feel the need to blame others for their boredom, such as parents and teachers.

Searching boredom

Searching boredom is also categorised by negative emotions but with a creeping disagreeable restlessness. People with this kind of boredom will often focus on other activities in order to relieve the discomfort.

Apathetic boredom

Apathetic boredom is the most recently *discovered* type and is categorised by feelings of helplessness. In a paper published in 2013, Thomas Goetz and colleagues from Germany, Canada and the US, reported on a series of studies utilising experience sampling techniques to establish the reasons why people (in this case university and high school students) get bored and, more importantly, if previous research that identified four types of boredom stands up to further experimental scrutiny (Goetz *et al.*, 2013).

Goetz and his team supplied each participant with a Personal Digital Assistant (PDA) loaded with specially designed software. The PDAs would then emit a number of audible sounds throughout the day and participants would complete a questionnaire that appeared on the screen (the procedure was slightly different between the two groups – university or high school students). The questionnaires required scaled responses to identify levels of boredom, wellbeing, satisfaction, enjoyment, anger and anxiety. If they identified themselves as being bored, they were asked a second set of questions on arousal and valence (the extent to which they were attracted or repelled by the task).

Results indicated the existence of a fifth type of boredom – apathetic boredom, which appeared widely prevalent amongst both groups of students. The interesting point here is that the team identified apathetic boredom as possessing characteristics related to learned-helplessness (a condition associated with depression and discussed in Chapter 2), making apathetic boredom a very unpleasant experience indeed. The implications for teaching and learning are as yet unknown but might suggest there is a learning process involved in certain types of boredom. On the other hand, there might also be some speculation involved in the findings and the *types of boredom* might simply be the result of the statistical analysis rather than anything *real* (so-called *reification*). Nevertheless, the mere suggestion should ignite further research, certainly in terms of pupil wellbeing and factors such as day-to-day resilience.

The positive side of boredom

So far we have only thought of boredom as being a negative emotion, but are there any benefits to being bored? From an existential point of view (remember Schopenhauer?) it's highly likely that boredom pushes us to find meaning in our lives. This is certainly a laudable activity and fits in with certain types of boredom. However, can boredom serve an educational function, or more specifically, can boredom benefit learning? You'll recall that emotions can be both positive and negative as well as activating and deactivating, so at the same time as being a negative emotion, boredom could serve an activating function (like spurring us on to find the meaning of life). Certainly, boredom could act as an alarm bell for teachers. Boredom, as we have already discussed, is not the same as not being interested, the emotions underlying boredom are screaming out for stimulation – it's Audrey from Little Shop of Horrors shouting 'Feed me now!' – and while it's far beyond the realms of possibility to engage all students all of the time, if a teacher looks out onto the classroom and sees the majority of the class nodding off, it's pretty clear the game needs to change. But such a positive outcome doesn't mean that boredom itself is inherently activating.

Sandi Mann at the University of Central Lancashire wondered if boredom could actually make people more creative (Mann & Cadman, 2014). Mann conducted a number of studies where participants were given either a boring or a control activity followed by a creative task, such as coming up with as many creative uses for an everyday object as possible. Those given the boring task were able to offer a greater number of uses than the control group, leading Mann to suggest that the boring activity allowed participants to let their mind wander and activate deeper levels of creativity. Studies like these are beginning to change the way in which we view boredom and related activities that are seen as serving little purpose. So what are we doing when we are bored that could activate our creativity and is it only our creativity that is being stimulated?

Daydreaming and mindwandering

One of the most interesting things we do when we are bored is allow our mind to wander beyond the parameters of the task. Daydreaming, mindwandering or task-unrelated thought often takes place during automatic behaviours such as driving a car or other attention demanding tasks. Mindwandering is also tied up with affective states other than boredom. This decoupling of thought from the current task onto more internal mental events is the bane of many teachers and is often seen as behaviour associated with laziness and inattention. Certainly, mindwandering has been linked to a number of negative outcomes including increased error rates, poor working memory function, decreased knowledge retention and comprehension problems (Xu & Metcalfe, 2016). Sigmund Freud associated it with infantile thinking, a return to a child-like state, but recent research suggests that in some circumstances mindwandering can have certain cognitive benefits.

There is a common-sense assumption that when we are doing nothing our brain is in some kind of stand-by mode; it's just sitting there, waiting for stimulus. Furthermore, there also exists the view that teachers can and should prevent students from daydreaming. There is certainly a valid case for this position; after all, mindwandering can lead to negative consequences. The problem is that it's very difficult to prevent anybody from daydreaming and many of us engage in such activities much more often than we might think. In a study conducted by Matthew Killingsworth and Daniel Gilbert (Killingsworth & Gilbert, 2010), 2,250 volunteers were contacted at random intervals via an iPhone app and asked about their current state of happiness. Mindwandering was reported in over 46 per cent of samples, suggesting that most people spend a huge amount of time daydreaming. Data also found that people reported being less happy the more their mind wandered from the task they were engaged in (but mindwandering was less likely to occur during sex). This points to a clear relationship between daydreaming and affective state (the subjective emotional experience). Neither does daydreaming represent *doing nothing*; in fact, the brain is still hard at work. Kalina Christoff and Jonathan Schooler placed participants into an fMRI scanner and asked them to engage in a tedious task. It took only seconds for the volunteers' brains to begin to wander, during which time the cortex was consuming huge amounts of energy. Analysis of the scans found that participants were awake but not really present, existing somewhere between sleep dreaming and focussed attentiveness.

Mindwandering is therefore an intensive process with many negative outcomes. However, research carried out at Meta Lab, based at the University of California, Santa Barbara, has found that people who engage in more mindwandering also score higher on a number of scales used to measure creativity. Daydreamers are therefore more creative, suggesting that mindwandering might be linked to creative thinking. The problem is that not all daydreaming is equally effective and people who are most aware of their own mindwandering seem more able to use the experience effectively. The important element here is something called meta-awareness; it's all well and good zoning out but unless you are able to recognise the idea or the revelation when it arises, the experience has little value. People can, however, develop the skill of meta-awareness and become more adept at grabbing hold of insight when it arises; they essentially get better at being bored (see Killingsworth & Gilbert, 2010 for a more complete discussion of these and other relevant studies).

During periods of distraction, we loosen our thought processes in order to find solutions to problems using previously unexplored options. Daydreaming can allow us to reach more creative conclusions by facilitating a period of incubation. This is perhaps why Mann found that bored people are more creative. Daydreaming also enhances our sense of identity, often through what cognitive scientists call *Future Orientated Cognition* – we recall our past and envisage what our futures might be like or imagine alternative scenarios dependent upon the choices we make. Interestingly (and incredibly sad at the same time) people with dementia are unable to daydream and to forecast the future due to damage to the default mode network.

Boredom, therefore, can have positive consequences due to its activating qualities. The positives are perhaps more due to the propensity for daydreaming that arises while we are bored, and it's unlikely that making lessons boring would in any way enhance learning outcomes. Nevertheless, there is a strong suggestion here that cognitive downtime could help complex ideas and concepts to incubate, leading to a deeper understanding through creative thought processes. The upside is that when students appear disengaged, there is a likelihood that they are far from it, but rather working through ideas that they don't yet fully understand.

Coping with boredom

It might seem odd, but students don't always cope with boredom in the same way. It might also seem odd to suggest that they indeed need to cope; after all, boredom doesn't necessarily require us to do anything, right? As I've already mentioned, boredom can be a psychologically painful and even physically disturbing experience, especially in the closed system of the classroom. Students don't want to be bored and they employ a number of strategies to prevent the discomfort that can arise (some adaptive and others maladaptive). Studies have found that bored students roughly fall into one of three categories:

- *Reappraisers* – This is the most effective coping activity whereby students respond to boring tasks by increasing their focus on the potential value of the task or activity. These students find the task boring but are able to find some kind of value in it, such as a particular topic in a history lesson being able to provide a better understanding of a separate, more interesting topic.

- *Criticisers* – These students attempt to actively change the situation by expressing their frustration towards the teacher and asking for an alternative activity. Criticisers might complain that the task is stupid or pointless and suggest more interesting topics or activities.

- *Evaders* – The most destructive of the three strategists, evaders, will employ a number of avoidant strategies in order to relieve the boredom. Younger children might chat to their classmates while older ones might resort to using phones and other electronic devices.

Dealing with boredom in the classroom

The classroom environment

Classrooms need to be free of distractions. Strict *no phones* policies and noise control is essential. Chatter from other classmates can distract those whose attention has wandered through boredom. Research has also identified wall displays as distractions to learning, contradicting the view from many teachers that they are learning tools. I have mixed feelings concerning the use of tablets in the classroom, but this is a personal opinion rather than being based on any real evidence. Certainly tablets and other electronic devices can be distracting if classroom management is poor. I have seen some classrooms deal very effectively with the use of tablets and others, well, less so.

Challenge

Students who feel challenged are more motivated and less likely to get bored. Sure, those students displaying a performance-related orientation do have a tendency to opt for less challenging activities because they are more concerned with proving their ability rather than learning a new skill. Nevertheless, these students are much more likely to display the negative symptoms of chronic boredom. Think about what keeps a teenager engaged for hours with a computer game. It's rarely about the game per se, but rather about challenging themselves to get to the next level. They may have to repeat the same stage again and again until they succeed, but this doesn't necessarily lead to boredom, rather, gamers almost seem to accelerate to a state of *flow* where time dissolves and they are motivated towards a single goal. Some might wince at the gaming analogy, but rarely do we witness such intense and determined focus from a teenager as when they are engaged in these activities. We do see it in other activities such as sports and music, but gaming allows us to witness goal achievement first hand.

Under-challenge will bore while over-challenge can lead to a feeling of helplessness. Pitching challenge correctly is vital in order to engage and motivate, but the teacher must also take into account individual learners' abilities and where they currently fit with their learning. Some students might have grasped the concepts presented in the lesson better than others, so the challenge level will differ as will individual learning goals.

Columbia University researchers Judy Xu and Janet Metcalfe call this the Region of Proximal Learning (RPL); that *sweet spot* where challenge is pitched just right. They found that remaining within the RPL increased engagement and reduced mindwandering (the tendency to daydream). Furthermore, working with a student's RPL encourages a mastery orientation (Xu & Metcalfe, 2016).

Task value

Ask yourself: 'How can I add value to the task?' With exam classes, stressing that the task will help them in the exam often works well as does the suggestion that students will be tested on the material later. Linking the boring content to other content and stressing that it will help them better understand related concepts can help with reapprais-ers who will already be trying to figure out the value of the activity. Teachers can also attempt to make the content personal by, perhaps, linking it into the experiences of students.

Goal directed learning

Emotions are goal directed, even boredom. The main goal of boredom is to escape it, so setting goals allows us to 'see' our way out and put in place strategies to get there. Sharing the timeline of a topic helps students to see the bigger picture and envision the end stage. This is more important for younger children whose concept of time can often be distorted (anyone who has ever taken a long journey with young children will be more than aware of the 'are we there yet?' syndrome). Breaking goals down into smaller chunks also increases the feeling of achievement while at the same time reassuring students that the boring bits will not last forever. I discuss goals (specifically *personal best goals*) in a more detailed section in the final chapter.

Regular low stakes testing

I'm firmly of the opinion that children (especially in the UK) are tested excessively for no good reason. However, high stakes testing is here to stay so educators need to ensure that students can cope with the pressures of exams. Regular low stakes testing (or quizzes) also helps to break up academic topics and provide an end point (or *closure* if you prefer). Testing in chunks also works well with anxious students (see the previous chapter) and also those with a propensity towards boredom.

Making use of downtime

Learning new facts and solving complex problems form the backbone of learning, but reflection is often required to consolidate newly acquired memories. Reflective activities needn't be directly related to the content learned as the brain often requires time to embed information and related information can often prevent this. As we have also seen, creativity often comes from not doing anything. While strategies such as *spaced learning* have been shown to be effective, it isn't always practical. *What if?* scenarios related to the content can be useful and allow students to engage in short bursts of discussion.

Chapter summary

- Students become bored for many reasons. Teachers often don't see themselves as the cause of boredom, but students do.

- Boredom arises through a combination of external (e.g. quality of teaching) and internal (e.g. feelings of task usefulness). Even if the quality of teaching is good, students can still feel bored because they are unable to see the utility in what they are learning.

- If appropriate, making learning relevant can reduce the instances of boredom.

- Regular low stakes testing can give students something to aim for and reduce the instances of boredom.

- In some circumstances, boredom can increase creativity.

References

Berlyne, D.E. (1960). *Conflict, Arousal and Curiosity.* New York: McGraw-Hill.

Daschmann, E.C., Goetz, T. & Stupnisky, R.H. (2014). Exploring the antecedents of boredom: Do teachers know why students are bored? *Teaching and Teacher Education* 39, pp.22–30.

Fisher, C.D. (1993). Boredom at work: A neglected concept. *Human Relations* 46, pp.395–417.

Goetz, T., Frenzel, A.C., Hall, N.C., Nett, U.E., Pekrun, R. & Lipnevich, A.A. (2013). Types of boredom: An experience sampling approach. *Motivation and Emotion* 38(3), pp.401–419.

Killingsworth, M.A. & Gilbert, D.T. (2010). A wandering mind is an unhappy mind. *Science* 330(6006), p.932.

Mann, S. & Cadman, R. (2014). Does being bored make us more creative? *Creativity Research Journal* 26(2), pp.165–173.

Nederkoorn, C., Vancleef, L., Wilkenhoner, A., Claes, L. & Havermans, R.C. (2016). Self-inflicted pain out of boredom. *Psychiatry Research* 237, pp.127–132.

Pekrun, R., Frenzel, A.C., Goetz, T. & Perry, R.P. (2007). The control-value theory of achievement emotions: An integrative approach to emotions in education. In P.A. Schutz & R. Pekrun (eds) *Emotion in Education* (pp.13–36). San Diego, CA: Academic Press.

Pekrun, R., Hall, N.C., Goetz, T. & Perry, R.P. (2014). Boredom and academic achievement: Testing a model of reciprocal causation. *Journal of Educational Psychology* 106(3), pp.696–710.

Xu, J. & Metcalfe, J. (2016). Studying in the region of proximal learning reduces mind wandering. *Memory & Cognition* 44(5), pp.681–695.

Interest and curiosity

Study hard what interests you the most in the most undisciplined, irreverent and original manner possible.

(Richard Feynman)

It's not a silly question if you can't answer it.

(Jostein Gaarder, *Sophie's World*)

The life of Richard Feynman is perhaps defined by his incredible intellect and by his Nobel Prize for physics. What has always struck me about Feynman (and Einstein for that matter) was his intense curiosity. He wasn't born into an academic elite, but his father (a salesman) instilled within him a questioning mind; a series of *what if's* and *how come's*.

In the opening scene of the 2013 TV mini-series *The Challenger Disaster* we see Feynman, brilliantly portrayed by William Hurt, enter a lecture theatre and attach a bowling ball to a chain. He then holds the ball up to his face and lets it swing into the audience. The ball sails into the mystified crowd before returning, stopping only centimetres away from Feynman's (Hurt's) head before sailing away again, losing momentum as it did so. The demonstration concerned the conservation of energy, but rather than begin with a complex equation, Feynman chose to begin his lecture with a theatrical display of how things work in the real world. This, of course, was a scene from TV but Feynman was famous for such demonstrations, the kind that enthuses and lights the spark of curiosity.

In Jostein Gaarder's book *Sophie's World*, 14-year-old Sophie Amundsen discovers two pieces of paper in her mail box; on one is written 'Who are we?' and on the other 'Where does the world come from?' These two questions lead Sophie on a journey through western philosophy with the mysterious Albert Knox as her guide. Knox must have learned the art of teaching from Feynman because he first feeds young Sophie's curiosity and then maintains it as it grows into a fully engaged fascination with human thought and ideas. I read *Sophie's World* before I became a teacher, and I truly believe it had some part to play in the educator I would become. I don't think I would have ever read it at all were it not for my friend and work colleague, Sue, recommending it to me with gleeful enthusiasm.

When we are curious about something we find that we are motivated to pursue it. The more we pursue the more our interest grows. Interest, of course, wanes and we might find that we move onto something else. At other times, the interest is maintained towards the point of obsession (Star Trek fan Tony Alleyne turned his apartment into a detailed replica of the Starship Enterprise). Oddly, children and young people are often accused of not being interested in anything; what adults really mean by this is that they aren't interested in the same things or the things that are deemed important. Any parent will know that a child's interest can often verge on the obsessional, and parents whose children have collected the likes of Pokémon cards (yes, I've been there) will understand how passionate younger children can become over collecting such items. Teenagers as well can easily become obsessed with the latest band, collecting memorabilia and covering their bedroom walls with posters of their music idols. Young people often have a greater passion for and more intense interest in things than adults. This kind of obsessional interest, however, rarely translates into the classroom; furthermore, the behaviour teachers witness in lessons is often far removed from behaviour outside school.

This interest rarely includes academic subjects, the exceptions being the likes of sport, music, drama and art. When interest does strike, it can be a powerful force indeed. Passionate pupils exist in school – just ask a drama teacher who organises the annual school play and you'll no doubt hear stories of young people staying to rehearse late into the evening, long after other students and staff have gone home. I used to occupy a classroom above the music department and on days when I stayed late for meetings or parents' evenings my chair would vibrate with the sound of the amplifier powering some up and coming rock star's guitar. These students had no obligation to still be in school, but their passion for music drove them to stay late into the day and they were happy that they were able to make use of the facilities available to them. Unfortunately, most students (and especially older students) separate school content from personal interest, deeming schoolwork to be conceptually different to outside interests and hobbies. The short-term fix to this problem is often the introduction and implementation of extrinsic reward systems, which could be as simple as offering merits or certificates for good behaviour or sophisticated systems offered by outside companies involving the accumulation of credits that can be exchanged for products such as CDs, DVDs and computer games. This kind of solution, however, causes added problems (especially if the system of reward is withdrawn) and studies have found that they don't always work in the way the providers hoped. I have discussed this in depth in Chapter 5.

Enjoyment plays a major role in motivation – we often feel as if our independence is being eroded when we are compelled to do something (even if we previously found that very same activity enjoyable). A stereotypical teenager might lie lazily on their bed thinking 'I must really tidy this room', but when Mum or Dad appears at the door demanding that the room be tidied, the teen loses all motivation and reacts negatively to the request. Psychologists call this phenomenon *reactance* – as human beings we value our independence – try and take it away and we'll react with hostility and rebellion. Of course, it can also work the other way. In Mark Twain's classic novel, Tom Sawyer was ordered to whitewash Aunt Polly's fence. Tom eventually managed to persuade his friends that fence painting was so enjoyable that they actually paid him for the privilege of completing the task. The so-called *Sawyer Effect* might have less of an impact in the real world, but the results can still be powerful depending upon the circumstances. Interest and curiosity are two emotions that allow for sustained engagement and motivation and both have been associated with higher academic success and positive school experiences. Unfortunately, both these emotions appear to wane in later childhood or are directed away from the school environment.

Interest and curiosity as emotions

Classifying interest as an emotion is problematic and controversial, but then again, so are theories surrounding what constitutes an emotion. There are, however, a number of criteria that we can refer to in our attempt to declare interest emotional. Generally speaking, for interest to be an emotion it should fulfil the following criteria: it should bring about physiological changes in the individual experiencing it; there should be visible facial and vocal expressions; there should be identifiable patterns of cognitive appraisal and it should be adaptive throughout the lifespan. Social psychologist Paul Silvia believes that interest fulfils all these criteria and manages a very convincing argument in favour of the emotional components of interest (Silvia, 2006).

Silvia cites work by other highly influential researchers who have described interest as having:

- a stable pattern of cognitive appraisal;
- a subjective quality;
- an adaptive function;
- physiological and expressive components associated with orientation;
- activation, concentration and approach-orientated action.

Furthermore, the movement of the muscles in the forehead and eyes are those that are typical of attention and concentration, and vocal expression is at a faster rate with a greater range of vocal frequency. In other words, we can tell when someone is interested in something; they might scrunch up their face, furrow their brow or even stick out their tongue. When they talk to us about what they are interested in their voice might speed up or their pitch change – when you are interested in something it excites you and you can't hold back your expressions.

The advantage of having a classroom full of interested students is obvious, even though the occasion rarely arises. Interested pupils are:

- more engaged;
- more eager to learn;
- more able to manage fundamental goals by being more motivated in their learning and more open to exploration;
- more intrinsically motivated and less influenced by extrinsic rewards;
- more likely to persist longer at learning tasks, spend more time studying, read more deeply and remember more of what they read;
- more likely to gain higher academic grades.

Carol Sansone and Dustin Thoman at the University of Utah also found that interest not only enhances motivation and performance, it also triggers strategies to try and make boring activities more interesting (Sansone & Thoman, 2005). We can therefore think of interest as an activating-positive emotion because of its ability to motivate and engage. Interest also has a positive impact on views of failure and, more importantly, the fear of failure (see Chapter 10). A teenager, for example, obsessed with playing the guitar is more likely to work through difficulties and setbacks in order to play along with his favourite band. Similarly, a student might attend early morning football training to master ball control in an effort to be selected for her local team. Academic interest is, of course, much more complicated, as students will view some subjects and topics within subjects as being more or less interesting than others. They will also view some subjects and topics as being more or less relevant to their wider needs, goals and conflicting interests. When I first became a teacher, I was drafted into delivering a few religious education lessons a week and it was often difficult to justify to young learners the relevance of teaching about faith and belief – such things, they felt, had little relevance to their actual lives. Almost every lesson I would be asked by students why they needed to *do* RE when the majority of them had little or no contact with religion or religious institutions. At times, the students did become animated and show a degree of interest, especially when we discussed ethical and moral dilemmas because they saw these as more relevant to their lives. Interest would, therefore, wax and wane and was highly dependent on the topic being taught. It would appear then that not all interest is the same and, indeed, it can shift considerably based on environmental and internal circumstances.

The difference between interest and curiosity

In everyday language usage we tend to use the terms curiosity and interest interchangeably. If we do make a distinction between the two, then it's usually in the region of curious being used to denote an upcoming event and interest a current event. We also might talk of being curious about or interested in something, but such distinctions are more a matter of language usage rather the conceptual differences. Suzanne Hidi suggests that they do differ and that while interest is imbued with pleasant feelings, there is something aversive about curiosity. Todd Kashdan and Paul Silvia describe this view of curiosity as being like a mental itch that needs to be scratched (Kashdan & Silvia, 2012). When we are curious about something it causes an almost unpleasant feeling, a need to relieve discomfort by *finding out*. It's like watching that TV programme and recognising one of the actors but not being able to work out where from. You find that you can't concentrate on the storyline because your brain it so busy flicking through your mental collection of everything you've ever watched. Eventually you succumb and Google it, feeling a wave of pleasure when you discover that they were also in CSI (because everyone's been in CSI, right?). Experimental psychologist Jordan Litman has suggested that curiosity can be seen as either a feeling of interest or as a feeling of deprivation and that people either seek out information out of interest or seek it out of frustration caused by not knowing (Litman, 2005). Litman's model would further suggest that curiosity has an aversive element, yet does little to convince us that interest and curiosity are distinctly different.

Sometimes there is little benefit in agonising over definitions and conceptual differences that might not exist. It's better perhaps to let the academic discussions continue and adopt the route of least resistance by assuming that interest and curiosity are generally conceptually the same thing. This is certainly the position adopted by many researchers due to the lack of scientific evidence to the contrary, and because of this uncertainly I'll tend to use the terms synonymously.

The downside of curiosity

Emotions can, of course, have activating and deactivating qualities and curiosity is no different. From Pandora to unfortunate cats, curiosity has been associated with both positive and negative outcomes. The benefits of curiosity to human existence and survival are beyond reproach, but the itch (as Kashdan and Silvia describe it) can also lead us into difficulty. Indeed, a 2016 paper written by researchers at the University of Chicago Booth School of Business and the Wisconsin School of Business, describe a study that has discovered the downside of curiosity (Hsee & Ruan, 2016).

In this most recent study, researchers tested the willingness of student participants to expose themselves to a situation that was potentially unpleasant. Why, you might ask, would somebody do this? Well, sometimes we just need to satisfy our curiosity even though the consequences might be unpleasant. When I was young my friends and I would grab onto the electric fences used by farmers; we morbidly desired to feel the jolt of the current. The feeling is incredibly unpleasant, but understanding that didn't quell our need to experience it. Not surprisingly, this study also involved electric shocks.

The students in one version of the experiment were shown a pile of pens that the researchers claimed were from a previous experiment. The interesting part was that half the pens would deliver an electric shock when clicked. Half of the participants were told which pens would deliver the shock while the remaining half were told that only some of the pens were electrified. When the students were left alone in the room, the participants who did not know which pens were rigged clicked more pens and received more electric shocks than the students who knew what would happen.

Curiosity, therefore, has the capacity to drive us towards our own destruction (just like the poor cat) even though curiosity is essential for scientific advancement. So-called *morbid curiosity* is one such example, especially with often graphic and disturbing images shared through social media. In a final experiment conducted by the same team, however, asking participants how they would feel after viewing an unpleasant image made them less likely to view the image. Thinking about the long-term consequences of our actions appears to strengthen our resistance to morbid curiosity.

This most recent study adds to the growing body of evidence in support of the view that emotions aren't intrinsically good or bad. Emotions can be both functional and dysfunctional dependent upon the situation. Emotions are, therefore, based on utility and the ability to activate or deactivate certain behaviours.

Catching and maintaining interest

Assuming that curiosity and interest are activating and positive, the question of how we can catch and keep (or maintain) interest becomes a high priority. Educational psychologist Suzanne Hidi has spent much of her career studying, researching and writing about the psychology of interest (for example, Hidi & Renninger, 2006). Hidi believes that interest can be roughly divided into two distinct components, consisting of *situational* and *individual* interest.

Situational interest

This tends to be spontaneous and transitory, it's that *hook* that many teachers use to catch the attention of young minds. The transitory nature means that it can disappear as quickly as it appeared if interest isn't maintained. A science teacher, for example, might start off a lesson with a dazzling display of explosions to grab her students' interest, but once the whizz-bang excitement of the demonstration is over interest begins to wane as the class gets down to the complex nature of the chemical reaction.

Individual interest

This kind of interest is much less spontaneous; it lasts longer because of its personal value (it's the child who can tell you all about the vast range of Pokémon, their strengths, weaknesses and evolution). Individual interest is activated internally with close ties to intrinsic motivation – it's the student with an interest in chemistry who witnesses the whizz-bang of the demonstration and goes home to Google it in greater depth. Situational interest is important because it has the ability to facilitate individual interest, so we can think of situational interest as the *catch* and individual interest as the *hold*.

Situational and individual interest both enhance learning in different ways and it would be erroneous to suggest that one is superior to the other. Situational interest is effective in increasing learning when the task or the information to be learned is novel or when the information is specifically relevant to the task or learning outcome. Individual interest, on the other hand, positively impacts learning through increased engagement, the acquisition of expert knowledge and by making seemingly mundane tasks more challenging. Furthermore, Suzanne Hidi and her colleague Ann Renninger have discovered that individual interest mediates the relationship between situational interest and long-term mastery and learning within a specific domain. Both types of interest, therefore, work together in order to transform short-term and long-term resources into viable learning outcomes.

It's clear that interest can enhance motivation and that this in turn leads to higher achievement outcomes. There is also strong evidence suggesting that individual interest plays a facilitating role in academic self-regulation (for example, being self-directed rather than having to be led or told what to do). Woogul Lee, Myung-Jin Lee and Mimi Bong found that individual interest played a role in the prevalence of self-regulation in Korean students and that self-regulation could be encouraged through the promotion of individual interest (Lee *et al.*, 2014). The assumption here is that students who are intrinsically interested in a particular subject or topic are better at regulating their own learning. This is a promising yet problematic suggestion. Some students are more adept at self-directed learning, but even these students could find it difficult to self-direct if they fail to be interested in or to see the value in what they are doing. There is also a greater emphasis placed on extrinsic motivators than intrinsic ones; what is taught and what is studied must have some kind of outcome reward, so many students might feel unmotivated even if they are interested in a topic that won't be in the exam. This is the point made by psychologists Paul O'Keefe and Lisa Linnenbrink-Garcia (O'Keefe & Linnenbrink-Garcia, 2014). They stress that self-regulatory behaviours can only provide optimal benefit if the task provides the student with a feeling of personal significance.

As we have already seen, emotions also impact on cognitive processes, and individual interest appears to help hold this relationship together. Interest, therefore, enhances cognitive ability and encourages the efficient processing of information. People remember the facts about things that interest them and often fail to recall facts about things that don't, suggesting that memory is at least in part related to relevance. Indeed, the relationship between interest (as well as relevance) and increased memory recall has been seen in a number of studies. Although some research has found that interest is more strongly associated with better memory in older people, there remains a general consensus that the effects remain relatively stable across the lifespan. This is certainly the case for text-based material, with research finding that subjectively interesting text is more accurately recalled than text deemed to be less personally interesting. Even more interesting perhaps is that in some studies participants have been able to predict the information they will recall better based on subjective judgements of interest and relevance.

One particularly interesting study found that not only do curiosity and interest boost memory and learning, they also make it easier to remember unrelated information presented at the same time. Matthias Gruber, Bernard Gelman and Charan Ranganath asked participants how curious they were to find out the answer to a number of trivia questions (see Hsee & Ruan, 2016). Participants were then placed into fMRI scanners and shown the trivia questions with the answers, followed by the image of a person's face. After this, participants were given a surprise test on both the trivia questions and their ability to recognise the faces. Gruber and his colleagues were interested in two things: would people who displayed higher levels of curiosity recall the answers to the trivia questions more accurately (and what would be the impact of the unrelated faces) and what parts of the brain were displaying the greatest activation during the task? Results showed that curiosity really did increase memory recall, even after 24 hours had passed. Surprisingly, however, curiosity also enhanced the recall of the unrelated material, indicating that curiosity actively makes the brain more engaged and that interest to learn is better overall. Furthermore, when curiosity is stimulated there is an increased activity in the hippocampus (the region of the brain associated with memory) and an increased activation in brain regions associated with reward (see Hsee & Ruan, 2016).

The study conducted by Gruber and his colleagues is relevant for a number of reasons. First of all, it supports the view that interest acts as an intrinsic reward – the *finding out* components actually measure as a pleasurable event, activating the brain's reward system. It also suggests that curiosity triggers learning in general, not just learning for content that the person views as personally interesting. This study also poses a number of interesting dilemmas. Because curiosity triggers the brain's reward system, do those students who are more curious require as much direct teaching as those who are less interested? Could it be that extrinsic rewards are best left to the less curious, while the more curious are best left to their own devices? Additionally, the more interested student might become more frustrated in situations utilising direct instruction, while the less interested might benefit more from such methods. Self-regulated learning is tricky, and leaving students to direct their own learning and development can be disastrous in the wrong circumstances. However, being able to identify those students who are adept at self-regulation because of their levels of curiosity and interest could help solve some of these contentious issues.

A model of interest sustainability

Interest either develops or it withers and dies. Many factors go into the sustainability of interest and students can be very fickle indeed. Interest in a subject might wane or increase when a teacher changes or the dynamics of the class alter. Situational interest doesn't simply miraculously transform into a sustainable individual interest and many students will fall by the wayside. Suzanne Hidi and Ann Renninger (2006) have developed a model of interest development that attempts to fill in some of the missing pieces. Their four-stage model breaks the components of interest down into triggered situational interest, maintained situational interest, emerging personal interest and, finally, well-developed personal interest.

Triggered situational interest

This is the spark; the point at which attention is grabbed as a direct result of some temporary change. It could be the stimuli itself, the environment or something about the information that needs to be learned that temporarily changes a student's view of it. The information might appear highly relevant (for example, a topic on the D-Day landings might trigger something in a student whose close relative was involved). Alternatively, the information might be surprising, the 'I never realised that' kind of moment. It could be the enthusiasm of the teacher for the subject or for a particular topic, but whatever it is it has that grabability, a certain something that pulls students in.

Maintained situational interest

This is when the attention becomes focussed on the task, resulting in a growing personal investment – getting down and actually doing the hard graft or understanding the content. Some students might fall by the wayside at this point while others begin to go beyond the externally influenced and turn their interest inwards, passing from extrinsic to intrinsic factors. This is the stage known as emerging individual interest.

Emerging individual interest

Interest in the topic or task begins to become part of the student's disposition. These changes are supported by increased curiosity and greater domain knowledge – the student might consider engaging in wholly independent study beyond the classroom.

Well-developed individual interest

Further development leads to the final stage and an increase in positive affect, intrinsic motivation and extensive knowledge as well as an increase in the ability to monitor and self-regulate future development in the topic or subject area.

Interest and personality

Anthropologist Clyde Kluckhohn and psychologist Henry Murray suggested that every person is in some aspects like all other people, like some other people and like no other person (Kluckhohn & Murray, 1953). Human beings are in many ways identical – that's what makes us human beings. However, there are some people we are more alike – perhaps we were born in the same country, speak the same language or support the same football team. But in other ways each one of us is unique; we are moulded by different experiences and our reactions to those experiences and the elements of our biology and personality we have inherited from our parents. I, for example, am a human being with all the universally held qualities that all human beings share. I am also a father (not all human beings are fathers) but I am also a single father, a group within a group. My experiences of fatherhood have partly shaped me into the person I am, and many of those experiences are unique to me. We often refer to individual differences in psychology because there is recognition that people won't always react to the same things in the same way. There is also a recognition that not all brains operate in exactly the same way; some people might have better memories than others, shorter attention spans or score differently on measures of intelligence.

Interest is also common to all people and some people appear to have more of it than others. We can therefore say that there are two main aspects to interest: aspects that are common to many and aspects that are unique. In this respect, we can think of interest as a trait (a characteristic or disposition of an individual that remains relatively stable over time). Traits are common to many but not to all. While some traits are universal, the traits themselves may vary, so a person might display a trait for conscientiousness but this might manifest itself slightly differently when compared with others who also display the trait. If, therefore, we view interest as a trait, we discover that individuals differ in terms of their breadth, depth, levels of sensation seeking, proneness to boredom and openness to experience. We also need to consider the extent to which interest is state dependent or trait dependent (is it something about our personality or something about the environment that fuels curiosity?).

Models of curiosity

There are many ways to assess and classify trait-based curiosity, many of them reliant upon self-report measures (asking people to complete questionnaires about their own level of curiosity). It's useful to describe a couple of these very briefly and I have chosen two from opposite ends of the spectrum so to speak: Spielberger's Optimal Arousal Model and the Personal Growth Facilitation Model that grew out of the Positive Psychology movement.

The Optimal Arousal Model

Spielberger's model grew, in part, from an earlier model proposed by Daniel Berlyne (see Litman, 2005). It is based around four collective variables of curiosity: novelty, complexity, uncertainty and conflict. The model distinguishes state (S) curiosity from trait (T) curiosity and suggests that high levels of S-curiosity indicate a desire to seek out, explore and understand new things and environments. T-curiosity, on the other hand, highlights individual differences in the disposition to experience S-curiosity when presented with a novel stimulus. In other words, the prevalence of high trait curiosity allows individuals to experience greater levels of state curiosity and to sustain these levels for longer. The model also assumes that curiosity is bound by anxiety, in that the same stimulation that fuels curiosity also fuels anxiety if stimulation passes a certain level. This is what is known as the inverted U, whereby as stimulation continues to rise so does curiosity and the optimum level is at the highest point of the inverted U. After that, it's down hill all the way as anxiety kicks in due to over stimulation (see Chapter 6 for a more in-depth review).

The Optimal Arousal Model is useful in a number of ways, mainly because it allows us to predict the outcomes of the interaction between trait curiosity and trait anxiety. Curiosity and anxiety work in opposite ways; while curiosity promotes exploration, anxiety inhibits it. Therefore, people with the same level of trait curiosity will behave differently if they differ in their levels of trait anxiety. This suggests that anxiety actually prevents students from making use of their high levels of curiosity. When faced with uncertainty, those students high in trait curiosity and low in trait anxiety will be more curious than those high in both trait curiosity and trait anxiety. Spielberger's model makes a great deal of intuitive sense, despite the theory being largely untested.

The Personal Growth Facilitation Model

The most recent addition to the study of curiosity has come from the likes of Todd Kashdan and Positive Psychology in the form of the Personal Growth Facilitation Model (Kashdan *et al.*, 2004). Kashdan describes curiosity as a positive emotional-motivational system associated with recognition, pursuit and self-regulation of novel and challenging opportunities. Curiosity arises, not from anxiety but from a person's *self development project*. This is in line with the Positive

Psychology framework and its emphasis on personal growth and well-being. Curiosity, therefore, is a tool used to facilitate personal growth and meaning and purpose in life. The model uses a self-report measure know as the Curiosity and Exploration Inventory (CEI), freely available online, and consisting of only seven statements measured on a sliding (Likert) scale, including:

When I am participating in an activity, I tend to get so involved I lose track of time.

Everywhere I go I am looking for new things or experiences.

The CEI correlates positively with a number of other attributes, including positive affect, vitality, wellbeing, hope and optimism. I have also found that it correlates well with resilience and academic buoyancy (albeit with relatively small sample sizes). It correlates negatively with boredom proneness, neuroticism and social anxiety. The CEI is certainly an interesting measure as it allows us to make predictions about how curiosity (as measured by the scale) should and shouldn't impact learning.

Self-report measures are useful for obvious reasons, but they can be highly problematic as well, especially when used with young people. While very young children might not understand the wording and meaning of the questions, older children are susceptible to peer pressure and social desirability – even if anonymity of results is emphasised, people still have an annoying habit of being less than truthful at times. Wallace Maw conducted a study into curiosity in 1971 and, rather than use self-report questionnaires, chose instead to rely on teacher and peer reports. Like many other of the studies we have glimpsed, Maw used his own behavioural definition of curiosity.

According to Maw, an elementary school child was said to demonstrate curiosity when he or she:

- reacts positively to new, strange, incongruous or mysterious elements in his or her environment by moving towards them, exploring them, or manipulating them;
- exhibits a need or desire to know more about him or herself and his or her environment;

- scans his or her surroundings seeking new experiences; and/or
- persists in examining and/or exploring stimuli in order to know more about them.

In Maw's study, teachers were asked to give assessments based on the above criteria for each child. Additionally, the children were asked to assess their classmates using a *who shall play the part?* instrument. The instrument described eight different characters that displayed either high or low curiosity behaviours. The children's task was to nominate a classmate to play the role. Maw then sorted the children into high or low curiosity groups based on the teacher and peer ratings.

The results of Maw's analysis revealed that those children displaying high levels of curiosity also differed in terms of personality, displaying higher self-esteem, a greater sense of personal worth, better adjustment and a stronger sense of belonging. They were less prejudiced and more democratic and gave themselves higher scores for curiosity. There were also significant behavioural differences in terms of how the children asked questions, how they found absurdities, how they remembered unusual information and how they solved mazes and puzzles. Maw also found a significant correlation between curiosity and intelligence, which would certainly make sense seeing as interest and curiosity would encourage more diverse and exploratory experiences resulting in a growth of competence and intelligence. However, we could also explain this link by suggesting that intelligent children would feel more able to involve themselves in more complex tasks and feel confident that they would understand more ambiguous situations. This would then promote curiosity. The problem is that Maw used tests that also measure intelligence (such as memory and problem solving) so intelligence could have actually confounded the results. In fact, when John Coie conducted a similar study a few years later he included measures of intelligence. Coie found that teacher ratings of curiosity were heavily influenced by perceptions of intelligence. Importantly, however, Coie didn't use peer ratings (see Silvia, 2006 for a more in-depth analysis).

Interest in the classroom

There has been much debate over the insistence or otherwise that lessons should be exciting or interesting and the views of teachers often run counter to those of policymakers. A great deal of this derision is bound up in ideology rather than evidence and not all evidence supports the view I have presented here. After all, research is often messy and contradictory. Direct instruction has its role and rote learning will always produce results specific to certain situations. However, humans are curious beings, as any parent who has gone through the 'Why?' stage will tell you. We are natural explorers, full of the desire to expand our experiences and our minds in many different directions. While we might argue for a correspondence theory where school relates directly to the world young people will be ejected into once they are old enough, reality is quite different. To a greater extent, adults have more of an opportunity to nurture their interests in specific domains either by taking a job that fits or moving on to specialist study at university. Schools, however, are charged with providing a well-rounded education based on a limited set of criteria and young people will inevitably find themselves studying subjects that they both love and despise. Research is fairly consistent in the view that we learn best when we are interested in what we are learning and if we are not our learning is impaired. Interest and curiosity engage our brain, motivate us and help us to bounce back when things don't go the way we expected them to. Teachers will always have to teach content that pupils find uninteresting just as teachers often have to teach material they themselves find less than stimulating. Making such material interesting is a difficult task, especially when teachers are restricted by syllabi and exam criteria.

Hooks or attention grabbers are important but not vital. Some students will not find material interesting for many different reasons and some will hide their curiosity for fear of losing credibility with peers; these are the students who will benefit most by direct instruction and more didactic teaching methods. Nurturing, encouraging and sustaining interest in more curious pupils involves a degree of letting go, of testing and stretching their self-regulatory skills. Not all students react in the same way in identical situations and identifying their emotional states can help ensure that all students succeed.

Encouraging interest

Making it relevant

Hooks are good but interest needs to be maintained. Making topics relevant is the more straightforward way of maintaining interest. 'Have you ever wondered?' type questions are useful here especially for very young children. For older children there are more options and this is why the *Horrible History* series of books have been so popular. Many of my A-level students could recall studying Pavlov and classical conditioning at GCSE, but only in a vague way. When I informed them that Pavlov actually surgically removed the oesophagus from his dogs in order to collect the saliva they tended to show even more interest. If I explained to them that he conducted similar experiments with orphan children they were really hooked. The macabre can be a very effective hook.

I never knew that

I never knew that moments and *Did you know?* statements can also maintain interest. Again, informing students that Pavlov never actually rang a bell in his experiments (he used a metronome and other devices, but never a bell). Interestingly, they quickly check their textbooks and tell me that I am wrong because most books make the bell error. Challenging the facts works wonders for both engagement and interest and allows students to feel that they know something the textbooks don't.

Let the interested run

Don't bore those students who are already interested. We often assume that our students know little about what we are teaching them. This is often the case, but I have met many students who already have a deep interest in the topics I am covering and their knowledge is sometimes better than mine. Gauging interest and current understanding can help to differentiate and allow some students to regulate their own learning. This then gives us time to concentrate on the less knowledgeable and least interested. Some teachers might also see benefit in handing parts of the teaching over to the more knowledgeable students.

Interest, the overlooked emotion

The main takeaway from this chapter is *don't overlook interest*. There remains a certain assumption that students (especially teenagers) are reluctant to be curious about the subjects they are engaged in. This is certainly true in some, but not all circumstances. Many teachers are experts at igniting curiosity and maintaining interest in their students, and I have witnessed some amazing lessons, from physics to English, that manage to do just this. Interesting, however, isn't synonymous with fun and often teachers fall into the trap of expending much time and energy on a variety of activities that may see short-term benefits but ultimately fail in the longer term as fun is replaced with work (and, yes, even younger children can see the difference, disengaging when lessons no longer fall into the fun category).

Curiosity and interest feed motivation and engagement, especially the all-important intrinsic kind. Those students already interested don't need the extra shove but the majority will. Emotions are about individuals (what makes us different) and we can't expect all students to react in the same way to the same things.

Chapter summary

- Curiosity and interest have been associated with more positive attitudes towards learning.
- Interest can be divided into situational (the catch) and individual (the hold) interest.
- Curiosity can be seen as a positive activating emotion.

- Teachers can nurture curiosity and interest by making topics relevant and creating the element of surprise or awe.

- Those students who display high levels of interest in a particular area could be given more autonomy so that interest is maintained.

References

Hidi, S. & Renninger, K.A. (2006). The four-phase model of interest development. *Educational Psychologist* 41(2), pp.111–127.

Hsee, C.K. & Ruan, B. (2016). The Pandora Effect: The power and peril of curiosity. *Psychological Science* 27(5), pp.659–666.

Kashdan, T.B., Rose, P. & Fincham, F.D. (2004). Curiosity and exploration: Facilitating positive subjective experiences and personal growth opportunities. *Journal of Personality Assessment* 82(3), pp.291–305.

Kashdan, T.B. & Silvia, P.J. (2012). Curiosity and interest: The benefits of thriving on novelty and challenge. *The Oxford Handbook of Positive Psychology* (2nd ed.), pp.367–375.

Kluckhohn, C. & Murray, H.A. (1953). Personality formation: The determinants. In: C. Kluckhohn, H.A. Murray & D.M. Schneider (eds) *Personality in Nature, Society and Culture*. New York: Knopf, pp.53–67.

Lee, W., Lee, M.-J. & Bong, M. (2014). Testing interest and self-efficacy as predictors of academic self-regulation and achievement. *Contemporary Educational Psychology* 39(2), pp.86–99.

Litman, J.A. (2005). Curiosity and the pleasures of learning: Wanting and liking new information. *Cognition & Emotion* 19(6), pp.793–814.

O'Keefe, P.A. & Linnenbrink-Garcia, L. (2014). The role of interest in optimizing performance and self-regulation. *Journal of Experimental Social Psychology* 53, pp.70–78.

Sansone, C. & Thoman, D.B. (2005). Interest as the missing motivator in self-regulation. *European Psychologist* 10(3), pp.175–186.

Silvia, P.J. (2006). *Exploring the Psychology of Interest*. Oxford, UK: Oxford University Press.

9 | The emotional teen

Like its politicians and its wars, society has the teenagers it deserves.
(J.B. Priestley)

> When you hear the word 'teenager' what images does it conjure up? Do you think teenagers are more problematic than younger students?

Young people caused as many problems in Aristotle's day and in Shakespeare's day as they do in the twenty-first century; adults will always criticise them and demonise them, forgetting that they, too, once walked in the same shoes. Teaching teenagers can be difficult (as can raising them) but that doesn't stop them from being amazing, funny, complex and highly resilient additions to our society.

Although emotions play a role in all learning (from early childhood to old age), the teenage years are perhaps more emotion-driven than other stages, and this is why I have decided to devote an entire chapter to this oft-misunderstood yet highly important stage of development. While this chapter emphasises the role of emotions on the teenage learner, there is much that the teacher of younger children might also find useful.

Teenagers are often described in less than favourable terms and parents often dread the impending arrival of the adolescent years. Teenagers are lazy, arrogant, disrespectful and argumentative, leading Socrates to write that they are inclined to 'contradict their parents' and 'tyrannise their teachers'. Teenagers, it would seem, have changed little since ancient times and the adolescent years are often spent dab-bling in risk and stretching boundaries. These are also the times when we begin to detect the signs of early chronic psychological conditions such as schizophrenia and depression, so it would seem that teach-ers, who work more closely with teenagers than anyone else, would benefit from having a greater understanding of normative adolescent development and growth.

The American psychologist G. Stanley Hall described adolescence as a period of 'storm and stress' characterised by, at one extreme, intense moments of sociability and inquisitiveness, and at the other extreme, aggressive and uncontrollable outbursts (Hall, 1931). Hall was writ-ing in the early years of the twentieth century, but many teachers and parents will recognise such behaviour in the teenagers of the twenty-first century. He believed that the adolescent years were essentially the re-enactment of a more primitive evolutionary state, while some con-temporary psychologists have even claimed adolescence to be a period of temporary insanity. Many teenagers, however, manage to survive the adolescent years relatively unscathed; nevertheless, the teenage years do present specific challenges for teachers. There is little disagreement that the years between puberty and adult independence can be difficult. This is a time of rapid change both physically and socially; from significant physical change to major milestones such as going to secondary school and preparing for life-changing exams. During the ages of 11 to 16 a teenager will begin to develop a sense of purpose and self-worth; body image is examined and re-examined and sexual awareness becomes a component of friendships. How extreme these differences are varies between individuals, as do the ages at which these changes take place. Girls tend to mature faster than boys, but there are as many differences within genders as there are between them. Only around 15 per cent will suffer extreme psychological problems, although this figure does vary and currently appears to be on the rise.

Adolescence

So what exactly is adolescence? When does it begin and when does it end? The answers to such questions are grounded in both biology and society and, unfortunately, there is no clear-cut answer. The biological stage of puberty occurs at different times in different individuals, and the process of maturation differs both between and within genders as well as between cultures. From a social perspective, adolescence is governed by a set of laws and traditions specific to particular countries and cultures (for example, the age of consent, alcohol purchase, the age at which a person can drive and, of course, the age at which young people can legally leave full-time education). While puberty signals the biological beginnings of maturation, societal pressures govern its duration in a different way; girls are often able to carry a child from the age of 12 or 13, but society restricts the age at which a person can engage in sexual activity.

Puberty is a time of rapid physical change in both the reproductive and endocrine systems. For girls, this change begins to take place at around 11 years old, but boys must wait around another two years before they grow at the same rate. In industrialised countries menstruation can begin as early as 10 years old and as late as 16, due to a wide range of factors including diet and family background. Studies have found that girls who grow up in families with high levels of conflict or where the father has been absent for some time, begin menstruation earlier and that this can lead to the early onset of behaviours more often seen in older girls such as smoking and drinking. Those girls who do mature early are more likely to mix with older girls and be seen as popular by those nearer their own age. Early maturation in girls has been linked to problems with negative self-image while early maturation in boys is more likely to result in other outcomes such as higher levels of self-esteem.

The teenage brain

Recent advances in brain imaging have more recently allowed neuroscientists and cognitive psychologists to examine the rapid changes that are also taking place in the teenage brain. Researchers such as Sarah-Jayne Blakemore and her colleagues at University College London have spent a great deal of time looking at the way the teenage brain develops in comparison to the brains of younger children and adults. Blakemore and her team use a technique known as Functional Magnetic Resonance Imaging (or fMRI) to examine the inner workings of the living human brain. Before the introduction of fMRI, the only way psychologists and neuroscientists could investigate brains without surgery was through post-mortems of the recently deceased. So the main advantage of fMRI is that researchers can now study living brains while they are in the process of remembering, deliberating and making decisions. It was generally considered that the crucial period for brain development was the first three years of life and, certainly, there are many major changes taking place during this period, changes that include the growth of specialist cells known as neurons.

As we learn new things, be it reading, writing or riding a bike, a new connection between neurons is made and the more often the activity is carried out the stronger the connection becomes. This is why the more we repeat a procedure the easier it becomes to do (in some cases such as driving the car to work and back each day, our actions become so automatic that we often forget having carried them out). This increase in connections during the early years of life is called *synaptogenesis* and can last for several months depending on the species of animal. Astonishingly, the number of connections in the young brain is so vast that synaptogenesis is followed by a period where many unused connections are eliminated through a process known as *cognitive pruning*, which continues for a number of years. Once the process is complete the density of the connections will have reached adult levels. Studies conducted on monkeys have found that such density declines to adult levels at around 3 years old, the point at which monkeys reach sexual maturity. Of course, monkeys aren't humans and it would be highly erroneous to suggest that the development of a human infant mirrors that of other primates. Because the monkey develops faster, reaching sexually maturity at around 3 years of age, we must assume that the human infant develops somewhat more slowly.

This view is astonishingly recent, and prior to this it was assumed that humans, like monkeys, had reached maturity in terms of brain structure in early infancy. Unfortunately, this error led to the view that infants reach a critical stage in development, after which they might not be able to learn certain skills vital to human growth such as language learning. A more probable situation is that infants pass through a sensitive period where certain aspects of learning are easier to achieve. Studies of feral children, those children who spend the first few years of life raised in the absence of human contact, have discovered that even if they fail to master language in early infancy, these skills can be obtained later in life – albeit with extreme difficulty. In fact, rather than brain development reaching full term in early childhood, Blakemore has discovered that teenage brains are still developing; it's just that development is only taking place in certain brain regions. This has actually been known since the 1960s, but it is only now that researchers have access to fMRI scanners that they can support these views with stronger evidence.

The human brain matures at different rates; for example, the visual cortex should be in place by about 10 months. After about this time synaptic density declines (unused connections are cut away through cognitive pruning), reaching adult level by about 10 years old. However, development of the frontal cortex appears to last well into the teenage years and the pruning process is much slower. In fact, synaptic density doesn't peak until about the age of 11 years and the pruning process continues into the early twenties. This late stage of brain development may go some way to explaining teen behaviour but, before we get excited, there are a great many other factors to take into consideration.

Essentially, there appear to be two major changes that occur before and after puberty. First, during this period, the actual volume of the brain tissue appears to remain stable; however, there is a significant increase in the amount of white matter in the frontal cortex of the brain. As already explained, neurons are continuing to develop and new connections are being formed during this period. The neurons themselves are busy building up a layer of fatty tissue called myelin on the axon of the cell. The axon is responsible for carrying electrical impulses away from the cell body of the neuron, down the shaft of the axon towards the dendrites, causing one cell to communicate with another. Myelin acts as an insulator and increases the speed of the electrical transmission between the neurons. The fatty tissue of the myelin shows up white under a microscope (hence *white matter*) and would suggest that the speed at which they communicate with each other significantly increases after puberty.

The second major change was first identified by Peter Huttenlocher of the University of Chicago. Development in the brains of children leads to a major increase in connections (synaptogenesis) in pre-pubescence followed by a major decrease in the density of synapses after puberty (Huttenlocher, 1979). This supports other studies which have concluded that while unused connections are pruned, those that are used are strengthened. This indicates that teenagers (and only teenagers) go through a process of brain *fine-tuning* in the frontal cortex throughout the teenage years. The frontal cortex (literally the part of the brain at the front of the skull) is the home of what cognitive psychologists and neuroscientists call *executive functions*. These executive functions are involved in a number of activities including our ability to anticipate the consequences of our own actions, our capacity to decide between good and bad actions and the ability to suppress unacceptable unsocial behaviour. It is also concerned with what is known as *social cognition*, which involves the way in which we cooperate and communicate with others so that we can successfully exist with members of our own species. The frontal cortex also allows us to modify our emotions so that they can fit within socially accepted norms.

Could this later stage of brain development explain why some teenagers can become so difficult during this period of rapid and complex change? American psychologist Mike Bradley seems to think so. In his 2009 book *Yes, Your Teen Is Crazy*, Bradley has even gone so far as to suggest that adolescence is a form of mental illness caused by the immature yet rapidly developing state of the teenage brain. While many would pour scorn on Bradley's suggestion, it does appear that something is occurring in the teenage brain that compels them to behave in a certain way, a way that many adults might view as unacceptable. Essentially, the teenage brain is in a state of intense flux, which probably accounts for much of the behaviour teachers witness at secondary school. Attention levels can vary and motivation can dip as well as peak. Hormonal changes (although not as influential as we were once led to believe) can impact behaviour and emotions and make certain emotional states more visible (inexplicable crying or sudden bursts of rage, for example). Brain changes also go some way to explain why teenagers are more likely to take risks than older individuals and why their peers so heavily influence them.

Using evidence collected from brain scans is still in its infancy and it would be erroneous to claim that neuroscience can explain all behaviour. Nevertheless, researchers have managed to compile a convincing set of evidence to support the view that much of the behaviour we see in teenagers is the result of these rapid changes in brain structure. A particularly interesting and pertinent argument is that teenagers are risk takers and that brain development is not only responsible for risky behaviours but that peers also influence such behaviours. This is certainly relevant to teachers; we have all witnessed young people who seem to change personality when in the company of their friends, and others who have acted in ways that are uncharacteristic because others have led them on. Teenagers might experiment with alcohol, tobacco and other drugs and the older ones might engage in risky sexual behaviour even though they are fully aware of the dangers of cancer, addiction and sexually transmitted infections. There is compelling evidence from neuroimaging that many of these seemingly destructive behaviours are the by-product of brain development, especially the development of areas of the brain responsible for emotion.

Regions of the brain dedicated to the processing of emotion and reward (essentially the amygdala) mature earlier than those regions that protect against social anxiety and inhibit risk taking. What this means is that the teenager is able to process that rewarding feeling that comes with taking risks but is unable to stop themselves from taking risks because that area of the brain is still under development. Teenagers, therefore, might be aware of the consequences and dangers of certain behaviours such as smoking but can't escape the desire to experiment; teenagers are more sensitive to positive emotional feelings but are less inhibited when it comes to taking risks. Furthermore, this mismatch makes teenagers more vulnerable to social influence and peer pressure, and studies show that they are much more likely to take risks when their friends are around.

Peer pressure and risk taking

Peer groups are vitally important to adolescents, much more so than for adults. While adults aren't always worried about not fitting in with their peer group, teenagers possess a heightened desire to be accepted by and into the group. Social exclusion causes them anxiety and we have already seen how anxiety can impact young people's wellbeing and academic achievement. Teenagers cause no end of frustration for teachers and parents due to their change in behaviour when they have been excluded from a friendship group, and while we might comfort them there is little that can be done to calm the anxiety exclusion can cause. This anxiety (or the attempt to prevent it) coupled with a brain unable to inhibit risk taking, means that teenagers are highly influenced by the group they are worried about being excluded from. Psychologist Catherine Sebastian wanted to investigate the impact of social inclusion on young people. Sebastian and her colleagues used a computer game that could simulate social exclusion and tested the impact of social exclusion on participants of different ages. The participant played online with two other people who had the power to include or exclude the participant from the game. Results showed that younger adolescents in particular showed a greater decline in mood than adults following simulated social exclusion (Sebastian *et al.*, 2011).

Risk taking has been found to increase when under the influence of peer pressure. Lawrence Steinberg and Jason Chein use driving simulators to examine risky behaviour in teenagers and adults (for example, accelerating at the sight of a changing traffic light). Younger adult drivers are much more likely to be killed or seriously injured on the roads, partly through lack of experience but also due to their risky behaviour, especially when driving with similar aged passengers. Indeed, the results of Steinberg's and Chein's studies find that when adults and teenagers use the simulator alone they engage in similar risky activity, but when they use the simulator with friends watching, teenagers are three times more likely to take risks than the adult participants. These results are in keeping with other data showing that teenagers are more at risk of road traffic collisions (both involving others and stationary objects like trees and lamp posts) when they are carrying members of their own peer group (see Albert & Steinberg, 2011 for a review of research into adolescent risk taking).

Teenage behaviour is, therefore, more than hormones and the social environment. The development of the brain is an adaptive, natural and inevitable process with evolutionary advantage. Rather than viewing the teenage years as risky and problematic, it seems much more likely that this social and exploratory behaviour has many benefits. Certainly, if behaviour is linked to peer approval and the avoidance of social exclusion, it would seem like a good idea to use this in more academically advantageous ways, perhaps through peer learning and mentoring.

Teens in the classroom

While teenagers do appear to take more risks, there remains one important caveat: in classroom situations teenagers are less, not more, likely to take risks. There appears to be a contextual issue involved here, in that the classroom isn't necessarily the place in which risks should be taken. Indeed, as we have already seen, students safeguard their self-esteem and self-worth in the classroom; asking and answering questions appear to be risks not worth taking. The desire to be accepted by peers seems to override risk-taking behaviour where school is involved. This then relates to our earlier discussion on self-esteem and academic self-concept and there seems to be something about the classroom (the combination of a formal environment and the presence of peers) that inhibits certain risky behaviours.

But answering a question in class isn't the same as running a red light or experimenting with alcohol, right? We know that students might withhold questions and answers due to their desire to safeguard their self-esteem, and every teacher has had that sinking feeling when they ask a question and the entire class falls silent. This silence, of course, can be the result of many different factors including the social dynamics of the class and individual personality traits. Several years ago, I taught a year 13 sociology class consisting of only five pupils (all girls). They all had very similar personalities and could all be described as introverted, so there was little opportunity for discussion or debate. I have also taught much larger and more diverse groups and have encountered exactly the same problem. Anecdotally, this might sound familiar to many teachers. The majority of my teaching career has involved the education of young adults (16 to 18 years old) but I have also spent considerable time teaching younger learners. The younger children (typically around 11 or 12 years old) are much more eager to put their hand up and often long to be called upon to answer a question; however, as they progress through secondary education they become more reluctant to stand out from the crowd, to ask and answer questions. It's as if we can see the changes taking place as the teenage brain develops, from plucky hand-raising year 7 to fearfully reluctant year 10 and beyond.

Sleep and the teen brain

A final curiosity thrown up by the developing teenage brain is related to a biological mechanism know as the circadian rhythm. All living organisms have very specific cycles, from migration in birds and hibernation in other animals to patterns of heart rate and temperature. The circadian rhythm is concerned with our 24-hour cycle. Our body keeps a relatively stable cycle throughout the day in terms of sleeping and waking; for example, in the absence of light the pineal gland in the human brain begins to secrete a hormone called melatonin which makes us feel drowsy and prepares the body for sleep. In the morning, secretion is suppressed and we begin to feel more awake. Humans tend to have similar sleep–wake cycles, but these can be disrupted by air travel or shift work. Long haul flights can cause havoc to the circadian rhythm, resulting in the discomfort of jet lag where the body is out of sync with environmental cues. Some people might also have damage to certain parts of the brain and this can lead to an inability to maintain a steady cycle. It would also appear that the teenage brain is out of sync with adult cycles and those cycles of younger children, resulting in an adolescent who is alert later on into the night but finds rising early increasingly difficult. While this out-of-sync state might not be directly related to emotions and learning, sleep deprivation most certainly is.

If the neuroscience is correct (and at this stage there is very little to suggest that it isn't), the current school day is encouraging sleep deprivation in our teenage students. Lack of sleep impacts emotion, which in turn impacts learning; emotional regulation becomes problematic when you haven't had enough sleep. This has led to some UK schools shifting start times to later in the morning (between 10 a.m. and 11 a.m. appears to be optimal) with some surprisingly positive results.

Solitude and emotional regulation

Peers are vitally important for teen development (as we have seen), and they can act as both a positive and negative influence. Family is often relegated to third place due to the amount of time teenagers spend on their own. Influential American psychologist Mihaly Csikszentmihalyi, along with Reed W. Larsen of the University of Illinois, found that teenagers spend a similar amount of time on their own as they do with their friends and peers (see Larson, 1999). Paradoxically, many parents and teachers might worry that some teenagers are often alone or locked away in their bedrooms, only surfacing in order to eat or leave the house to meet with friends. This behaviour has perhaps become more of a concern due to technological advances, with teenagers able to access most of their needs from a computer screen, tablet or smartphone. Solitary teens are often thought of as lonely, and self-imposed isolation viewed as symptomatic of some deeper psychological problem. Indeed, it does appear that teenagers who spend more time alone than with friends and family do grow up displaying a certain amount of maladjustment, including difficulties with social integration and finding and holding down romantic relationships.

The desire to be alone is a behaviour found more in teenagers than in any other group (and is rarely seen in preadolescent children). Teenagers, however, are full of contradictions (as any parent or teacher will tell you) and their desire to be alone is matched only by their desire to socialise. David C. Geary of the University of Missouri suggests that evolution has in some way pre-programmed teenagers to be highly sociable; this would make sense from an evolutionary point of view as traditionally this would have been the time when human biology would compel individuals to seek out a mate. While many worry about the use of technology by teenagers, and the jury will be out for some time on its benefits in the classroom, such advances have taken the social teen in a new direction where even the introvert can discover new ways of interacting with their peers.

So why do teenagers choose to spend so much time on their own, and what is the impact on psychological wellbeing and academic achievement? Unfortunately, solitude in teenagers has received minimal attention from academic researchers, but we can begin to piece together the link between the desire to be alone and emotional regulation from some of the small number of theories and research studies. Solitude, of course, isn't confined to teenagers and has been used for thousands of years for personal insight and religious adherence. In their 1982 book *In Search of Intimacy*, Carin Rubenstein and Phil Shaver suggest that solitude can play a positive role in healthy psychological adjustment in adults, while Alfons Marcoen of the University of Leuven, Belgium and Luc Goossens of the University of Antwerp, Belgium have gone further by suggesting that changes in cognitive, psychological and developmental aspects of growth allow teenagers to use solitude in constructive and emotional ways (see Larson, 1997).

Being alone in childhood isn't always the same as being alone in adolescence, and while solitude in childhood (that is, pre-puberty) can have a negative effect on development (and is usually a symptom of shyness or social exclusion), it doesn't appear to have a particularly negative impact on teenagers. Jane Kroger of the University of Tromsø, Norway used a sentence completion task to assess younger children's attitudes to being alone. She found that the children frequently used negative themes to express their view of solitude, suggesting that they viewed the idea of being alone as bad or unusual. However, when Kroger used the same technique on teenagers, she found that they responded more positively, suggesting that adolescents view solitude very differently (Kroger, 1985). The assumption here is that those who took part in these studies fully understood the terms being used. Evangelia Galanaki of the University of Athens, Greece is unsure if younger children are able to distinguish between solitude and loneliness, suggesting that teenagers are able to tell the difference and give an accurate account of how they view solitude in their lives (Galanaki, 2004).

A particularly interesting method used to study individual emotional experience is known as experience sampling. The experience sampling method (or simply ESM) was originally developed by Larsen and Csikszentmihalyi and involves participants providing self-reports by means of a pager or alarm watch and allows researchers to gather specific information at any moment in time. With the rapid growth in technology, ESM has become much more sophisticated, and the widespread use of smartphones has made the process more straightforward. I have used ESM on a number of occasions with varying degrees of success, but it remains a powerful tool to collect very large sets of data that map the moment-by-moment emotional states of learners. Larsen was able to gather data in situ when participants were actually alone, rather than expecting them to comment on past events. He wanted to collect data pertaining to a number of situations in order to obtain a picture of the participants' daily lives. The study not only concerned itself with when the teenagers were alone but also on how they felt (their affect) when they were alone and how they felt during a period of solitude. Larsen believed that teenagers would show low affect while alone (even if the solitude was self-imposed) but that the period of aloneness would have a generally positive affect over the longer term. The fundamental attribute here is one of volition – that is, the teenagers' conscious choice to be alone (what I have described previously as self-imposed isolation). While it seems evident that young children suffer negatively from loneliness, Larsen suspected that teenagers would gain from solitude. In the case of teenagers, previous studies have supported the view that solitude can be of benefit to long-term wellbeing, and while teenagers often report that they feel more cheerful, alert and involved when in the company of others, these feelings are stronger when the previous two or more hours have been spent alone. This indicates that teenagers aren't necessarily happy when alone, but they do notice a wider feeling of wellbeing if they spend time outside the company of others. Solitude in teenagers, therefore, does appear to serve a purpose in that it allows for emotional release and self-renewal, a kind of *downtime* which gives them the opportunity to recover from a busy social life – a social life that is, in itself, a necessary development process.

As we are beginning to see, teenage behaviours are closely related to emotions and to emotional development. So what do teenagers do when they're alone? Media of all kinds has become a major part of a young person's life. More than any other group, teenagers are using media in order to regulate mood and escape their sense of self. The reflective parent will be more than aware of the struggle to coax the teenager from the room when all they want to do is lie on their bed and listen to music. Such solitary activities can cause concern. Music is often a highly emotive topic within families and the persistent wearing of headphones can also cause friction at school. Like daydreaming and fantasising, being transported by music into imagined situations may at first appear maladaptive, but according to some researchers the ability to do this could have a major impact on current and future well-being and emotional stability. Dara Greenwood of the University of Michigan, alongside Chris Long of the Ouachita Baptist University in Arkansas have suggested that people turn to different types of media in three emotional states: a positive mood, a negative mood or out of boredom (Greenwood & Long, 2009).

Media is used for tactical reasons, including daydreaming, relaxation, self-reward or distraction. Mood regulation is also more important for teenagers than other groups and would appear to be related to self-imposed isolation. While some behaviour (for example, the insistence on wearing headphones even during social occasions) is often construed as arrogant and antisocial, the act itself might not be intended as such, but rather as a way of withdrawing from a situation with a highly negative social association. Greenwood and Long have suggested that this use of media is related to the inability or difficulty to regulate emotion, in other words, when we are presented with a situation we have little or no control over, we attempt to regulate these feelings by withdrawing into certain types of media. Because the teenage years see an increase in emotional instability, teenagers are more likely to employ tactics that appear antisocial but are, in reality, important for regulating certain emotionally related states.

Why teenagers need to regulate their emotions

We all need to regulate our moods at some point or another and we all need to take time out from friends and family at some point. For teenagers, such a need is bound to be more intense, partly because of the rapid developmental changes taking place and also because adolescents are deep in the process of self-building. The development of what psychologists call the self is a far from easy task, and while teenagers strive to be individuals they usually end up more like their parents than they would care to admit. Nevertheless, the experience (or journey) of self-building is a vital part of a teenager's development and we still don't really understand the mechanisms involved as well as we would like. Coping with new experiences leads to the experiences of new emotions, experiences such as pressure from peers and family, the pressure to conform and the inevitable conflicts, first-loves and break-ups. While teachers exist to educate, their invisible remit extends far beyond this. Ultimately, the emotional turmoil and instability makes its way into the classroom, and teachers often have to cope with tearful or aggressive students. While the incidence of physical aggression towards teachers remains relatively low, many teachers have witnessed or been victims of violent behaviour. This behaviour impacts on learning, not only the learning of the individual involved but also those in the vicinity or those within certain peer and friendship groups. It's often all too easy for situations to escalate due to errors in judgement or misread signals and although behaviour management remains beyond the scope of this book, there is still an obvious link between it and the emotional learner.

Working with the teenage brain

Working with these changing states is likely to cause less frustration and heartache than working against them. It can be difficult at first to think of teenagers as going through an important developmental process and much easier to label them as moody, lazy and deliberately confrontational. While these behavioural labels are often accurate (even though many teenagers will never display these behaviours), the reasons behind them are grounded in brain development and other biological and psychological processes. Working against the grain, so to speak, can only cause problems for both teacher and teen. Working with these changes can represent both small (individually based) and much wider (whole school based) strategies with some being more practical than others.

Turn peer influence on its head

We have seen that teenagers are highly influenced by peers and that this influence can lead to a rise in risky behaviours outside of the school environment, but reluctance to take risks in the classrooms. We also know that many classrooms and groups contain a hierarchy based on a number of variables including social and academic status as well as popularity. Persuading those students at the higher end of the hierarchy to model behaviour, such as asking and answering questions in class or leading discussions, can release certain behaviours in other students.

Avoiding verbal responses

While teenagers often view verbal responses as a risk too far, written responses are not. Mini whiteboards, post-it notes and the like are powerful tools when used well. Students can hold up their answers on the whiteboards, allowing teachers to test understanding (although a student of mine once chose to draw the most beautiful picture of a giraffe instead). While some might pour scorn on the post-it lesson, those little sticky pieces of paper are rarely seen as threatening to students. I would, however, suggest that such strategies are short term and should be used while simultaneously encouraging academic risk taking.

Later start times

On a more school-wide scale, changing the times of the school day is beginning to reap some rewards. The optimum starting time for most teens appears to be 10 a.m. or 11 a.m. This isn't always practical for either teachers or parents, however, and many schools might determine any costs outweigh the benefits.

Amazing teens

Teenagers are, put simply, quite amazing and can be thought of as a special case when it comes to learning and emotions. Adolescence will always be seen as a problematic and potentially volatile time of life and advances in science are managing to map these dramatic changes with sophisticated scanning technology. What we used to think was all about the hormones turns out to be far more complex, as new neural connections are formed while others are pruned. This then impacts on behaviour and reactions to peer pressure and risk taking, leading to high levels of peer fuelled risky behaviour outside but not inside the classroom. The process of self-building often encourages teenagers to seek solitude, a place away from a vibrant and complex social life and the use of music and other media in attempt to regulate emotion. It's a wonder, sometimes, that teachers manage to educate teenagers at all and yet they are all too aware of the emotional complexity of the teenage years. Within this milieu are a multitude of individual differences: personality types, socio-economic background, family differences and so on, further adding to the complex navigation of this fascinating developmental stage. Of course, adolescence need not be a time of storm and stress and in most cases, we will all survive relatively unscathed, but forewarned is forearmed as the saying goes.

Chapter summary

- The development of the adolescent brain can lead to difficulties when teaching teenagers.
- Even though teenagers are more likely to take risks, such risk taking doesn't always follow them into the classroom, making them less vocal.

- Changes in self-concept during the adolescent years can lead to teenagers being more self-conscious and engaging less.

- Teenagers are more vulnerable to peer pressure; this can be advantageous in the classroom if used strategically.

- The teenage sleep–wake cycle differs from that of older adults and, consequently, many teenagers are more alert later in the day.

References

Albert, D. & Steinberg, L. (2011). Judgment and decision making in adolescence. *Journal of Research on Adolescence* 21(1), pp.211–224.

Bradley, M. (2009) *Yes, Your Teen Is Crazy: Loving Your Kid Without Losing Your Mind*. Gig Harbor, WA: Harbor Press.

Galanaki, E. (2004). Are children able to distinguish among the concepts of aloneness, loneliness, and solitude? *International Journal of Behavioral Development* 28(5), pp.435–443.

Greenwood, D.N. & Long, C.R. (2009). Mood specific media use and emotion regulation: Patterns and individual differences. *Personality and Individual Differences* 46(5–6), pp.616–621.

Hall, G.S. (1931). *Adolescence*. New York: D. Appleton and Co.

Huttenlocher, P.R. (1979). Synaptic density in human frontol cortex: Developmental changes and the effect of aging. *Brain Research* 163, pp.195–205.

Kroger, J. (1985). Relationships during adolescence: A cross-national comparison of New Zealand and United States teenagers. *Journal of Adolescence* 8, pp.47–56.

Larson, R.W. (1997). The emergence of solitude as a constructive domain of experience in early adolescence. *Child Development* 68(1), pp.80–93.

Larson, R.W. (1999). The uses of loneliness in adolescence. In: K.J. Rotenberg & S. Hymel (eds) *Loneliness in Childhood and Adolescence* (pp.244–262). Cambridge, UK: Cambridge University Press.

Sebastian, C.L., Tan, G.C.Y., Roiser, J.P., Viding, E., Dumontheil, I. & Blakemore, S.J. (2011). Developmental influences on the neural bases of responses to social rejection: Implications of social neuroscience for education. *NeuroImage* 57(3), pp.686–694.

10 | Fear of failure

Of course to adhere to standards, to idealism, to vision in the face of immediate dangers takes great courage and takes self-confidence. But we also know that only those who dare to fail greatly, can ever achieve greatly.

(Robert F. Kennedy, Day of Affirmation Address, 1966)

There is only one thing that makes a dream impossible to achieve: the fear of failure.

(Paulo Coelho)

Failure is so important. We speak about success all the time. It is the ability to resist failure or use failure that often leads to greater success. I've met people who don't want to try for fear of failing.

(J.K. Rowling)

> **What are your own experiences of failure? How well do you overcome setback and what strategies might you use to keep going?**

I've lived in Harrogate for most of my life. If you've ever visited Harrogate you'll be familiar with it as an affluent bastion of the blue rinse brigade and home of flower shows and tea rooms, nestled deep in the beautiful Yorkshire countryside. For a few days in July 2014, however, all this changed. Gone were the coach loads of pensioners making a bee-line for the world famous Bettys tea rooms to partake of Earl Grey and Fat Rascals and instead there were hordes of Lycra-clad cycling enthusiasts. The Tour de France had come to town and the population of Harrogate exploded virtually overnight. What made this event even more significant was that British boy wonder Mark Cavendish has a connection with the town through his mother's family and he was quoted as saying that winning this stage was extremely important to him. Even a local pub near the finish line had temporarily changed its name to the Cavendish and Horses.

My son Ethan and I set off that Saturday morning in July to walk the short distance from our home into town where the first stage of Le Grand Depart would conclude. We walked along roads and through streets devoid of traffic and noise apart from the occasional support vehicle carrying spare bikes and equipment for this team or that team. Once in the town centre it seemed as if the entire world had descended. We squeezed our way through the crowds, searching for the one place where the police were allowing the public to cross the wide tree lined boulevard that, in a few hours, would see Cavendish sprinting for the finish line and victory. What should have taken us only a few minutes took us more like forty-five, but we eventually found ourselves on the right side of the road. Another diversion brought us out about halfway down Parliament Street, a relatively steep incline a few hundred yards away from the finish line. People lined the road, hung out of windows and sat on roofs, endeavouring to get the best view of that all important sprint finish.

It turned out to be a long wait. Every now and again there would be an update from someone in the crowd, informing us all of the where-abouts of the peloton. Then the support vehicles began to emerge, along with a cavalcade of sponsor vehicles with waves and the honking of horns and the throwing into the crowd of free samples of tea and sweets and all manner of merchandise.

Then the leaders, so fast that Ethan could barely catch a photograph as they whizzed past us, up the hill towards the finish line where the Duke and Duchess of Cambridge waited to greet the winners. What happened 250 metres from the finish line has now entered cycling lore.

Desperate to be the first across the line, Cavendish appeared to collide briefly with the Australian rider Simon Gerrans, shoving him with his head and shoulders, before hitting the ground hard and dislocating his shoulder. German Marcel Kittel took the victory we all hoped belonged to Cavendish, who instead was forced to exit from the 2014 Tour de France.

How do you pick yourself up from that?

World-class athletes know more about failure than most of us. Whether it's tripping at the last moment in the sprint or hitting the deck metres from the finish line in the world's most famous cycling road race, the best athletes in the world are also experts in getting up, dusting down and getting on with the job in hand. Failure is an unfortunate part of life; an experience that makes us learn from mistakes and ensures that we do better next time. Stressing that it's okay to fail is part of the battle, but we also need to be able to use that experience in a positive and constructive way. In a society where exam results are so highly regarded and success is often measured by how many qualifications you have, it becomes even more important to think carefully about those youngsters who struggle to meet the high standards society and parents have set (and indeed the standards they have set for themselves). Giving youngsters permission to fail is just the beginning and telling them to work harder or comforting them by explaining that they can re-sit an exam or two becomes part of the problem rather than part of the solution. Success and failure are ingrained within our culture and society; we can never wipe away the stigma that comes with failing to succeed, but we can smooth the path a little and shift perception a little bit.

So what is the solution? We can learn a great deal from athletes – nobody understands better about what it's like to miss out on the gold medal or fail to hit the back of the net in a penalty shoot-out. But athletes are a particular kind of people with a skill-set often very different from students who are struggling to understand complex issues and motivate themselves to succeed. We can't necessarily generalise in such a simplistic way. The truth is, of course, that we all fail at something or other at several different points in our lives – the thing is, we all deal with it differently. We must also be careful not to belittle failure or the devastating impact it can have on a person's life. Failure to read or write can ruin lives and the failure to care properly for others can often end in tragedy, while failure to win an Olympic gold is not, in itself, life threatening. In the same way, product failure (such as defective design) can lead to devastating situations such as aircraft disasters and other huge losses of human life.

What we mean by 'failure'

Individual failure is subjective and relative. It can best be described as finding ourselves in a state or condition that does not meet our desired or intended outcome. Failure is therefore about outcomes and goals, about what we want to happen and hope will happen, and then does not happen in the way in which we hoped. This kind of failure leads to disappointment and a feeling that perhaps we are not good enough, intelligent enough or worthy enough. Self-esteem takes a battering and we might stop trying in an attempt to ensure that we never again have the opportunity to fail, a situation that could ultimately lead to learned helplessness (which I discussed previously). J.K. Rowling is right when she claims that failure often leads to greater success; you have to fail first. This might seem very dramatic and not all individuals will react in this way to minor setbacks. Nevertheless, the current trend in education, where young people are rarely told they are wrong and success is seen as a right rather than something obtained through effort, places youngsters in a position which prevents them from seeing the lack of absolute success as some kind of total and complete failure.

Failure might also make us feel rejected, a feeling that we are somehow unworthy to take up our place in society or the feeling that our opinions aren't valid. Teachers are more than aware that some students rarely volunteer answers in class, not because they don't know the answer or understand the question, but rather because of that nagging feeling in the back of their minds that they might be wrong. Rather than risk the embarrassment of being incorrect, these students stay silent and, as result, their potential is rarely recognised. In my time as a teacher I have attempted to adopt strategies that circumvent this issue, with varying degrees of success, only to find that some young people will risk the embarrassment of staying silent when asked a direct question rather than the perceived greater fear of being wrong. Even though many teenagers may appear intimidating and overly self-confident in the street, when it comes to the classroom many guard their self-esteem with tight lips and frozen gazes.

When I think about this fear of answering a question and getting it wrong, I often think of Becky. Becky was an exceptionally capable sixth form student who excelled in sociology; she was also a perfectionist who demanded constant encouragement and advice (which she usually rejected) in order to bolster her self-esteem. Becky wasn't unusual in her behaviour; it was just that her behaviour was more extreme than similar young people I have taught. Despite being a high achiever, she was also lacking in self-confidence – if she didn't achieve an A grade then, in her eyes, she was a failure and failure was something Becky wanted to avoid at all costs. One thing Becky would never do was answer questions in class, which would drive me to distraction and I'll admit to losing my temper with her on a number of occasions. When I did ask her a question she would stare at me and then answer with a simple 'I don't know'. Even if I asked her a very basic question that she was guaranteed to know the answer to she would still reply with 'I don't know'. At first I interpreted this as arrogance (Becky had a certain demeanour that said 'Go away, I don't want you to single me out, you know I can answer these questions so why bother asking me?'), but as time went by and I got to know her a little better, it occurred to me that she feared getting the answer wrong and, in her own mind, not knowing the answer was preferable to giving the wrong answer. The fear of failure had begun to overwhelm her; her perfectionism had made her less confident in her ability to succeed.

While rejection and failure are at times synonymous, both are situations that are dealt with very differently by different individuals with varying character traits. While athletes have to deal with failure, writers need to deal with rejection. J.K. Rowling famously had the manuscript for the first Harry Potter book rejected by 12 publishing houses before finally being accepted by Bloomsbury; James Joyce had to suffer 22 rejections for his work *The Dubliners*. Other rejected manuscripts include *The Diary of Anne Frank*, William Golding's *The Lord of the Flies* and George Orwell's *Animal Farm* (which was rejected by the then director of Faber and Faber, T.S. Eliot). Many established authors will say that getting published is more to do with dogged determination than talent, and the only possible course of action once a manuscript has been rejected is to submit it immediately to another publisher. In the end, it is often the most persistent writer who gets published, not necessarily the most talented. Writers (at least the successful ones) have found a way of getting around failure – sticking at it and never taking no for an answer.

People cope with failure in different ways; their behaviours, responses and emotions differ, often due to the nature of the specific failure. In his book *On Writing*, Stephen King tells of the time when, as a young boy, he had sent a short story to *Alfred Hitchcock's Mystery Magazine* for possible publication. The story was returned with a standard rejection slip and a hand-written addition that read 'Don't staple manuscripts'. It's safe to say that such a response doesn't represent useful feedback and yet it is quite typical in the publishing industry. When I first approached a publisher with the idea of *The Emotional Learner*, they at first seemed enthusiastic and asked me to send them some additional material (I had already supplied them with two draft chapters). I forwarded them a further seven draft chapters and waited around four months for a reply. Eventually a response came with the news that the book wasn't 'currently within our remit'. This isn't unusual in publishing either but, nevertheless, proves highly frustrating (some publishers don't reply at all). King's response to his rejection was to hammer a nail into the wall and poke the rejection slip onto it. By the time King was 14 the weight of the rejection slips had grown so much that he was forced to replace the nail with a spike. By the time he was 16 he was receiving rejection slips with hand-written advice. For King this was success, a sign that all his efforts were beginning to pay dividends.

That may seem simple enough – if you want to succeed just keep on banging away until you get it right (or at least until somebody notices you) and accept rejection and failure as part of the process. Of course, it may not be as simple as all that. After all, why is it that some people just keep going while others give up so easily? Are people born to succeed or is there something about their upbringing or their personality that makes them more resilient than others? Treating rejection and failure as a positive thing is very difficult. After all, the very idea of failure is so saturated with negativity that many people are unable to see it as a chance to grow and use the experience as a springboard for later success. King was young when he started writing and possessed the tenacity and the confidence in his own abilities to keep going, but he also listened to advice and worked at mastering his skill. Teachers see this all the time; some youngsters are devastated every time they fail to reach the goals they have set or the standards parents and teachers have set for them. Others use the situation as a way to improve; they take advice on board, seek extra help and slowly perfect their art (be it writing the perfect history essay, remembering how to use complex mathematical formulae or, well, creating an artistic masterpiece). So, what's inherently different about the latter student, and more importantly, can this attitude be learned and taught to others? The evidence suggests that the answer to this is a resounding 'yes', but I would add one important caveat: the words teachers and parents use can have a major impact on the self-worth of many young people (especially teenagers) and that which we spend years building can be destroyed in a heartbeat. While I would never advocate the use of undeserved praise, neither would I praise innate ability over effort. Be realistic about what can be achieved and work from there. The problem is that the current trend in education is to praise when no praise is due as a way of building confidence when the best way to build confidence is to offer praise when hard work and determination have led to positive outcomes. This might sound harsh but that need not be the case. Feedback and advice are the key (as many studies have found), along with the giving of the freedom that allows exploration and creativity.

Fear of failure as attribution

Why is it that some students can cope better with failure than others? Perceptions of failure are often tied up with ideas about why certain things occurred, that is, how we attribute success and failure. As the Austrian psychologist Fritz Heider indicated, we are all naïve psychologists with an innate desire to understand our behaviour and its outcomes. When people experience a desirable outcome such as success on a test, our attributions help us to understand the behaviour that led to that success so that we know how to experience it again; psychologists of the behavioural persuasion call this *positive reinforcement*. If outcomes are undesirable (failing a test, for example), attributions help us to identify and avoid this happening again. Attributions help shape emotional and behavioural responses.

Unfortunately, this process isn't always as simple as it appears at first sight. Our attributions are the product of two distinct processes: locus of causality and stability.

Locus of causality

Our locus of causality can be classified along a continuum ranging from internal to external. An internal locus of causality places the cause of an outcome within the person, that is, something about them. External locus of causality, however, views the outcome as caused by external factors. A student who fails a test might decide that he failed because he wasn't intelligent enough, while a student who is externally biased would be more likely to attribute failure to a particularly difficult exam or even the inability of her teacher to cover the material properly.

Stability

As well as internal and external, traits can also be either stable or unstable. Stable attributions are those things that we cannot change to any specific degree. This would include intelligence, certainly in terms of IQ points, as these figures tend to remain stable throughout the lifespan.

Unstable traits might include effort, so our student might have failed the test because they didn't put enough effort into preparation.

These attributions shape perceptions of success and failure and can have damaging effects, especially if attributions are inaccurate. A biased attributional style can lead to a fear of failure and learned helplessness. Attributional style can be divided into optimistic, pessimistic and hostile.

Optimistic attributional style

A student with an optimistic attributional style attributes positive outcomes to internal (often stable) components and negative outcomes to external (often unstable) components. This would lead to a student attributing success to something within themselves that is difficult to change, such as IQ.

Pessimistic attributional style

A student with a pessimistic attributional style attributes negative outcomes to internal (often stable) components and positive outcomes to external (often unstable) components. This means that they would attribute failure as being something about them (such as lack of intelligence) but success as something external, such as luck.

Hostile attributional style

A student with a hostile attributional style would be biased towards external stable attributions for negative outcomes. This student would also react to negative outcomes in an aggressive and hostile manner, perhaps by blaming the teacher for his or her failure.

Impact of attributional style

Clearly, attributional bias can be damaging. A pessimistic style assumes that failure has an internal cause that cannot be altered. This would certainly suggest a performance goal orientation and, what Dweck calls, a fixed mindset. Furthermore, attributional bias can quickly lead to learned helplessness due to the inability to see failure as something that can be overcome. Persistent failure results in despondency and the feeling that nothing can be done to alter the situation.

Fear as an emotion

The emotion here is fear, or more precisely, the fear of failure. Fear is an evolutionary necessity; it's what prevents us from being eaten by wild animals or placing ourselves in life-threatening situations. It can also provide that rush of adrenaline so prized by the likes of base jumpers and free climbers. Let's face it, jumping from a bridge with nothing but glorified knicker elastic tied around your ankles will automatically trigger a fear response, no matter how exhilarating you find the experience. While many fears are logical and rational, others retain a subjective, personal and often illogical flavour. These might include the fear of appearing incompetent, stupid or unpopular.

Young learners fear being seen as unintelligent by their peers and would much prefer to be seen as lazy. Being lazy isn't viewed by young learners as a direct attack on self-esteem, so *forgetting* to do homework is much better than doing it and getting it wrong; the best way to ensure that it isn't wrong is to not do it in the first place. This brings us back to what I have discussed in an earlier chapter – the use of activating and deactivating emotions. In this respect fear deactivates because it initialises other behaviours that lead to lower levels of motivation and engagement. Self-handicapping is a maladaptive behaviour that prevents adaptation due to the emphasis on the belief that we are unable to reach our goal, and while safeguarding self-esteem isn't necessarily maladaptive, when it results in the option to give up (or not even begin) then it's certainly far from useful. We could, of course, argue that our current system is so concerned with testing and success that we don't have the time to deal with those pupils who constantly dwell on possible future failure. In 2013, Oxford High School for Girls established a test where achieving full marks was impossible.

The justification for this was that many of the high achieving girls at the top private school had never really experienced failure and that this was making them less resilient and, to be quite honest, not a little bit arrogant. The notion that we should allow (and even encourage) learners to fail is an interesting one (although one that I am reluctant to support). The idea is that, by failing, they learn to cope and adapt and eventually become better learners; the important part, of course, is to ensure that support mechanisms are in place to help these pupils, as is the greater conceptual understanding of the processes involved.

The dynamics of failure

Continual failure can lead to learned helplessness and we can certainly see this in our students (and often in ourselves); it shapes our behaviour and the feelings we have of how we view ourselves as learners and educators. Andrew Martin, an educational psychologist at the University of New South Wales, describes the type of learned helplessness we see in our students as *failure acceptance*, a term which better captures the behaviour many teachers witness. For Martin (as well as many other researchers), failure acceptance is only one part of a larger body of behaviours known as *failure dynamics*. According to this view, learners are primarily motivated by the desire for failure avoidance, which involves a great deal of effort attempting to safeguard self-esteem. Because intelligence and academic ability are so highly prized in society, the last thing people want to do is look stupid. So, in an attempt to protect themselves from the feeling that others are judging them on their academic ability, they quite often find themselves employing a number of strategies to prevent this from happening; this is the behaviour known as academic self-handicapping. Essentially, we all fear failure and often go out of our way to avoid it. Eventually, however, learned helplessness creeps in and we find ourselves accepting the unavoidable truth that we will always be failures (Martin *et al.*, 2015).

Researchers have identified a typology of failure dynamics where individuals are either success orientated, failure avoidant or failure accepting. The latter two share a number of dynamic factors that we have already visited throughout this book. The first factor is anxiety, an emotion that often gets overlooked or can be downplayed in educational settings. The second factor, performance avoidance, implies that in order to avoid failure we simply have to avoid the situation that could give rise to failure: not turning up to an important test doesn't necessarily sabotage our self-esteem – after all, if we don't take the test, we can't fail it, right?

The third factor, self-handicapping, involves those pre-emptive strategies we employ to give reason to our possible future failures. I once taught a student who insisted on apologising for her poor attempt at homework the moment she handed it in; it was her way of safeguarding against the possibility of getting a bad mark. Others may claim that they didn't revise for an important exam. This type of behaviour safeguards self-esteem by ensuring that failure is the result of laziness rather than lack of intelligence – it's much better to look lazy than it is to look stupid. Finally, and possibly as a result of the other factors, we meet the teacher's nemesis – disengagement. Disengagement can occur for a number of reasons and not simply because the lesson or the topic of the lesson is boring – the suggestion that teachers should plan lessons that engage all students is, quite simply, nonsense because pupils become disengaged for reasons beyond anybody's control (see Chapter 7). There could very well be anxiety issues as well as a past that has led to failure acceptance.

According to Martin, failure avoidant students are more likely to display high levels of anxiety, so there is a strong indication here that those students who might show potential but don't achieve are victims of their own internal worry rather than laziness or disengagement (see De Castella *et al.*, 2013). They have simply become prisoners of their own anxiety and disengage in order to protect themselves from any more psychological pain. Martin Covington, Professor of Psychology at UC Berkley, suggests that failure avoidant students display uncertainty about their own ability not only to achieve success, but also their ability to avoid failure. In behavioural terms, such students have learned to avoid situations that might lead to failure in the same way as Seligman's dogs didn't bother to jump the partition because they were too unsure of their ability to escape the painful shocks – it was better to accept the pain than attempt to escape it. However, unlike the dogs, our failure avoiders even go so far as to actively sabotage their chances of success through holding back on effort and choosing disengagement. It's a bit like Seligman's dogs getting out of the box and making sure the switch was on before jumping the partition; 'see', they would bark, 'told you it was a waste of time'.

Avoiding failure

In attempting to avoid failure, students will apply a range of strategies that might have both positive and negative consequences. Ultimately, humans strive for self-acceptance and view this as a high priority. But the way in which we approach this can take a number of forms; we can strive to avoid failure or we can strive to approach success. These two methods might appear too similar to be worth a distinction but do, in reality, deal with different methods, one of which (failure avoidance) triggers fear while the other motivates students to discover positive ways to approach learning and more adaptive routes towards success. In school, self-worth is measured by the ability to achieve in exams and other assessed activities – the higher the stakes, the greater the fear or the desire to adapt our behaviour towards successful outcomes. Our main concern here is how students attempt to avoid failure and the methods they employ in order to avoid it, methods that more often than not increase the chances of failure and reduce the chances of success. The three most common failure-avoidance behaviours are defensive pessimism, defensive optimism and self-handicapping, all of which lead students to unconsciously alter the meaning of failure itself.

Defensive pessimism: aiming too low

Defensive pessimism involves the holding of unrealistically low expectations of tasks where there is a formal evaluation, such as an exam or a homework that will be given a grade. If we hold low expectations of our own performance, then these beliefs cushion us against anxiety because we create unrealistic targets for ourselves and it's not as far to fall when we do fail (yet it's a cause for celebration when we do better than expected based on our own low expectations). Essentially, we turn a failure into a success in our own minds. Defensive pessimism can manifest itself in several ways, such as telling yourself and others that you are going to fail the test even though past experience suggests that failure is far from inevitable. While some may think of this as a reasonable strategy, unconsciously there is a real danger that it will reduce motivation and engagement due to the complex relationship between our thoughts and our behaviours. In other words, we end up convincing ourselves that failure is the most likely outcome even though we have displayed a history of success. If we lower the bar, we make failure less likely (in our own eyes at least), which in turn lifts some of the anxiety associated with the fear of failure. Aiming for failure allows us to revel in success, even if that success is below expectations. Students might also aim lower than their academic history suggests them capable of, for example aiming for a grade C when all indications suggest that an A or a B is a more likely outcome or deciding not to apply to a prestigious university even though current levels indicate the high likelihood of acceptance.

Lucy, for example, excelled in her GCSE exams and began her A-levels with high target grades. During discussions around performance and outcomes she would insist on telling me that she had been lucky in her GCSEs and that her success had little to do with her ability. She was frightened of A-levels because they seemed so much harder than her GCSEs and her high target grade in psychology filled her with dread because she feared that she would never be able to reach such a standard and would be 'lucky if she passed' (she had adopted a pessimistic attributional style). There was always a suggestion here that Lucy felt like an imposter, someone who didn't deserve to be studying for A-levels simply because she 'got lucky' in her GCSE exams. Lucy's low expectations of her success were unrealistic; she had obtained As and Bs in her GCSEs and teaching staff viewed her as a very capable and hard working student; however, Lucy knew that failure would be a dramatic fall from grace and she was very anxious about the possibility that she wouldn't be able to maintain the high standards that others had placed on her, high standards that she believed were due to luck rather than effort.

Intervening with such students is difficult and few schools are equipped to deal with such issues. By continually presenting Lucy with the evidence of her ability, she gradually became more confident in her ability to do well, and in the end, she had little choice but to accept this. She still felt a little like an imposter but was ultimately very successful, attending a prestigious university and graduating with a first class degree.

What we need to emphasise here is that this type of pessimism is unrealistic because it isn't supported by previous experience (Lucy had a history of success but, despite this, still expected to fail). This might cause problems for educators because they need to walk the line between realistic and unrealistic expectations and gauge the level at which they offer encouragement; aim too low and we feed into that unrealistic pessimism, aim too high and we might encourage the fear of failure where previously none existed. Students who are fearful of failure are more motivated to avoid it by adopting a pessimistic outlook despite previous successes. These students don't view previous success as an indication of future success so adopt unrealistically low expectations of their ability to do well. Defensive pessimism is more common in females than in males and is also more relevant in western countries and those countries that place a higher emphasis on success through examinations. Defensive pessimism is also associated with a lower grade point average and higher life stress and dissatisfaction as well as higher incidents of psychological problems. While defensive pessimism is employed as a self-protective strategy, in reality consistent negative expectations will take their toll over time, reducing the rewards success can bring and leading to poorer academic outcomes.

Defensive optimism: aiming too high

While defensive pessimism leads to students pitching themselves below their ability, defensive optimism exists at the other end of this continuum. Defensive optimists set unrealistically high goals and expectations for themselves even though past experience and evidence suggests that they are unlikely to reach these levels. Students who are predicted Ds and Es, for example, might set their sights on an A despite having only achieved Ds in tests and other assessed work. They may also choose to embark on subjects at higher levels despite only mediocre success at lower levels. We often find this during the transition from GCSEs to A-levels and although many schools will discourage or bar some students from taking certain subjects at a higher level, others have more flexible entry requirements. A student who has only managed Ds in science subjects might then wish to take A-levels in Physics and Chemistry even though prior attainments in these subjects has been low. This often leads to these students struggling and eventually leaving the course. Schools, therefore, need to be careful that they assess students in terms of prior attainment and ensure that minimum standards are upheld. Teachers want students to remain optimistic about their chances of success and realistic optimism should be encouraged; however, defensive optimism doesn't represent a realistic position due to the evidence for success being absent.

Defensive optimists display certain behaviour that betray their thoughts. These might include:

- striving towards an A grade when previous assessments have placed them closer to a D;

- choosing books, texts or other information that are far beyond their capabilities in terms of their previous attainment. For example, our struggling physics student might select a textbook aimed at first year undergraduate students. This would raise his self-esteem because others might assume that he is able to handle more advanced studies;

- applying to the top universities even though they are highly unlikely to obtain the required entry grades.

The problem here is not the optimism, but rather the unrealistic nature of the optimism. Certainly, students should be encouraged to aim high, but also be encouraged to aim high within realistic parameters. Rather than aiming for an A (when the current level is closer to a D), students should be encouraged to aim for the mid-range and raise in increments once the evidence is able to support higher expectations. In a similar way, when students begin to think about university, discussing their interests, desires and current attainment helps them to make more realistic decisions. Is the student, for example, the kind who might be more suited to a smaller university closer to home rather than a large campus university at the other end of the country? More prestigious universities simply don't suit some individuals, due not only to their ability but also their personality. A mismatch so often leads to higher rates of non-completion.

It seems logical that students might downplay their ability in an attempt to feel good about a lower grade. But why would a student overestimate their ability? This is indeed a curious thing. After all, isn't the defensive optimist simply setting themselves up for a fall? The most probable reason for such a destructive strategy involves our thinking about short- and long-term goals and our perception of time, as well as failure and academic insecurity. The fear of failure problem can easily be resolved – by simply refusing to accept failure as a possibility, even when evidence suggests that our belief in success is so far removed from the evidence. Although defensive optimism represents a defensive mechanism rather than a cognitive bias (although the two can be thought of as closely related), it does display similarities with the Dunning-Kruger effect that states people will overestimate the abilities and under evaluate their ineptitudes despite evidence to the contrary. If students refuse to accept the evidence of failure as a possible outcome, then the beliefs created by such a refusal protect them from anxiety and fear associated with failure. As we have seen, fear and anxiety have a negative impact on self-esteem and wellbeing, as well as on academic achievement. Removing the fear in such a way helps protect self-esteem in the short term due to the protective nature of the illusion; however, as reality begins to bite, the fear and the anxiety can become overwhelming. Defensive optimism can also be used as a way of excusing poor performance by blaming high expectations rather than accepting that it was down to ability or effort. Explaining away poor performance by accepting that your expectations were too high doesn't necessarily represent an attack on self-worth.

Academic self-handicapping: sabotaging success

Why would students actively go out of their way to fail? I have taught many students over the years who rarely hand in homework and some who have even failed to attend practice tests and, on the odd occasion, missed important high stakes exams. As teachers, we've heard a vast array of excuses from the very basic to the incredibly complex and outlandish (although nobody has ever declared that the dog ate their homework). If students get so anxious about exam success, why would they go out of their way to jeopardise their chances?

Consider some of the following statements:

- I have a very bad memory;
- I didn't understand the question;
- I'm not feeling very well but I'll take the test anyway.

I hear the first statement quite often. Memory is a topic taught in A-level psychology and many students pride themselves on informing me that their memory is very poor (and that's why they're so bad at exams). On hearing this, I quickly point out that the majority of the population has pretty much the same ability to retain and recall information, although there are a relatively small number of people who have exceptionally bad memories, usually as the result of brain injuries or developmental disorders; there are also a tiny number of people who have exceptionally good memories. They might actually believe that their memory is very bad and indeed it could be (although this is more often due to attention than it is to memory processes), but the reality is that by blaming their memory they are giving themselves permission to fail in a way that safeguards self-esteem. Most of us experience nerves when we submit something that is going to be assessed or opened up to possible criticism. Those involved in the arts know this better than anyone else; the book you've just published, the artwork that's just gone on display or that part in the play at the local theatre all conjure up fears that someone will criticise. We all find ways of dealing with such things, either by ignoring the hecklers and the critics or concentrating on the positives and ignoring the negatives. Some people, however, avoid the critics by never doing things that will open them up to such criticism. I'm sure there are millions of wonderful writers, artists and actors in the world who are stuck in jobs they hate because they fear being knocked back should they decide to pursue their dreams. You can't fail if you never try, so not trying becomes the fall-back position.

These are examples of self-handicapping, a strategy that deflects the cause of failure away from the student's ability and onto premeditated excuses in the event that failure occurs. A student might, therefore, think that if she leaves revision to the last minute, she will have an excuse for not doing well that safeguards self-esteem (she might be accused of being lazy, but at least people won't think she's unintelligent).

Common examples of self-handicapping strategies include:

- task avoidance;
- denial;
- deliberately withholding effort;
- procrastination;
- lack of practice;
- reporting illness;
- drug and alcohol use.

Another, potentially more serious, strategy involves students allowing themselves to become run down, for example by foregoing sleep or not eating properly. Rather than feigning illness, students are actively making themselves ill. In a small number of students this might also involve self-injury, deliberately causing physical harm in order to deflect the cause of failure away from the student and onto the injury.

A particularly curious strategy is false self-handicapping (often called Claytons self-handicapping). This is a particularly intriguing phenomenon whereby a student uses past experiences and current situations to avoid responsibility. For example, a student might claim to be highly anxious about an exam when, in reality, they are not.

Students might tell others that they haven't revised for an exam when, in fact, they have, or spent five minutes on the bus completing their homework when in reality they have spent all weekend perfecting it. In a similar way, a student might adopt a persona that appears laid back and relaxed about their ability to succeed or fail; however, when away from the school environment they spend all their time catching up on the work missed in class. Although this alternative form of self-handicapping might appear harmless, research finds that such students are more likely to engage in traditional self-handicapping in the right circumstances. In essence, these students have become masters of self-handicapping, altering behaviour and strategies to ensure that they can't be held responsible for their own failure. Furthermore, Claytons self-handicappers are just as likely to underachieve as traditional self-handicappers.

Krista de Castella and Don Bryne of the Australian National University, along with Martin Covington, have suggested that the absence of achievement goals can feed self-handicapping and that the fear of failure is strongly associated with a number of maladaptive behaviours including self-handicapping (De Castella *et al.*, 2013). There are certainly some complex emotional behaviours at play here and it would appear that even when important exams are at stake, some learners will continue to defend their self-esteem at the expense of academic achievement. Self-handicapping isn't as common as defensive pessimism, but does appear more prevalent in boys. Like defensive pessimism, however, self-handicapping predicts a number of maladaptive behaviours such as low self-esteem, poor self-regulation and lower academic achievement. The emotional complexity with which learners approach their fear of failure leads to the utilisation of a number of strategies, both adaptive and maladaptive, and recognising these strategies can prove useful. Certainly, approaching success from a realistic angle rather than instilling false hope can help reduce some of these destructive strategies (particularly defensive pessimism and defensive optimism); however, the emphasis on personal success rather than comparison with others has been found to significantly reduce the adoption of such strategies.

Reducing the fear of failure

Increasingly, studies are beginning to show the damaging impact of classroom and school comparisons of performance, and if we return to our discussion of professional athletes, we find that many sports women and men are as much concerned with personal bests as national and international rankings. The emphasis of ranking students based on performance merely feeds the fear of failure because it acts as a direct assault on self-esteem and self-worth, which can indirectly impact on self-concept. More damagingly, it nurtures performance-learning orientations and hinders mastery (see Chapter 2 for a more comprehensive discussion). Some schools might publicly rank student performance by placing lists in classrooms and corridors in a misguided attempt to increase motivation through competition. While competition can be an effective motivator if approached carefully, there remains a very thin line between it and public shaming.

Fear of failure is often fuelled when comparisons are revealed, even though parents and students are often eager to know their position within the class or year group. However, comparing individual past performance with present performance and future goals (*personal bests*, discussed in detail in the final chapter) have been shown to be better indicators of motivation than wider comparisons (Liem *et al.*, 2012). Nevertheless, the use of personal bests can cause further issues, especially as data shows that progress is rarely linear (around 10 per cent of students make linear progress between key stages), so it's highly likely that personal bests will not always be met and, in reality, progress can slow and even reverse before leaping forward.

More recently, research has found that including details of the failures and setbacks of significant individuals can increase motivation and possibly help students to reframe how they view such events. Xiaodong Lin-Siegler and colleagues discovered that rather than concentrating on the successes of important scientists, highlighting their failures, setbacks and struggles results in higher levels of motivation in high school students. While many school science textbooks describe famous scientists as extraordinarily talented, few treat them as ordinary individuals, prone to the same mistakes and failures as the rest of us (Lin-Siegler *et al.*, 2015). This creates the view that effort and the ability to carry on despite adversity aren't part of what made these individuals great, in the same way that we often see successful people from J.K. Rowling to Bill Gates as being in some way special and immune from the anxieties that affect the rest of us.

This chapter has investigated failure and, more specifically, the fear of failure. We have seen how fear operates as a negative deactivating emotion and how it fuels maladaptive and often destructive strategies. In other circumstances fear of failure can motivate to a degree by encouraging learners to work harder to avoid possible disappointment. As we have seen, however, human behaviour is less predictable than some would have us believe, and students, particularly teenagers, devise their own personal strategies in an attempt to prevent themselves from looking unintelligent in a society that values high academic standards. The problem here is that often self-esteem and how we think others view us hijack the resources needed to achieve academically, pouring effort into safeguarding our fragile selves.

Chapter summary

- Failure is an important part of the learning process, yet many students view it as a personal indictment.

- Students use a number of strategies to avoid failure, including self-handicapping, defensive optimism and defensive pessimism.

- Often, these strategies impact negatively on academic performance.

- Taking a pragmatic view, based on the evidence of individual success and failure, can nurture a more realistic view of personal achievement.

- Teaching students about the success and failure of others can help reframe their own setbacks.

References

De Castella, K., Byrne, D. & Covington, M. (2013). Unmotivated or motivated to fail? A cross-cultural study of achievement motivation, fear of failure, and student disengagement. *Journal of Educational Psychology* 105(3), pp.861–880.

Liem, G.A.D., Ginns, P., Martin, A.J., Stone, B. & Herrett, M. (2012). Personal best goals and academic and social functioning: A longitudinal perspective. *Learning and Instruction* 22(3), pp.222–230.

Lin-Siegler, X., Ahn, J.N., Chen, J., Fang, F.-F.A. & Luna-Lucero, M. (2015). Even Einstein struggled: Effects of learning about great scientists' struggles on high school students' motivation to learn science. *Journal of Educational Psychology* 108, pp.314–328.

Martin, A.J., Nejad, H., Colmar, S., Liem, G.A.D. & Collie, R.J. (2015). The role of adaptability in promoting control and reducing failure dynamics: A mediation model. *Learning and Individual Differences* 38, pp.36–43.

Teaching with emotions in mind

I think of myself as an intelligent, sensitive human being with the soul of a clown which always forces me to blow it at the most important moments.

(Jim Morrison)

In my mind their life narratives will always remain incomplete just as mine will in theirs.

(Tim O'Brien, *Inner Story*)

Learning is a cognitive, emotional and social process. Learning doesn't take place in a vacuum; we can't realistically claim that learning is simply a cognitive process because in order to learn we have to be part of the world, we have to interact with others and experience both interpersonal and intrapersonal feedback. *Thinking* involves complex emotional processes as well as complex cognitive ones. Things are attached to emotions; not just the memories of past experiences but also faces, voices and detached sounds. Emotions have a huge controlling influence over our behaviour, they can motivate, engage and help us achieve or they can demotivate, disengage and send us on unfavourable trajectories. Teachers accept the challenge to educate and nurture, but there appears to be a growing tendency in education to view young people as feral and in need of training in the ways of society. In this respect, young people become seen as something less than human and, rather, creatures whose futures can only be guaranteed through behavioural and cognitive modification. Teaching with emotions in mind allows us to retain a sense of purpose and humanity; it allows us to accept that each student in the classroom is a unique and amazing human being with complex needs and desires.

Tim O'Brien, a psychologist who has spent much of his professional career working with elite athletes and top businessmen, sums this up nicely when he states that we all have two stories inside our heads; one is about our lives (our experiences of life itself) and the other story is controlling our lives – our *inner story*. Emotions form part of this inner story and are responsible for influencing the way we see the world in both healthy and unhealthy ways. If your inner story isn't working for you, suggests O'Brien, then change it. Teachers have the power to help young people change their inner story, to reduce the fear of failure, to find passion in what they learn and do, to master the skills they need, not for recognition or wealth, but because it makes them feel something deep down in their bones. Like O'Brien says, teachers only glimpse the inner stories of their students, our contact with them ending when they move on to secondary school or complete their exams and head off on a different path. It's only in rare cases and much later when we might get the opportunity to realise the impact we have had in the writing of their story and them in the writing of ours.

Life offers us myriad affective experiences; we love, we grieve, we are joyful and sad, aggressive and passionate. But one thing is clear – we can't escape our emotions; they are a vital part of who we all are. Classroom settings are no different. In classrooms across the planet young people experience life through anxiety, fun, frustration, fulfilment and pride. Such complex cognitive-emotional experiences are bidirectional; while they concern the appraisal of academic success and failure and the internal analysis of pleasant and unpleasant personal and social encounters on the one hand, on the other we experience emotions that energise or restrict achievement and motivation. During the first two decades of life, educational settings are one of the most important sources of affective experience. Not only that, teachers' affective states are influenced by their success and failure as teachers, so perhaps we should also accept the existence of the emotional teacher in our discussions of the emotional learner. The affective states of teachers, after all, moderate evaluations and attributions and, in turn, impact teaching behaviour.

Of course, teachers don't have control over the emotions of students any more than any of us has any significant control over our own emotions. Teachers have more control over what psychologists call *specific emotions* and that is what the majority of this book has been about. We often know where specific emotions come from and why they arise in the first place, because they are bound by a specific stimulus context; embarrassment might arise from the experience of failure (like getting an answer wrong in class and feeling the silent ridicule of our peers). Mood states are trickier because they are of indeterminate origin; they are often unspecific yet enduring – when we are in a bad mood we are often unable to identify the source of the mood but it can remain with us all day.

What we know

Perceptions about ourselves impact on learning outcomes. While self-esteem has no direct relationship to academic success, more specific self-concepts do. The positive impact of higher self-esteem in some areas (happiness), however, might be negated by other less helpful outcomes (poor self-judgements). Higher academic self-concept is positively correlated with better exam grades, but this is state rather than trait specific, meaning that levels of academic self-concept are likely to be spread unevenly across school subjects. Mastery orientations impact more positively on academic attainment than performance orientations; viewing intelligence as malleable (incremental/growth mindset) is preferable to viewing intelligence as unmoving (entity/fixed mindset).

Learning involves complex interactions between cognitive states, emotional states and social contexts. It also appears clear that positive and negative emotional states influence learning behaviour in intricate ways. In this respect, the early Positive Psychologists were undoubtedly wrong about the way in which positive emotions help and negative emotions hinder. Later Positive Psychologists such as Todd Kashdan and Robert Biswas-Diener accepted this notion (see Further reading).

It's becoming clear that the positive–negative emotion distinction is unhelpful and that it's more appropriate to view emotions in learning as either activating or deactivating.

Motivation and engagement aren't about making lessons fun, but rather about making content personally significant. While some students are intrinsically interested in some content, others need help to internalise extrinsic motivators. While enthusiastic and passionate teachers can make a real difference, effective pedagogy and the skill of educators bind the whole together. However, remaining mindful that some students will never find some content interesting allows teachers to use extrinsic rewards as a fall back position.

High levels of anxiety are detrimental to learning, but lower levels are helpful. We also know that many schools aren't very good at identifying and helping highly anxious pupils. This in itself is an interesting debate, especially when some sections of the teaching community claim that the rise in levels of anxiety amongst pupils is the result of everything from pandering to the so-called *snowflake generation* to the abolition of corporal punishment. While many might deny that a mental health crisis exists in our schools, the evidence from a number of different agencies and research institutions paints a very different picture.

Boredom can be both damaging and constructive; the disengaged brain isn't necessarily in stand-by mode. Furthermore, teachers rarely see themselves as a source of boredom, and students might be bored for personal rather than academic reasons. Interest and curiosity, on the other hand, promote engagement and intrinsic motivation. Sometimes, unfortunately, some students' boredom cannot be attributed to a specific cause.

Interest and curiosity enhance learning and reinforce cognitive processes. Catching and maintaining interest, however, remain problematic. Situational interest, carefully nurtured, can allow individual interest to grow and be reinforced by stronger intrinsic elements. Understanding the process by which this occurs allows for possible planning of lessons towards maintaining interest and the internalisation of extrinsic rewards.

The teenage years involve a high degree of brain rewiring and this can impact on learning and behaviour in a number of complex ways.

Teenagers are highly influenced by their peers and this is as much a biological reality as it is a social one, leading to high degrees of risk taking in their personal lives but not within the classroom environment. We are also confident in the suggestion that the process of self-building during the teenage years impacts on behaviour and emotions, but is also an important part of the developmental process.

Fear of failure can lead to the implementation of strategies and behaviours that sabotage learning outcomes. Promoting specific strategies (such as confronting beliefs about personal strengths and weaknesses) allows students to reframe not only the nature of failure but also the nature of their own academic ability and critically examine personal learning strategies.

What we can speculate

Emotions impact memory through the complex communication of different regions of the brain. Memory for emotionally significant events can reinforce the memory trace but is still vulnerable to the processes that impair retention and recall. The brain also has an annoying habit of plugging the gaps in our memory with information that doesn't belong there, creating false memories that are indistinguishable from the real thing.

Emotional images can enhance memory consolidation and strengthen the testing effect. Images can be imagined or real but must elicit an emotional response (negative images appear to work best but neutral images have no impact). Even when answers are incorrect, reconsolidation allows for greater recall once feedback has been given. More research needs to be conducted in this area before it can be applied to learning environments.

What we can reject

The assumption that learning is a cognitive only process should be rejected. While cognition plays a larger role than any other factor, it doesn't operate in the absence of affect.

That we all learn in the same way should be rejected. While we can wholeheartedly reject the idea of individual learning styles and similar unsubstantiated theories, we must accept that different students will react in different ways emotionally to similar situations. This doesn't necessarily refer to outwardly emotional reactions such as anxiety or excitement, but rather to internal neurological processes and the areas at which cognition and emotions transect.

Emotionally positive classrooms

The social nature of the classroom means that emotional responses are often the result of what is happening within the group rather than within the individual. An environment of trust, support and collaboration creates a classroom in which students feel safe and valued. It's also important, especially for younger children, that classrooms are seen as places where emotions can be expressed and that teachers value and listen to these emotions. Furthermore, the appropriate reactions to such emotions should also be encouraged as a way of nurturing appropriate methods of emotion regulation. This would include the appropriate display of destructive emotions such as anger and less problematic ones such as excitement.

We can distil the emotionally positive classroom down to a small number of specific yet interrelated components:

- *Caring* – Relationships are strong and students feel safe, trusted and valued. Teachers are nurturing, supportive and sensitive to the needs of the students.
- *Pro-social* – Teachers and other students are supportive and accepting of diversity. Students care for and support each other and encourage their classmates when things become difficult.
- *Learning-focussed* – Students share a common purpose and common values. Teachers and students are goal-directed and everyone is clear about the goals they are working towards.

Emotions in mind

As already noted, emotions can be slippery things. Learning can influence many feelings both positive and negative, and it would be unfair to suggest that teachers and other educators need to take every emotion of every student into account. Furthermore, emotions can arise as a result of learning and as a result of indirect factors emanating from beyond the classroom (hunger, sleep-deprivation and those inexplicable bad moods are just some examples). Of course, some emotional behaviour can be related to more serious conditions such as abuse or underlying mental health problems, but these factors are beyond the scope of this book.

Others such as test anxiety are manageable under the right conditions but often exacerbated when handled badly. Being aware of these emotional responses in no way encourages or promotes the behaviours of the so-called snowflake generation (if such a thing even exists). Neither does it assume a traditional versus progressive dichotomy, in fact, because emotions are so closely linked to cognition and behaviour, it spans the ideologies that often lead to derision on both sides of the education debate. Whether we are attempting to master the complexities of advanced algebra, getting to grips with the causes of the First World War or learning a piece for the classical guitar, emotions are going to emerge and often need recognising and dealing with in young people who are often unprepared for them. The component that links all these things is the way everything we learn requires effort towards a goal and while the journey itself can be worthwhile on its own, it's much more satisfying if we eventually reach our destination. Nevertheless, before the jubilation of reaching our goal, we all need to experience the emotional rollercoaster of the journey, with all its leaps forward and falling backwards, slow-downs and dead stops.

Progress is rarely linear

One of the many changes to impact education has been the emphasis on progress. Students are expected to make progress within and between key stages and to display progress in lessons. It seems fair enough that learning needs to be seen to be happening, but there are some major problems with this.

Progress between key stages is rarely linear. In fact, fewer than 10 per cent of students show linear progress between key stages. Learning is punctuated by peaks and troughs and at times some students might even appear to be in reverse. These bumps in the road can occur for many reasons, including the difficulty in maintaining consistent effort and motivation over long periods of time, personality differences, personal problems and the inevitable problems of growing up and existing in the world. I've looked at some of these factors in more detail and concentrated on the pertinent ones such as boredom, anxiety and curiosity. Students reach their destinations by many routes, routes that are often stalled simply because life has an annoying tendency to get in the way sometimes. These bumps in the road often go undiagnosed and overlooked and most of the time present few difficulties to the learning process over the long term. However, for some students, the inability to resolve these issues can lead to underachievement and maladaptive strategies that exacerbate the situation. Additionally, the interactive nature of learning means that it is rarely the student alone who is either the cause of the problem or, indeed, the solution to it.

Focussed solutions

Throughout this book I have hopefully shed some light on a few of the more complex emotional aspects of learning. In this final chapter, my hope is to narrow the focus and offer a few practical solutions grouped into five broad areas: adaptability, mastery, relationships, support/feedback and regulation. These solutions can be applied to both teacher and student alike because, as I pointed out, there is a deep social and interpersonal factor to both teaching and learning.

Adaptability

Adaptability refers to the capacity to respond to and manage new, changing and uncertain situations that arise. In a broader sense, adaptability also involves the capacity to change when current behaviours aren't working for us. This broader definition is perhaps more difficult because it requires people to take a critical look at the way they do things and the way they think about their personal circumstances. Adaptability also involves the admission that something that we might feel comfortable with and cling to is actually doing more harm than good. Students who insist that their exam preparation is effective even though evidence suggests otherwise are probably clinging to the familiarity of a strategy rather than taking into account its efficacy. Similarly, false confidence arises from our ability in one particular subject area so, for example, a student might continue to revise the circumstances that led to the outbreak of the First World War and to test themselves on this rather than moving onto the causes of the Great Depression. Knowledge of something raises our confidence, but moving onto something we are less knowledgeable about can have the opposite effect.

Recognising what doesn't work for us is about identifying our own inner story. O'Brien states that it's our inner story that has the capacity to control our thoughts and behaviours, some of which might be positive and others that might be holding us back. A student, for example, might see him or herself as less intelligent or less academically able than others in the class or particularly bad at a particular subject. This is often the case with subjects like maths and people often reveal their inner story by telling everyone how bad they are at it. Maths is a particularly interesting area because it tends to be the subject in which people are less confident, despite evidence to suggest that there is no logical reason why some people should be any worse than others (barring any specific disorder such as dyscalculia). If our internal narrative insists that we are bad at maths, then we need to change it. Easier said than done perhaps, but challenging assumptions often leads to rapid change and teachers are best positioned to challenge such beliefs.

Mastery

A mastery orientation drives the desire to become skilled in a particular area while a performance orientation involves the desire to be successful in comparison to others. Mastery approaches are preferable because they allow motivation and engagement to be sustained over extended periods of time and also encourage longer-term goals. As we have seen, there is a close relationship between emotions and goals, so concentration on goal achievement allows the teacher to accommodate emotional states with broader success criteria.

Andrew Martin's work in Australia supports the use of what he calls *personal bests* or PBs. We can think of PBs as growth goals rather than achievement goals because they operate in increments rather than ultimate long-term goals. Working towards long-term goals is hard for many people and young people especially. This is why incentive schemes requiring the accumulation of points that count towards future rewards often fail. The longer the interval between the behaviour and the reward, the less likely the two will be seen as related. This is partly a psychological aspect of the measure of time and has an impact on related motivational behaviours such as procrastination. Long deadlines, for example, encourage people to put the task off for another day and when a deadline spans more than a week, procrastination is more likely. This is essentially to do with the way in which we perceive time. In a similar way, lengthy goals such as target grades are too far in the future to have any real meaning, and when progress towards that long-term goal isn't met, the goal appears even farther away and unachievable. Strategies such as PB goals break these larger long-term success criteria into smaller short-term components in a *better than the last time format*. In the same way, elite athletes will work towards exceeding their personal best, PBs in learning take the current personal achievement level and look towards obtaining a small increment within a time-bound framework. A student who, for example, is currently hitting consistent C grades might set a target of a B to be achieved by the end of that term, even though the target grade might be higher. All along the way, guidance is given and strategies towards beating PBs is discussed, followed by an audit of why the student might not be achieving this.

Encouraging mastery over performance works with emotions on a number of levels. First, mastery and growth goals reduce the destructive impact of failure fear. Because we begin at a realistic position and use smaller increments to measure success, the leaps forward are seen as more achievable and strategies agreed upon between increments can be more carefully focussed. Second, anxiety is reduced because success criteria don't represent high stakes situations. If teachers also include a number of low stakes tests in between the evaluation of PBs, tests become the norm and fear often subsides. With smaller groups tests can even be tailored to individual students, reducing the tendency towards performance orientations.

Relationships

Despite the suggestion that teacher–student relationships are important to success, there is often precious little advice on how they can be nurtured and sustained. I have already implied that the connection between the teacher and the learner is often critical to positive achievement outcomes through processes such as motivation, engagement and interest. While the need for teachers to resist the temptation to be a friend, a nurturing and supportive relationship is important for students of all ages. Longitudinal studies have found that students, especially those who are faced with greater levels of adversity, tend to rely heavily on teachers and others in the wider community to assist them in coping with issues that can derail both their academic success and general wellbeing. Positive relationships also have other indirect implications including increased resilience to general life setbacks and also to specific school-related resilience (so-called academic buoyancy). Many of us can recall that one inspirational teacher (and perhaps more than one) who just *got us* somehow. They were able to engage us and support us when things went wrong. Such teachers were often the ones who didn't accept our rather pathetic excuses and instead made us believe that we could succeed (no matter who we were).

Interestingly, there also appears to be a dearth of research relating to the impact of the teacher–student relationship on academic outcomes. This is perhaps the result of such things being very difficult to measure and establish accurate causation. Many different variables influence academic outcomes and students will inevitably be taught by many teachers throughout their school life. Often, it's only in retrospect that students are able to identify those teachers who made the greatest impact; we might recall some teachers as being fun and the lessons being exciting, but these factors might not reflect favourable academic outcomes. It's only much later that we are able to fully appreciate such factors. During my first couple of years of teaching I taught a very capable and amiable young man named Zac. He was an avid reader and possessed a veracious appetite for philosophy and the theories lying on the fringes of psychology (the subject I taught him). He began his studies with me having already dabbled in Jung and Nietzsche and was fascinated by the components and influences that made us human. Unfortunately, the deeply philosophical elements that so enticed Zac lay far beyond the confines of A-level psychology and he rapidly lost interest somewhere between attachment theory and research methods. Towards the end of 2015, I received an email from Zac in which he informed me that he was a PhD student in the psychology department of a prestigious UK university. Even though our relationship failed to result in high academic success at school, he cited me as one of the reasons he was now engaged in advanced psychological research. The way in which we measure outcomes is often simplistic and short term, and the way in which students view school now and in the future is equally problematic.

Positive relationships are beneficial in all walks of life, and close friendships are an important measure of psychological health and well-being. While teachers should avoid the friendship trap (your students will never be your friends), nurturing positive relationships is important. Harvard University researcher Hunter Gehlbach found that manipulating perceived similarities between teachers and students enhances relationships and improves academic outcomes (Gehlbach *et al.*, 2016). Certainly, humans are naturally social creatures and education is a process that involves a number of different relationships. Relationships, by their very nature, are emotional – when we think of a person we know we are rarely ambivalent and are more likely to think of them in terms of a like–dislike continuum. Indeed, research has consistently found that those children who thrive are those who are able to cultivate positive relationships with parents, peers and teachers. Gehlbach believes that by leveraging individuals' perceptions of similarity, we can improve positive teacher–student relationships. Similarity, of course, varies along a number of dimensions from the way people dress, their background, interests and hobbies – I once struck up a positive relationship with a particularly difficult student because he liked my shoes; I recall my son responding positively to a teacher because they happened to mention that they were attending a Slipknot concert. Decades of social psychological research has confirmed that liking someone is linked to compliance and pro-social behaviour, yet often teachers are discouraged from revealing anything about themselves that goes beyond the classroom environment. Furthermore, research has found that interacting with similar others supports our sense of self, our values and our core identity.

Support and feedback

This might seem obvious and is also linked to some of the other previous points. Nevertheless, it's worth stressing again and again. I also link them together, as feedback is best used when targeted towards goals and teachers support students in the achievement of such goals. As we have seen, positive teacher–student relationships impact learning but also make offering support less problematic. Negative relationships often result in students feeling as if they are being picked on or singled out for unjust criticism so those engaged in a more positive teacher–student relationship are more likely to view feedback in more positive terms. Feedback has also been found to be one of the most effective routes to academic achievement.

During my teaching career, I've tried many different methods of written feedback. Early on I quickly realised two things:

- most students don't read feedback;
- all students read the grade they have been awarded for the task.

This is in itself an interesting observation, seeing as research (Harks *et al.*, 2014) has discovered that so-called *grade-orientated feedback* is far less effective than *process-orientated feedback* (the latter emphasising the type of feedback that aims to improve outcomes by giving specific targeted and goal-orientated advice). Furthermore, process-orientated feedback not only has a positive effect on achievement, it also positively impacts on emotionally based processes such as interest.

In an attempt to curb this, I have, over the years, omitted the grade and given process-orientated feedback only, but because students often appear to be more concerned with how well they have done rather than how they can improve this tended to lead to criticism from students, parents and (on one occasion some years ago) school management. More recently I instructed students that they could have their grade only if they came to me to discuss the feedback – needless to say, few were motivated enough to follow up on this. The unwillingness to discuss the feedback is related to fear of failure (they actually didn't want to know the grade because they feared one that questioned their ability) so that their actions constitute a method of self-handicapping rather than genuine laziness.

Feedback should be elaborated sufficiently to help the learner change erroneous knowledge components and, thus, improve achievement (Harks *et al.*, 2014). Feedback should also offer information that contributes to the satisfaction of the student's basic need to feel competent (Ryan & Deci, 2000). Feedback, therefore, has both meta-cognitive and motivational components, so content should reflect both of these. John Hattie has suggested that process-orientated feedback should ask the following questions:

- Where am I going (learning intentions/goals/success criteria)?
- How am I going (self-assessment/self-evaluation)?
- Where next (progression/new goals)?

All the above points support the *personal best* strategy of Andrew Martin and were discussed earlier. Useful feedback allows students to understand where they are, where they need to be (and when they need to be there) and how they are going to get from where they are to where they need to be. Knowledge of this kind reduces fear of failure and anxiety and makes maladaptive processes such as self-handicapping and defensive optimism/pessimism less likely.

Regulation

In Chapter 1, I introduced you to emotional regulation and stated that people attempt to cope with their emotions in the following maladaptive ways:

- distraction;
- rumination;
- worry;
- thought suppression.

Those individuals skilled in regulating their own emotional responses adopt more adaptive cognitive strategies, including reappraisal, distancing and humour.

Reappraisal

Reappraisal is essentially taking a step back and attempting to see the bigger picture. Adopting a 'what's the worst thing that can happen?' approach allows students to think more rationally about their fears within a context of the pursuit of long-term goals, rather than imagining short-term catastrophes.

Distancing

Distancing is adopting an independent third-person perspective to allow for a more objective evaluation of the situation. Asking students to adopt the position of *good friend* can be helpful. Ask them 'If your friend came to you with this problem, what advice would you give them?'

Humour

Basic but effective, humour is a great stress reliever and allows people to cope better with anxiety-inducing situations. Smiling and laughing leads to the release of hormones related to happiness and wellbeing and the reduction of symptoms of anxiety. So-called *gallows humour* is perhaps the most common.

As well as cognitive changes, emotions can also be regulated through activities or *response modulators*, including:

Exercise

The psychological *cure-all?* Certainly, not all negative emotional states can be treated through exercise but there exists substantial evidence that it can reduce the symptoms of conditions such as anxiety and depression.

Sleep

At a time when studies indicate that the vast majority of young people are sleep-deprived, taking care of your snooze time has never been more important. Sleep provides us with downtime, with recent research supporting the view that it also helps with the ability to solve seemingly unsolvable problems.

Concluding remarks

The purpose in writing this book was to take the reader on a brief tour of what we currently understand about emotions and their impact on learning and achievement. It doesn't provide a blueprint for practice, neither does it claim to have all the answers. It assumes that teachers are skilled enough to identify what might be useful to them and apply chosen methods appropriately regardless of personal ideology.

Emotions are important but their nature is often misunderstood or viewed as something problematic that needs to be curtailed. Emotions guide and often determine behaviour, they are ever-present, often hidden from conscious awareness but influencing our actions nevertheless.

Hopefully *The Emotional Learner* has gone some way to redress the balance between cognition (thoughts) and emotions, where cognition is often viewed as the determining factor in learning.

Chapter summary

- We are yet to fully understand the role emotions play in learning, but what we do know can be successfully applied to the classroom.
- Adaptability, mastery, relationships and support/feedback are the key ingredients of emotionally aware classrooms.
- Emotional regulation is another key ingredient in ensuring that students flourish.

Further reading

The Learning Brain (2005). Sarah-Jayne Blakemore & Uta Frith (Blackwell).
Building Classroom Success (2010). Andrew Martin (Continuum).
Inner Story (2016). Tim O'Brien (CreateSpace).
Drive (2010). Daniel H. Pink (Canongate).
The Power of Negative Emotions (2015). Todd B. Kashdan & Robert Biswas-Diener (Oneworld).

References

Gehlbach, H., Brinkworth, M.E., King, A.M., Hsu, L.M., McIntyre, J. & Rogers, T. (2016). Creating birds of similar feathers: Leveraging similarity to improve teacher–student relationships and academic achievement. *Journal of Educational Psychology* 108(3), pp.342–352.

Harks, B., Rakoczy, K., Hattie, J., Besser, M. & Klieme, E. (2014). The effects of feedback on achievement, interest and self-evaluation: The role of feedback's perceived usefulness. *Educational Psychology* 34(3), pp.269–290.

Ryan, R.M. & Deci, E.L. (2000). Self-determination theory and the facilitation of intrinsic motivation, social development, and well-being. *The American Psychologist* 55(1), pp.68–78.

Index

Note: Page numbers in **bold** refer to tables; page numbers in *italics* refer to figures.